The

KALI

Project

Invoking the Goddess Within
Indian Women's Voices

Conceptualized and Edited By
Candice Louisa Daquin
Megha Sood

Praise for The Kali Project

(The Kali Project) "hits you with its immediate and striking relevance as protest art and underscores the point that Indian women, in every generation, have to discover their own ways of being and becoming; that the quest for a life of dignity is a Sisyphean journey. Steeped in the empowering mythos of the demon goddess Kali. . . bringing about the integration of the human and the divine and pointing the way out of the nexus of victimhood, into the urge to take control of one's own destiny."

Charanjeet Kaur, Academic, author of *ror Image & Other Poems*

(The Kali Project) "brilliantly gathers the voices of silence and sadness, helplessness and fury of feminist thoughts in powerful, simple and heart-wrenching verse. The poems nestle up into the folds and hems of the mythical mother- goddess, Kali. The poems in this collection deal with an array of themes, ranging from female foeticide to kanyadaans, marital rapes, bride burning and dowry deaths. It screams against the patriarchal penchant to invade and claim the female body as if it were an instrument of pleasure to be used and discarded or a possession to be bidden, sold and burnt.

. . . The poems in this anthology appear equipped with ten heads, ten arms and ten legs like Goddess Kali carrying the pain and ravages of broken spirit and psyche. Each representative poem spits blood, bile and tears and is a soul-rending cry for equality and harmony. The angst one feels is both personal and universal."

Pushpa R. Menon, Teacher, Academic, Writer, Poet

"The Kali Project is a unique piece of art. It stands testimony, bridging the gap between India and the rest of the world, informing the ignorant and aware alike, of the power and enduring talent of Indian women.

. . . I suspect all women can tap into Kali's positive energies and relate to the value of her fierce, unrepentant feminine energy. I appreciated this the most, reading The Kali Project; the convergence of women pulling together, creating, birthing, speaking without repression. . . We are all Kali."

Dr. Belinda Román, Economist/Researcher/Historian

"When one woman speaks her truth and is heard, the world is altered. When hundreds of these voices join together in declaring that truth, the moral axis of our existence shifts. This is the power of the collective voices of The Kali Project poetry anthology."

Rebecca Huston, Screenwriter, *Prytain, the epic untold stories of the first female rulers of ancient Britain*

"The Kali Project left me at times in tears, the intensity of emotion outpoured by brave Indian poets was almost overwhelming. But this was not a negative experience at all. I felt a lot of hope in reading the courage and resilience within those poems. We avoid raw truth but sometimes it is necessary to wake people up."

Selene Crosier, Contributing poet & artist: *As the World Burns*

"What I find unique in this collection is its ability to navigate reality using the cornerstones of myth and religion. Our objects of worship speak something of the substance of our humanity. The collected stories and wisdom of the ages prove to be flexible in what they admonish and offer believers. The confrontation with age-old claims on women's bodies and psyches is expressed within these poems with clarity."

Dustin Pickering, Poet, Editor, Publisher, Musician, author of *The Forever Abode*

"The Kali Project is timely and wise in its publishing on the world stage. The world really can do with more projects like this that helps those that have never experienced a lot of hatred against them due to gender, sexual preference, color or race, to gain understanding and empathy. The Kali Project brings empowerment to women in India in a totally different way."

Hanlie Robbertse, *Wishes of Hope, Chapbook of Poetry*

The

K A L I

Project

Invoking the Goddess Within
Indian Women's Voices

Conceptualized and Edited By
Candice Louisa Daquin
Megha Sood

INDIE BLU(E)
PUBLISHING

Havertown, Pennsylvania
United States of America

The Kali Project: Invoking the Goddess Within / Indian Women's
Voices
Copyright 2021 Indie Blu(e) Publishing

For information, address
Indie Blu(e) Publishing
indieblucollective@gmail.com

ISBN: 978-1-951724-06-1 (paperback)
ISBN: 978-1-951724-07-8 (hardcover)
Library of Congress Control Number: 2021930348

Conceptualized & Edited By: Candice Louisa Daquin &
                             Megha Sood
Cover Design: Mitch Green
Title Page design: Tejinder Sethi
Interior Artwork: Lakshmi Tara Chandra Mohan
Interior Formatting: Christine E. Ray

Dedication

"It was all the world that told us we were women not fit to look into their eyes, / women who could not think or stand up in the middle of a room with men, speaking about how to bury dead uncles. / They said only men could talk. Only men had voices."

—Arathy Asok, A Poem For My Sister

The Kali Project, Editors Introduction

"Inside every woman, there is a Kali, a Hindu goddess who morphed into seven hidden beings to win a battle. Do not mistake the exterior for the interior".
— *Jennifer Beals*

Dear Readers,

We are living in the 21st Century, yet constantly witness a continual violation of female rights; sexual and gender-based violence, threats to reproductive rights, female infanticide, domestic violence, acid attacks, prejudice against the LGBTQ community, honor-based killings, sexual assault, rape, mutilation, and child abuse. Not to mention basic inequalities like wage and healthcare discrepancies.

To voice and curate the experiences of Indian female poets and truly celebrate their magnificent achievements and brilliance in creative art, we put out a call to women writers of Indian heritage to submit work that resonated with their desire for equality; illustrating their struggles, angst, and pain in attempting to carve an equal position in patriarchal Indian society.

"The *Kali Project,*" was born. Deriving inspiration from the Indian Goddess "*Kali*" and her various manifestations. Kali represents the perfect metaphor of the great dissenter which we desperately need in Indian society, to rise above patriarchal and subjugate society, laced deeply in Indian culture for generations. Goddess *Kali* is an embodiment of the unfettered, uncontrolled energy which speaks to her ambivalent nature. Like nature, she can create and destroy with equal ease.

Rage against these atrocities against the female has birthed and empowered Indian women's movement for equality, liberty, and choice. Indian women are shouldering their additional responsibilities in today's times whilst simultaneously breaking the glass ceiling set by patriarchy for generations and all of this, while pushing against the rigid opinions of Indian society, en mass.

Crimes against women have always had a heinous history, with rapes leading to mutilation and worse. Recent cases like *Hathrus*, *Kathua*, and *Nibhaya* are shameful examples of such enduring atrocities. *Kali* is the perfect feminist icon for women then and now. The representation of *Kali* in mythology is the very concept of femininity. Kali is very different from the concept of a demure, disciplined, and dutiful woman. She is the quintessential embodiment of the *Shakti*, the feminine power. She is scary, bloodthirsty but also the ultimate protector against evil. She is frightening, uncontrolled, and at the same time awe-inspiring and maternal. This ambivalent nature and the multiplicity in her nature as the Goddess draws a stark reflection with contemporary Indian women.

This anthology is a deep exposition of the struggles carried by Indian women for generations. It encapsulates angst, rage, passion, and creativity, transforming it into potent poems, and striking representative art. It is a summation of the myriad ways; women are claiming their feminist power. Our collection of poetry and art bears a stark reflection of the immense vigor carried in the brave voices of its contributors and reiterates the immeasurable power, all genres of art possess.

The Kali Project celebrates the writings of well-established writers and emerging writers with equal respect. Featuring authors as young as nine through to our golden years, demonstrating the myriad incantations of the modern Indian woman and her enduring value at any age.

Hoping that this collection infuses you with the same formidable strength, healing, and immense courage that the goddess imparts.

Megha Sood, *Co-Editor — The Kali Project*

Foreword to The Kali Project

I am a Shakta and Vajrayana practitioner. With the blessings of my Gurus, I will speak of the Tantric Kali. She eats time (Kala/time+i/) and thus makes one fearless. Her fierce black female form is the Void (*shunya*) from whom the dualities of Shakti and Shiva, Prajna and Buddha arise. Prajna is wisdom and Buddha, compassion/ skillful means. She holds this female and male dyad as one within her womb. Here Shakti/power and Shiva/awareness are one, "non-duo" (*advai*).

I learned from my Vajraguru, Kulavadhuta Satpurananda, that Kali's well-known icon with Shiva under her feet is an image of a dynamic samadhi. Shiva is *shava* or dead body without Her touch. When all disturbances of the elements we are made of, body (earth), emotions (water), mind (Fire), and intellect (air) evaporate, one enters the fifth element (akasha/space) of samadhi. This is a dynamic equilibrium of Mahamudra where samsara and nirvana are one. From the perspective of the Kali tradition, all life is sacred. Nothing is denied or disparaged. Buddhists call it Sarvastivada, way of all yes.

There are many Kalis: aesthetic, imaginal, geometric. Among Kali's many forms, one is Kamakhya that represents the intensity of desire. Flip side of desire that brings life is death, and Kali dances in the cremation ground, her auspicious altar. Sexuality is a divine gift and the very root of all life. There will be no life without sexual energy, but it must be enclosed in the ethics of compassion and respect for all bodies. Violation of a female body is the greatest crime against the Divine Mother, but no amount of violence can ever desecrate a female body as it mirrors the Goddess. Women need to internalize this, not Brahminic patriarchy's devaluation of their form as maya or mere unconscious prakriti.

Although suffering enters the very cells of the body, one can transcend that suffering on the path of Tantra. Yeshe Tsogyal, a female Buddha, was gang raped under severe Tibetan patriarchy, but with Guru Padmasambhava's grace she awoke as the luminous Guru Dakini and transformed the rapists themselves. On the path of Kali, one neither accepts injustice nor reacts violently against it;

instead, one responds with clarity and fierce compassion. One needs to practice deep meditation and observe one's entire being without judgement to accomplish this.

Kali is the fiercest aspect of the Divine Mother in her mythic aspect. She arises out of Durga's forehead in the *Devimahatmya* to destroy the demon Raktabija or blood seed. Each drop of blood that falls on the ground creates another demon, so Kali laps up all the blood before it falls on the ground. These blood seeds represent our uncontrollable and scattered mind as Prithviraj Banerjee shows in his book, *Chronicles of Kali: Secret Book of Asurs*.

Kali is known as Mahaprajna as the great wisdom among her thousand names. Wisdom effortlessly inhabits the female body which is her most gracious temple. She is also Prakriti (Nature) in her kinetic, enchanting, and whirling form. In the end, even the Purusha/Ishwara or the witness consciousness of a god/great being vanishes in her dark womb; hence She is the Mother of God. Then a *Sadyojata* or newborn being awakens from the womb of Tara, her savior form.

At that point in sadhana, nothing but a luminous and pulsating reality remains, and Her Mahakaruna or great compassion flows through one's being. Various forms of this awake being are called Shivas, Buddhas, Jinas, Christs, Nabis, and Krishnas that teach us the way of the Mother, here and now. All people, both men and women, are potentially awake entities. It is harder for many men under patriarchal delusion to awaken that Shakti; hence the methods are rigorous. Once their identities vanish in Kali, they are totally free to live life in spontaneous ease; this is Sahaja or Dzogchen in Tibetan parlance, Marifat in Sufism, and the way of the Dao.

I have described my experience of Kali as 'pregnant nothingness' in my books; I began writing a blog, Stand Under the Mother Principle, to give expression to Her grandeur. My family's female Guru Shiddha Ma performed Kali puja in my birth town, Dharmanagar in Tripura, not a male priest. My Vajraguru revealed that I received a powerful transmission from Shiddha Ma which was utterly terrifying, devouring and yet compassionate. It changed my life and set me up on a crazy ride. I am now slowly learning the luminous ways of Tantra beyond all religions.

Tantra, an ancient method, is about the alchemical transmutation of energies. For the tantrika reality is Feminine, and women in all their forms inhabit that reality as the magnificent expression of Her evolutionary expansion. Hence the first vow a tantrika must take is to revere all female forms. There is nothing but the Great Mother as the Void, the world her manifest aspect. Each individual *jiva* or being of whatever orientation is potentially a Buddha waiting in Her womb to awaken. However, one must die to one's self to experience the shocking compassion of Kali. Once Kali takes over the being, all identities in terms of gender, caste, race, nationality, everything evaporates.

On the tantric path, energies of sex, anger, and greed need to be faced and transmuted for us to roam free as a Sky Dancer or Dakini in the spacious consciousness. Tantra was suppressed, and Shakti was misappropriated by patriarchal power structures in India because it demolishes all social hierarchies and gives the reigns of yogic freedom to people themselves. Women's awe inspiring and gorgeous poetry and prose in this volume flow from the fierce Shakti in their veins. Kali here appears as the transformation of anger into divine creativity. According to Tantra, one must not suppress anger, or it will show up as dis-ease of the mind and body. All creativity is an articulation of energy as beautiful form.

Patriarchy is an aggressive expression of the bounded masculine mind as the dominator of a separate feminized reality. It is a deluded, desperate, and failed attempt to deny the truth of the Mother Principle, the source and bounty of life. Consumerist capitalism is an extreme manifestation of that dominating persona that turns us all into 'hungry ghosts' or *pretas* who are painfully and perpetually dissatisfied amid plenty. Exploitation of Mother earth is patriarchy's most devastating and self-destructive outcome. Men and women both unconsciously participate in this short-sighted system in a frantic effort to protect their anxiety ridden small self.

Fierce feminine energy of Kali is arising today so that we can save ourselves from total annihilation. This volume is a sublime expression of that emergence. Not all women are necessarily open to that creative and annihilating energy, and some sensitive men are. However, women have the Mother Principle imprinted in their being whether they choose to be biological mothers or not. But they must activate that fearless energy with a calm mind and a kind and blissful heart if they decide to follow Tantra. It is a difficult, but the most exalted path designed by awake beings to help us be truly human and enjoy life fully in its play of light and dark energies, an expression of the paradox of Kali, my 'pregnant nothingness'.

Dr. Neela Bhattacharya Saxena
Professor of English and Women's Studies at Nassau Community College, USA

Dr. Saxena is author of In the Beginning IS Desire: Tracing Kali's Footprints in Indian Literature and Absent Mother of God of the West: A Kali Lover's Journey into Christianity and Judaism
https://neelabhattacharyasaxena.com/ and a blog
http://neelabsaxena.blogspot.com/

Acknowledgements

Our greatest thanks are to all the contributors of *The Kali Project* who took the time & effort to create such beautiful works for this anthology. We are staggered by your talent & your commitment to this project. You are the reason why *The Kali Project* is so beautiful & will endure.

A huge thank you to Dr. Neela Bhattacharya Saxena for her invaluable guidance on the reality of Kali and her manifestations and for writing our powerful, guiding foreword.

Deepest thanks to Tejinder Sethi for the marvellous wording: *Invoking the Goddess Within / Indian Women's Voices.* We immediately loved it, and knew it should become our subtitle. Thank you also for the beautiful title page design and invaluable support of The Kali Project.

Thank you to Lakshmi Tara Chandra Mohan for her lovely artwork used throughout the anthology.

Thank you to Mubida Rohman for your passionate PR and marketing relating to Kali and your much appreciated support of the project.

Candice Louisa Daquin: Thank you to Megha Sood. My colleague & most of all, my friend. I have loved working with you, it is a true joy. I have admired you for the longest time & am so honored you agreed to work on The Kali Project with me. You are a true, dear friend.

Many thanks to Usha Akella and Nitya Swaruba for your support of *The Kali Project.* Thank you to Dr. Belinda Roman for helping me & always being smarter than I am. Finally, thank you to Christine E. Ray & Kindra M. Austin, my sisters at Indie Blu(e) Publishing, for publishing *The Kali Project* & for being bad-ass women who always come down on the right side of things that matter.

Megha Sood: I'm immensely grateful to my co-editor and friend Candice Lousia Daquin for her constant guidance and encouragement through the various phases of this brilliant project. I'm thankful to her for her unwavering faith in my abilities and for giving me the opportunity to work on this stunning anthology. Finally thanks to Christine E. Ray and Kindra M. Austin of Indie Blu(e) Publishing for believing in us and giving this anthology a home. The essence of sisterhood for standing proudly for things that matter is reflective in every single collaboration this anthology represents.

Contents

Aakriti Kuntal
Spit

"Nights, I squat in the cornucopia
Of your left ear, out of the wind,"

Nights, I squat in the cornucopia
Of your left ear, out of the wind,
The pearl shell of the flesh is where
The crooked teeth of the moon fell,
Collecting into the basin between
My mouth and tongue. My tongue
Hangs outward,
It is striped,
It hums and hums,
The mosquitoes saunter in its liquid
Saltiness. It kills and kills and kills,
This tongue. It is the nectar
That blinds the bees and breaks
The tension in the cold sweat of the night.
I am hanging,
In the middle of the night,
Catching sap and flatness,
Echoing the dizziness that is light.
The body plunges
Across the window, scratching
With empty fists at the
Hollowness that disassembles all things.
At the end of the night,
Where the blood squeals
beside the violet-green shrub,
There is the totality of loneliness.
The absurd, laughing face of life
That consumes
All it can.
The body detaches from its head

And walks into the cemetery of soil
Awaiting its miracle,
An empty promise
That spurts from all living things.
Dead seas sleep in my body,
Writhing in their strewn carcasses,
Condemning with their nighthawk eyes.
I'm a murderer, mama,
I kill the tiny birds who wish to fly,
I kill them with my switches
And the electricity that flows like a mad pulse
Across the chambers of my tin house.
We are murderers, mama,
As you are mine, how sweetly
You disassembled me piece by piece,
The cotton doll that you never wanted
To birth in the first place.
We are all murderers, mama,
Jostling for space,
Waiting for the night to chew us all out.

The poem is my humble attempt as an ode to Sylvia Plath's poetry.
It quotes her line:
"Nights, I squat in the cornucopia
Of your left ear, out of the wind,"
from the poem titled 'The Colossus'.

Chronic

Poppy seeds raining/ A snoring window spreads as the mouth of an eagle/ Dull yellow light-- melting butter-- dotted slime of air-- particles, and particles, and particles

None have dwelled longer on the visage of a window as the flapping beat of the lonely, one-seeded iris/ The body dwells inside its cave as a large trepidation / There is no tenderness in its felt/ Growing and burgeoning as mushrooms on a pallid wall/

One attaches all sorts of divine abilities to illness/ Woolf murmurs of its spiritual capabilities/ There is little purification like the tremors of the body from being beckoned into the night over and over and over/ An exorcism, perhaps? A body no more in unison with being or life becomes a snarly beast/ vicious/ seamless/ encapsulated in the thin sheet of skin/ The body is a forest and the quite croak of the dim morning light enters it as fine, emerald pills/ The body slices through it all and sits atop all emotion as a fat serpent, the body bites its own air/ While one may argue over the reign of the mind over the body but only the little child in the sweltering heat of red rain knows well—
as bright as a vowel, as sharp as human apathy, as ruthless as nature's food chain-- is the horror of the body/ The body bears in its enormous endlessness the ugliness of circumstance/ Its abject rejection from life and society/ One could never understand how one was lesser for suffering/ how guilt is endowed upon one for no act of one's own/ how one is taught from childhood that disability or sickness is something to be compensated for in the elite court of human beings/

The body squirms as a tiny bird in a duvet/ It is the blurring eye of the sun in the dawn's crooked mouth/ It is both terrified and beyond fear/ The body inhales death and life in one gasp/ The body is sore with desperation and yet absent of desire/ It is a language that no one comprehends/ The body is the flat line of the sky—

A tiny droplet inside the large echo of being, poised, calm, cold, and white in its eternal wait to be free

Hereditary

Orange seaweed. A garden in space. Bluebells swaying in the clay foliage of ear. Mother, the sky is a neat, yellow dress drying in the sun's angst. The city is a pinch of salt splitting between gargles of air. A thin line stretches from lip to lip, a diameter of strangeness tiptoes above the sea of endless noise. What clutches now? What holds on to the rinsed pockets of white, lily air? There's a bewilderment that rushes between the eyes and the vertical nose, an injection of blood. I squat on the cold, marble floor and bathe sometimes in the wavering chorus of nights. Its emptiness so large, it's almost freeing. There is an ugliness in my chest, it rises as a stinging vomit and floods the senses, the narrow nose, the tiny tracts to the ears. Blood swims along the valleys of the scalp, dancing and dancing in its sad, little song. What is this burden of life that doesn't break or detach, that spins forth and forth, eating and eating, never resting, this ugly being of might? Mother, the cold sun is coming to swallow us both. I don't wish to be left alive.

Aakriti Kuntal, aged 28, is a poet and writer from Gurugram, India. Her work has been featured in various literary magazines and anthologies. She was awarded the Reuel International Prize 2017 for poetry and was a finalist for the RL Poetry Award 2018. Her poem Lilith was nominated for the Best of the Net 2018-19 by the Pangolin Review.

Aaliya Baba
Equality

My dear
don't speak to me of equality tonight,
Let's try a lesson on anatomy...

Woman grows to bleed, and learns to smile through it,
In a culture of forbidden sighs!
You might help few with doses of pain-killers
for finding them crawling like one wounded pet!

Bearing a child then, is a bond with death
She is the last to wake up
to see what she had nurtured in her womb
In blood, sweat and excruciating labour
They cut her open to get the heir out of her.

Thus, you would say isn't this what they all go through?
Indeed they do...
Well, I thought the historical silence might speak to you of equality!

Born and raised in Srinagar, Kashmir, Aaliya Baba is pursuing her Ph.D. from the University of Kashmir on the politics and philosophy of Autobiography. Her poems have appeared in journals like Miraas, Sheeraza, Kashmir Lit, English Studies in India, and Setu (Pittsburgh, USA)

Aanya Sheth
Quest for equality...

When it was a girl born,
They were filled with delight
For them respecting every gender was absolutely right
As the baby grew up she had interest in athletics much
Convinced her parents for sports
To keep in touch
Once she read a poster,
"Race of Infoys"
They said it's only for boys
She raised her voice
It was a quest for equality
Opting a dangerous race
Teasing from boys she'd face
"Infoys" isn't a place for girls
Who are slow and filled with curls"
She was badly mocked.
Because of her brave aura, she stood firm not shocked
No sooner, authorities let her in
They all knew boys would only win
When the race started she beat them all
She believed in herself, her talent would never fall
At the end, she had won
Achieved a million ton
She was overjoyed fulfilled her only dream
Inspired people to focus on the save girls scheme

Aanya Sheth is an aspiring young poietria and reading has been her passion since she was 3. Always being inquisitive, she dived into writing poetry at the age of 7 with natural ease. Poetry became the rhythmical creation of her beautiful imagination and thoughts. Today, at the age of 9, Aanya has penned down several poems on distinct themes.

Aashika Suresh
Lingerie Shopping

for
breathable
      cotton underwear
a tiny bow
lace trimmings like snow
sans red
(so i will know i have bled)

there is
      a party
across the street i won't
attend

instead
i am out buying
this fresh
tight shield
no space for fingers

   especially his

nobody but i
will see me wear
this new pair

Aashika Suresh is a writer, dreamer, and sunlight seeker based in Chennai, India. She was shortlisted for the 11th Srinivas Rayaprol Poetry Prize (2019). Her poems have most recently appeared in Nether, Lockdown Journal Chennai, Under the Basho, Rigorous, Chestnut Review, among other places.

Abha Iyengar
A Woman's Cry

And then one day, we tried to change things,
Make them better for ourselves
Now we are single and alone
We've paid a heavy price for our freedom.

Slavery is hard to bear, so is freedom,
One finds you in chains,
The other delivers you to the world.
One makes you bear the onslaught of one on one,
The other makes you pit yourself against many
That's why so many surrender
Even after the battle is won.

Don't give up, fight hard,
It may destroy you,
But you are making the world a saner place
For the daughters that follow.

(First published online in ItsAboutTimeWriters, 2001)

The Ultimatum

If marriage was the ultimate
Destination
Why did you not prepare me, mother?
Why did you fill my head
With words like
Independence,
Self-worth,
Education,
Rights.

You taught me everything
that was wrong
For married life.

I bow my covered head
With a sari
And am covered more
With a feeling of dread
Of how much more
I will have to bow.
I will run away
Or take my life
Because this is not
The path you chartered for me.
No, this is not what
I was made to believe.

It is wrong now to tell me
To change direction.
I lay the blame at your door
For hiding the truth.
You showed me blue skies
And shaped my wings
And broke them then
When you placed my hands
In a steel cage.

(First published online in Kritya, 2005)

Finding Myself

I am all arms and legs entangled
Holding them around me
Strangled I feel, tying those
Knots myself.
Cares, needs, concerns
Me, mine, and the rest of the world.
Like a butterfly well-meaning
but rudderless.
Eyes darting, mind whirling,
With these arms and legs
Holding.
Grasping me, telling me
I cannot do so much without failing.
Falling. Falling.

And then you appear within me
A flood of waters raging.
Fill me with hope so much I emerge
a great tumultuous energy, wind
whipped hair and sailing.
Arms and legs open wide
wielding weapons of healing.
Compassion, love, desire, passion,
A kaleidoscope of feeling.

But, above it all,
red hot woman energy, all-consuming.
A sense of self in being and believing
Womanhood, creative spirit, justice
and freedom. A giving and receiving.

My limbs dance
manifesting your power.
My tongue speaks red and bright
River of joyful fire.
Rising. Rising.

I have become you.
O Kali Ma, I am you.

(First published online in Seeking Kali, 2010)

Abha Iyengar is an award-winning, internationally published poet, author, editor, and British-Council-certified Creative Writing mentor. She won the Kota Press anthology Contest (U.S.A., 2003). Her poems have been included in various journals like "Conversation Poetry Quarterly" and in anthologies, most recently Sahitya Akademi's, "The Lie of the Land" (2020). She was a Featured Poet at Prakriti Foundation's Poetry Festival, 2010. "Parwaaz" (her poem-film) won the Special Jury Prize in Patras, Greece. Her collection of poems is entitled "Yearnings" (Serene Woods, 2010).

Abhinita Mohanty

Another Mythical Story

Last year,
A girl with streaks of blue hair,
And a boy with big moustache,
were playing as usual,
On the patio after dinner,
Those boisterous siblings, you see,
Perfection.
The girl's blue hair drew some attention,
the boy's moustache, drew some admiration,

Their hijinks, weaved that mellifluous, into the dreary town folks

One day,
When the boy went on an errand,
the girl was not to venture beyond gates of their gilded home,
Then she saw,
A golden fish laying on the sand, on the road,
And went ahead, crossed the gates,
picked up the fish and nibbled at it!

Then there was another girl, standing by,
She smiled and held hands,
Off they went, near the seas,
They snatched a mountain here, a plain there,
Smelling the bazaar smells, colours,
Scarlet red skies, and then they toured a globe,
She returned later after sun is gone,
Found her brother never came home,
Next day, they all left to the hospital,
There he lay, with one leg mostly non-existent,
Lying on the bed,
Did you venture out yesterday, he said,

No, she said,
Good, dear, that's why you are safe.
She gave a smile, sly and cranky
And some flowers that said, "Get better soon, and try to tour the
world".

*(The poem above is roughly based on the Ramayana story involving a
scene of a 'Lakshman Rekha'. This one is rather a parody with a feminist
touch to it)*

A relationship

Their minds met, long before they knew,
That even their bodies are deemed profane,
If only they can touch other dermis, not akin to them,
Other burly arms to sleep on,
Then each other's little souls,
When the bells of the sacred,
Raised its iron clad head,
They once again pretended under the sun,
That they are mere friends,
Within the curtains though, shadows mate and played,
Forming pareidolia under the thin poles of street lights,
She moaned at her fluttering smile,
She dreamt of misty days under sickening heat,
Both together weaved a portal, underneath their floors,
Before sunrise, it summarised,
They washed face and 'sins'
And left the doorstep, as "just friends",
Until, the curtains and the heat of night,
Brought that familiar calmness again,
They knew someone will keep a gulag ready,
when their lips will flutter or touch another,
under that cruel sun.

Abhinita Mohanty hails from Odisha, India. She is pursuing a PhD in the Department of Humanities and Social Sciences, IIT Madras. Her works have been published in Outlook Magazine's Website, Feminism in India (FII), New Asian Writing, Tribune Newspaper, Green Ink Poetry, Bombay, Review, Punch Magazine India, Trouvaille Review, Ponder Savant, Ayaskala Magazine, sheepshead Review and a few others. When not busy pondering over her research, she loves to read, write and occasionally binge eats!

Aditi Puttige
Consent Not Found

Aditi Puttige is a 17-year-old student from India, studying in grade 12. She is keen to pursue a career in the field of design. A feminist who believes that there is beauty in imperfection, she enjoys playing the flute, sketching, reading, and photography in her free time.

Ajanta Paul
The Real You

Who says you look old?
Don't believe the mirror,
It has cracked at the edges
And it's silvering has worn off.
Those are laughter lines,
Not wrinkles around your eyes,
And your skin is a palimpsest of poems
In the wrought parchment
Of your face.

I stand on your shore
And realize with increasing clarity
That deep below the waves
Lies the tumultuous reality
Of your teeming ocean floor,
Vibrant in its unseen life
Where your story is written
In the vivid inks of inspiration -
Turquoise, indigo, aquamarine,
Purple, amethyst, and rose,
There your beauty reigns
In amazing agelessness.

I walk by your shore
And quietly explore
Your swelling littoral litany
And in my moment of epiphany
Perceive the wrecks
The ships and relationships
Yielding your buried secrets
To none but the intrepid explorer

Who risks his life
In search of your secret store,
To discover who's the real you?
The beautiful self true!

Ajanta Paul is a widely-published poet, short story writer, and critic from Kolkata, India who has been in academia for ages and has returned to her first love - writing. She did her Ph.D. in English from Jadavpur University in the 1990s and is currently working at Women's Christian College, Kolkata.

Akhila Rajesh
Flow Back, O Gange Ma!

O Holy Gange Ma
The eternal bearer
Of flowers and filth
Of sins and things unwanted
Of dead bodies and live babies discarded

Eons ago, under a flushed orange sky
Upon your overflowing bosom
An unwed teenage princess set afloat one in a basket
Result of a boon turned into a curse-
To beget a child from her favourite Dev
A princess, but where was her power?

What humiliation and wrath did she fear-
Her honour, her kingdom's honour-
More important than a tiny life in danger?
And what means did she may not have had
To at least secretly bring up the child
Than float it in water, hoping it will not die?
The eldest, but cut off like an inconvenient sixth finger?
But then I take back my words

Why secretly?
Why do the million fingers of the society
Always point to the unwed mother?
Unwed motherhood- a misconceived pleasure maybe, but certainly
not a crime
Illegitimate child - not a legitimate heir maybe, but certainly a
worthy life!

Eons change, but society's dual face remains
Just because the womb alone bears
Her honour is ripped thread-bare

45

Married - and a barren womb is a curse
Unmarried - and a nestling one is a worse curse
A childless father is free to remarry
But an unwed mother-
In her heart has burdens to carry
And a child to drown or bury;
All because of the depraved society
That cradles the betrayer
Castigates the unwed mother
And ostracizes the newborn flower

Today, society should change
Tomorrow, evolution should also change-
So that history doesn't have to chronicle bloodied rivers -
Nature should change, to make man the bearer;
And then an unwed father-
Will then society hold high the child and the father
And for betrayal, float upon you, O Ganga, the mother?

O Holy Gange Ma, for once change your course
Flow back the sins and filth into the human heart
Let them feel the stench of their sins
Let them absolve it with penance
Let them come to your banks with a pure conscience

Enough being
The eternal bearer
Of flowers and filth
Of sins and things unwanted
Of dead bodies and live babies discarded...

(Poem first posted on FaceBook poetry group – The Significant League)

Torn

Dear Society,
Don't blame her for her torn clothes
When you always wear a torn conscience

She has been shredded
Help her rebuild her torn confidence
Don't abuse her further with your stigmas
Stop blaming her, stop shaming her
After all, your mouths that mouth the blame & shame
Don't have an answer for her screams

Don't repress her in jails of your regressive thoughts
While beasts roam free with audacity
Help her salvage her future
Don't let the savage scavenge another prey from your midst

Don't define dignity by her clothes, for
Everybody has been naked at some time
Don't marry her for the chastity of her clothes
Marry her for the chastity of her mind

Accept her as she is, respect her for what she is.

Akhila Rajesh is an IT professional with poetry at her heart. Her journey with poetry began in her school days and continues to get intriguing each passing day. Her first published book of poems is – 'From Womb to World'. The second book 'Enchanted Verses' was a collaboration with fellow colleagues. Her poems have also been published in multiple anthologies of Poetry Society of India, Xpress Publications, The Significant League, Poetry Corner, Asian Literary Society etc.

Anita Nahal

Homo Sapiens and Hindu Goddesses in India and America

I left my India one score ago. Running from abuse, my son and I were. As we arrived at Dulles airport, a sense of excitement laced with trepidation engulfed. Seemed we had boarded a spaceship to another planet never to return. Return was no longer a word in my dictionary. I folded it neatly in the white handkerchief my father slipped into my hand at the airport between tears and smiles. My mother clasped my fingers, repeating, "I think you both will not come back to India." "Of course, we will," I sounded unconvincing.

> Folks say I am Kali, Durga, Laxmi, and Saraswati, and all other Hindu goddesses manifest in me. I am grateful yet I don't wish to float on high pedestals. I don't get human hugs often. That touch, that oxytocin making me feel grounded with love. And I don't wish for the mean and uncouth Homo Sapiens to pour milk over my statues or feed me heavy sweets while disdainfully shooing beggar children out their way. Or seeking blessings from me-a female- and then raping other females. I also don't want to float my goddesses as exotic to horny Homo Sapiens anywhere in the world.

I hid the handkerchief in my native memorabilia box taking a whiff or two every now and then. Fatigued tears drudge along from the sides of my eyes like broken subalterns returning from a long war. Mom and dad have long passed.

> I became all the goddesses when my son was born. I became all the goddesses when you tried to snatch him from me. I became all the goddesses when you abused me in public. I became all the goddesses when I rejected you. I became all the goddesses when I decided we must leave. I became all the goddesses when I fended alone for my son. I became all the goddesses when I did not compromise anymore. I became all the goddesses when I did not cry anymore. I became all the goddesses when I signed on the dotted line of our divorce papers in my America.

(Durga: Goddess of war, strength and protection;Kali: Goddess of the destroyer of evil; Laxmi: Goddess of wealth; Saraswati: Goddess of learning/education)

Finally, She Showered

The bed was quiet and neatly spread with arms inviting...and she wanted to sink deep into the satin covers. Wanting to shower and have a drink first, Priya turned the water on, waiting for it to be the right temperature. She thought about the last time she made love. Letting her *lehenga* fall she checked her breasts pressing them all over for any signs of a lump. Her son had got married today. Twenty years after they'd left India. Emotional refugees. As she aged, alchemists tugged at her sleeves often. And gypsies gestured to her, come join us in your years of autumn with graying hair at your temples, graying all over, including in the forest, which is normal, not rare. The aging, hopefully maturing her restless travels, her restless needs, her desires and wants now quietly straddling the times. No more fake agendas written by some men. No more equality diminishing. No more pendulum shaking Zen. No more fake standards lowering or raising. Why some men slouch on recliners, beer in hands? Why then they unbuckle their belt, zip open their pants? Why such exhibitions don't come from women? Are fertility eggs stronger than tasteless semen? Is exhaustion an excuse from housework? Seems their power egos tend to be on steroids. Men need to learn more about their tools before smearing those who learn to swim in the smallest of water pools. A deep sigh filled, letting out the tears under the steaming water, Priya finally showered.

(Lehenga: Indian ethnic dress).

(Accepted for an anthology on Searching for home, dignity, and value: Poetry of migration, work and belonging).

Kali asks, "Two, three, or karmic wrongs make it right?"

I am woken in the middle of the night by nightmares of fires raging, homes burning, smoke rising and rising...nowhere to go. I am woken up in the middle of the night by the shrieks of tornadoes and hurricanes volleying up their impenetrable bodies against weaker souls. I am woken up by screams, innuendoes, pleas and tears. Woken up by jolts of the human tongues spitting out the harshest words...to demean, to mock, to kill.

Two wrongs, three wrongs, repeated wrongs, karmic wrongs, the loop keeps looping. No one to pull, reign in or break the cursed circle to start afresh. My skin burns, my skin crinkles, my skin simmers. I don't give up. I am Kali and Parvathi and I am dark and a goddess too. I can control time. Alter time. Make time difficult for you. Take you away from time. I am magnificent. I forgive. I love. I have surging passion that is filled with Shiva's Tandavam. He may lay at my feet. He may seem in obeyance. He may seem asleep on purpose. Mistake not...he's very aware. Maybe in awe, in admiration, of my *shakti*, my love making that fills him. Rouses and arouses him. Keeps him dancing.

I come a full circle and ask you humans, do two, or three or any karmic wrongs that you so wickedly try for me to swallow condone your actions? Your words? I am modern. I am a traditionalist. I am a seeker. I am a giver. I am a destroyer. I love. And make love in all my forms and moods. And I am just. I am benign. I am me. I see much deeper than my third eye. I scratch the third often to make sure no scrap of knowledge is left untouched. I may not fully understand each entry in my brain cells. But I seek it out. Let it rest in the sun. Marinate. Not Curdle. I pat it. I goad it. I hope that humans would feel it too. Change. Improve. Become better.

I am a female goddess just sharing, honestly, what's circulating in my body, heart, mind and soul.

(Kali: Goddess of protector against evil; Parvati: Goddess of fertility; Shiva: God of destroyer; Tandavam: Cosmic dance performed by Shiva; Shakti: Power)

Anita Nahal, Ph.D., CDP is a poet, professor, short story writer, and children's books author. Currently she teaches at the University of the District of Columbia, Washington D.C. Besides academic publications, her creative books include, two volumes of poetry, a collection of flash fictions, three children's books and an edited anthology of poetry. She's just completed her first novel. Read more on Anita Nahal at: https://anitanahal.wixsite.com/anitanahal

Anju Kishore
Goddesses

He sees me in stone
And seeks succour on my sculpted lap
Blessings from my immobile lips
Bounties from my chiseled finger-tips.
Pouring promises and praise
He rallies flowers and fruit to the task
Of pleasing my gravelly heart.
Mother, he calls me
Assuring me of his insignificance
In my intricate scheme of things.

She awaits him with his baby on her lap
To serve a meal, painstakingly gathered
But the devotee smashes her lip
And bloodies her finger-tips.
So drunken are his drawls
She clasps in alarm, the infant's ears
Lest they leave a future scarred.

He has left another marred
By yanking her honour off her heart
While looming beastly large
Above her brutally pinioned lap.
Woman, he calls her
Crushing her flowers
With the fruit of his carnal wants.

He returns to me
A garland in his hands.
His eyes rise to mine.
Fire tingles in my breast
Within me, blood leaps.
But in stone.
Will the real goddesses rise, please?

Anju Kishore's poems have been featured in numerous national and international journals and anthologies. They have won many prizes in poetry competitions as well. Her book of poems inspired by the civil war in Syria, '...and I Stop to Listen' earned her a glowing review in Kendriya Sahitya Akademi's English journal, Indian Literature. She has been part of the editorial teams of four anthologies with India Poetry Circle and Kavya-Adisakrit Publishing

Anna Sujatha Mathai
Goddess Without Arms

My poetry didn't come
           full-blown,
a perfect flower,
every petal proudly placed.
It was never a goddess
     rising from the waters
seated serenely on a shell
or emerging from a lotus
       all arms gracefully extended,
a Canova Venus or a Saraswati,
resplendent in her plenitude,
     certain of her sovereignty,
No. It grew painfully,
       armless,
        limbless,
         somewhat blind,
    a few stray petals here and there,
       more like wounds.

But day by day,
    inch-by-inch

it gathered grace,
    arms, limbs, eyes...
       wholeness

Light

When I was seventeen
And dreaming of distant lands
And faraway loves,
My grandmother said
'Get her married
        before the light
                goes out of her face.'
The light in a woman's face
Should not be so brief.
It's meant to last a long time,
Nourished by the soul.
Well, they got me married,
and put out that light,
But I learnt to live in candle-light
When the other lights went out.
One learns by subtle contact to reach
Electricity at most mysterious levels.
Light goes from the face, but
Survival lends one light
        That shines most brightly.
She who seeks light,
Must learn to walk in the darkness,
On her own road.

'He who seeks light must learn to walk on his own road, alone.'
St. John of the Cross

Hysteria

Yes, for centuries we've been mute
Not that we're dumb, or our
tongues had been cut out. Not out
quite. We could prattle alright:
about recipes, about dust,
about our neighbor's daughter,
about our clothes, secrets about
how to stay beautiful, how to
stay young. We knew nursery
rhymes which we lisped to our
children, but never the dark
interiors of those stories, those
lay shrouded in sleep like the
Sleeping Beauty. Yes, we were
sleeping beauties, baby dolls,
we slept while our children
were branded with seals of ownership,
our names taken from us, we smiled
while others filled in forms for us,
others made laws that ruled our lives.
Yes. We were dumb.
except when we cried, which
was often; when we were ravished
as young girls, by strange, brutal men,
when we bore children and delivered them
in the agony of childbirth, When our husbands
and our fathers, our brothers, and our sons,
and even our lovers, if we dared have them,
struck us and betrayed us,
and sold us and wounded us.
We dreamed of gentle hands and loving words,
for were we not the soil filled with the ache
of longing for the seed, but instead, we were
coarsely used, our bodies brutalized,
                    our souls numbed.

And even our mothers denied us.
In the hour of darkness, they
cut off our hair, shaved our heads
burnt us on the funeral pyre,
burnt us in our homes,
our brothers inherited the earth.
We were disinherited of even our smallest
shreds of humanity, the day we were born.
Our parents cursed us. They educated
our brothers gave them the land
and the houses, and the future,
and the power and the glory.
We were married off, we were mere
pieces of property, passed from one family
to another, to work and bear children,
or if we didn't bear children,
to be cursed for our barrenness.
No one looked into our eyes with love.
If they had, they'd have heard our souls talk.
Instead, all they said was
She's hysterical. Women are like that,
especially when they menstruate,
especially when they stop menstruating,
especially as they approach death.

Anna Sujatha Mathai has been writing for many years now. She has 5 Books of Poetry in English. She has read her poems in many countries, including England, Sweden, Denmark at Struga, Macedonia, and at Centres and Universities all over India. In 2018, the Feminist Press, Women Empowered, awarded Anna Sujatha with the First Kamala Das Prize For Poetry.

Antara Banerjee
Botched Creed [Against Rape and Victim-Shaming]

'Look at me!
I am Medusa...
the most beautiful Gorgon of all.
My divine beauty,
now hidden,
under layers of scaled skin.
My lush tresses,
turned into
seething asps.

I dwell,
in this forlorn island,
banished
to this wretched existence
for no folly of mine.
Punished,
for being ravished
by a lustful god.

My laughter
echoes across the seas,
crashing at the feet of Parthenon.
Nay, these are shrieks,
my heart-rending calls,
to the virgin goddess.'
'Athena! You wronged me!'

So spake Medusa,
as she turned men to stone,
not by her gaze...
but by reflecting the story
of a wily world;
where the Gods

run amok
wielding their ugly manhood
and piercing innocent lives
with unabashed impunity;
where the Goddess of wisdom
is not a savior,
but a heartless dispenser
of irrational justice.

'Why question my virginity,
my dear goddess?
Wasn't my faith enough?'

'I pleaded and called out to you
as he thrust himself on me,
again, and again...
You failed me, Athena!
And so, did the world.'

A world,
that let you and Poseidon
remain divine.
The God and the Goddess
who preyed on the victim,
to push their divinity,
in a world
blinded by faith.
The wretches,
who pride,
in their twisted sense of justice!
And celebrate,
the death of innocence!

* According to the Greek myths, Medusa was the virgin Priestess at the Temple of Parthenon, to the Goddess of Wisdom and Justice, Athena. She was a legendary beauty with the most beautiful tresses

* She was raped by the God of the seas, Poseidon at the temple of Parthenon, The temple of the virgin goddess, Athena
* Athena had cursed Medusa to become a horrific creature, whose face was hideous, skin scaled and tresses, live asps. Her gaze was so dreadful that whoever looked at her face turned into stone.

Apocalypse [Embodiment of Mother Nature as an abused woman]

Mother earth is tired,
sick to her guts.
Disgusted,
with what she thought
was the best out of her womb...
She had birthed man
and placed him
in the cradle of nature,
lovingly.
Given him the best
she possessed...
Blessed him
with a million boons.
nurtured him
to be the worthiest of all.

Little did she know
that her favorite child
would grow up
to be corrupted by the
Oedipus Complex.
Consumed with a rabid desire
to consummate his libido
with its own mother,
the child would forge
its own death!

He ravages her
repeatedly
and loses one boon
after the other.
Million to thousands
thousands to hundreds...
the boons have eroded fast.
The shamed
and ravaged mother
tries to save her child
from her own wrath...
She lunges
to smother him
and yet refrains...
But each lunge
brings her closer to revenge...
the decimation
of her favorite child...
A lethal blow...
The Apocalypse!

Antara Banerjee is an award-winning author of the books, 'The Goddess in Flesh' and 'To be a Woman'. She is also a trilingual poet with the book, 'Pieces of a Tormented Mind' to her credit. Masters from Goldsmiths College, London and graduate from Presidency College, she is the recipient of Sanmarg Aparajita Award 2019, Young Achiever- Literature and Udaan Empowering Women Awards 2017, for her contribution in Women Centric Literature.

Antara Joshi
Changing Days...

Gone are the days when some of them would lock us up into darkness,
And treat us like the cattle stock by torturing us into silence.
Gone are the days when testosterone-fueled wars would spill so much blood,
While the dressed-up dolls would stay back home only to feed, nourish and love.
Gone are the days when precious girls would get gifted off to strangers,
And thank goodness gone are the days when living flesh was burnt on pyres.
But we also moved past the times when our opinion was a sin,
For we are not those dolls anymore who live just for their kin.
Our whispers found a voice,
Our open eyes so adamant,
The goddess within each of us is no longer so dormant.
We fought our way through thick and thin, to establish our individuality,
And make anyone ignorant, realise that feminism is about equality.
Times changed drastically and so did our men,
To our stories they gave an ear and showed that they too care.
Our choices, our genders and identities glistened,
Sexual and marital opinions were no more forbidden.
We set the chains in motion for even better days to come,
So our daughters from the future will be treated as equals on Mother Earth.

Antara Joshi is a 16-year-old writer, poet, and illustrator from Thane, India. She has an interest in languages and art. She is currently studying Arts in Jai Hind College, Mumbai. Antara's first illustrations were published in the book 'Yellow Butterflies: Tales of Love and Letting Go' by Dr Asha Deshmukh. Instagram ID: dontcallme_antara_ Art page ID: @strokesnstuff

The Face of Modern Kali

Antara Joshi

Anu Mahadev
Eight days till the new moon

1. She bites into a cheeseburger without realizing there's beef in it.
Will it be the cane or the boot, this time, she palpitates?

2. She agrees to anything he says. She'll change for him.
Gets her atoms ready in the reactor.

3. "So what is the big deal if you forget to shave your legs? Surely
the stubble won't hurt as much in bed?" She can't tell her friend
everything is always a big deal.

4. Her eyebrows are dense forests, mixed with blood. He wants her
to wax them. They hide her acne. Which he hates too.

5. Who invented this torture device, the cellphone? The Greyhound
takes four hours - Houston to Austin. He calls her an asshole for
four hours.
She cannot hang up. The bus has to keep moving.

6. Car dealerships are stressful for her. Car lingo, sales jargon, he
helps her negotiate. Hands the keys. In the car - he rams her head
against the steering wheel, till a satisfied grunt escapes his lips.
And then he looks for the GPS.

7. Winter months. She hovers near the fridge. Soup or candy bar?
A post-it is stuck to the handle. His neat writing - her weight on it.
She steps back, stumbles against the weighing scale by mistake.
Flees the kitchen.

8. He wants to get married. With a noose instead of a *mangalsutra*.
She stays up, writing pros and cons, like balancing an accounts
ledger

Rag dolls

Some girls   in a land of billions
lie in fields, lone, dark   with gashes instead of smiles,

stripped of tongues   mute, a garble of screams
silent.   These girls   with no important names,

news items for a day   fodder for talk shows,
protest marches will never know why.

They cannot change   their low caste origin,
       in a nation obsessed   with patriarchy, religion.

Labeled as sluts   since birth,   they are mere
sex toys   forced into   the vices of pedigree,

of bestiality.   There is substance in   the nine   rasas
     in dance   *bhayanaka*(fear), *bibhatsa*(disgust).   But true

class shows   in lust, greed, power. Who are these women   –
only nubile   virgins ripe for the picking,   never knowing

their past karma?   Why else would they be easy targets
to plunder,   their gouged eyes   no longer limpid pools

to cry in?   How can their bodies turn   against themselves
become enemies   to their own innocence, how

can they come marked   with a destiny to be violated
beyond recognition?   Questions.   Too many to answer.

We die a little with each roadkill carcass   we see,
but since when are we immune to a human

corpse, burned in contempt   hungry fires licking,
wiping away   their wounds, a final offering of bones and blood?

Sonagachi

her words – whatever erodes me/deposits this sediment, this
*   mixed identity,*
*   I stand before you, a jasmine in a field of violets.*

Her body — citadel, guards her cavernous womb — someone
forgets to shut the door. swirl, the wind's whiplash rushes in.

Night is a fortress; its jaded ramparts fail to keep intruders out.
This castle, built with a portcullis to a drawbridge, leads to her ruin.

Another like her, waits, in the moat of her amniotic fluid.
A woman-child, her trapped identity belonging to her vagina's
        highest bidder.

Her birth in the flesh market, in a makeshift room of stained
        sheets,
lust-cloaked air thick with mosquitoes and moisture, brings no joy.

No game of coquette here, no foreplay, only tears long dried,
buried under garish makeup, so many bills to pay.

She throws away the condom, refuses HIV testing, outranks the
        others' sales.

Another day, another batch of underage girls, trafficked into bonds
of slavery.

She envies their youth, wonders which one is from her native place,
        fingers a cheap ring, the only
link to her mother's betrayal.

No DNA test, no father figure, nothing to promise, nothing to
        forgive,
she wraps herself around her knees, conjures warrior names for the
        unborn,
Durga, Arjun.

her thoughts —born to sin, guilty without trial, burned
meteors under half the crimson sky.

Anu Mahadev is a left-brained engineer who morphed into a right-brained poet. She is a 2016 MFA graduate of Drew University, and her work has appeared in several journals and anthologies. She serves as Editor for Jaggery Lit, the Woman Inc., and the Wild Word. Her collection of poetry titled "A Mouthful of Sky" is upcoming from Get Fresh Books LLC.
She can be found on Facebook at http://facebook.com/amahadevpoet

Anuradha Vijayakrishnan
Saraswathi

Saraswathi lies open-mouthed and bleached
amongst condoms, bottles, needles, take away
boxes, rotting worm food. She is no goddess of words; her dead
words have leached, tongue bled blue and carmine
when she must have

screamed and screamed. They say she has other
names given by worshippers, all of them lost when
her skull caved in. Her hair is matted like her sister's,
the angry one. Saraswathi is gentle, kind to seekers.
She must have hoped for kindness too.

Where we found her, we found offerings of broken
bones, shredded skin, torn nails. As if animals
gathered to comfort her small feet, feed her
back into life. As if scavengers and predators knew
who she was and what had been done
to her.

What we found of her is enough
for a new myth.

Afterwards

They gathered me in cotton folds of hands, wiped me
clean of remembrance and blood, placed me against
the softest skin I would ever touch.
They called me by name and I wailed.
They wrapped me tight enough to breathe, kick
and scream till I slept, unborn.

Afterwards,
they led me to a wooden bench, clean white sheets for body's
shame, gauze pads for my wounds. I received gifts: soap and water,
hard scrubs, skin salves, towels, and plenty
of words. They took me into glitter of darkness, white
coated brightness where scalpels picked out
everything committed inside, needles
stitched me into shape till I
rose and walked, a story re-told.

Afterwards,
they framed me in polished teak, twelve by twelve.
They lit incense and strung me into memory
beads, kept some of my bones to be divided
among generations. Wore white, planted
a mourning tree where I was buried. Now my shadow dances
over their roof, my leaves spread into light. I will grow
so tall their arms will fall short.

Anuradha Vijayakrishnan I am an Indian writer and retail banking professional living in Dubai. My work has appeared in Asia Literary Review, Kenyon Review, Indian Literature, Eclectica, Guftugu, and Magma. My debut collection of poetry, The Who-am-I-bird came out in 2018.

Anushna Biswas
Ode To Clits

It relates to female sexual organ
A crimson, plume, tempting to patriarch
It menstruates per calendar
Since it is a part of me,
Ashamed I am not of its potential to procreate
It's my own self and natural identity.

You, you and you, the crude patriarchs
You are greedily tempted to claw it
Thinking you can corrupt me by muscular penetration
Thou art cowards, hypocrites
When act is over, crime done
And you tremble in fear
Then you worship the power of Kali and Durga
And visit Kamakkha temple to seek salvation
But there is none but hell
Yet you are the same men,
Who ravish women for lusts,
And stomp places with heads high!
Me not afraid of such sharks
Though loud they hark
To wipe out sins and wounds
Yet they can't hop out of its bounds!!!

Dr. Anushna Biswas Ph.D. In English, The University of Calcutta. Literary critic, Poet, Writer of several books of criticism, Contributed to literary and film anthologies, Contributing Literary Critic, The Indian Express Newspaper. Former Lecturer of Department of English, Distance Education, Rabindra Bharati University. (Tagore University), Calcutta, India.

Arathy Asok
A Poem for My Sister

When the railroads swept wind and dust,
my sister,
from the faraway country of snow and single rooms of struggle,
you ask me to write.

You say - write, write for me sister,
write for me something that will hold my hand,
the sun ahead is heat and the potatoes wait to peel.

You say write for me like Maya Angelou and I laugh;
I say you read Maya Angelou to read Maya Angelou,
I write like me.

But she says-like her sister, like her.

And after the dead night when I wake in the morning,
I know what you say, I see your eyes and I know their light.

They tell me of the rooms we have lived, the men we have loved, the
bodies we have carried inside our bodies
and I know suddenly what you tell me.

We have walked the roads they said we cannot walk.
It was not love that made us love.
It was need.
It was all the world that told us we were women not fit to look into
their eyes,
women who could not think or stand up in the middle of a room
with men, speaking about how to bury dead uncles.

They said only men could talk. Only men had voices.

We had small lives. Some called our breaths, school girl revolutions.

They called our mothers, sluts. They said our mothers destroyed us
by telling us to love ourselves, by telling us of the sky, the rivers and
the brown earth.
When we wanted to see the sky, they said we juggled our breasts to
show the men.

The men were around, everywhere.
We had to hide ourselves in downcast eyes, and dresses that
covered our brown arms and legs like water.
When we smiled to see an eye lifted to look at us,
we were crushed, crushed, crushed.

When there were leftovers on the table or father needed a glass of
water, they sat on cushioned chairs and let out a hand,
they read newspapers, walked on the roads and laughed aloud
in the open verandah.

What was left of us was a battered heart torn at the edges, that did
not know how to be happy anymore.

But we, my sister, we walked the nights in waters they did not see,
under our arms were daggers of steel.

Inside us we carry the bamboo winds of yellow light.

There is no poem I write to you.
I cannot write.

I only see you, walking in the snow,
alone, erect, a dot of red;
I only see me- walking this heat,
alone, erect, a dot of red.

(The poems were published in womawords literary press.
Link : https://womawordsliterarypress.home.blog/2019/07/30/arathy-asok-is-keralas-voice-of-reason/)

Arathy Asok is a bilingual writer, poet, and translator whose debut poetry collection Lady Jesus and Other Poems is described by the Journal of Commonwealth Literature as "Resistance poetry with a sharp edge" (2019, Vol. 54 4). Her most recent work is the translation work titled The Lost Heroine (Speaking Tiger Press, 2020). Recently a short story was included in the anthology One Surviving Story (icoe press, Australia).

Dr. Archana Bahadur Zutshi
The Unease of Light

A witch is deigned potent,
To be dismantled into impotence.
To make her crumble
 like a pack of cards,
From the pedestal.
 Shoved from sunlight
To the darkest hours
by desperate redeemer.
Hunted by packs,
 scaffolded they lie
In contrived pacts.
Witch old or modern
Is the Cinderella of daylight
Innocence.
Martyred for her prowess
For distancing herself from the gore.
They gore her for their guilt!
A girl is either a witch or goddess
Someone whose will and identity
Flickers in the dark unravelling
Of brute gospels created and fathomed
In make-belief.

The wind is mistaken
for the windmill.
The tale cannot be related
Without her part.
The daughter, disowned at birth.
An unseeming inheritor!
She must prove herself—
The 'instead'!
 As a misfit, or vice-versa —

Whose reckoning?
A mob is a freaking mob.
A witch is a witch...

Dr Archana Bahadur Zutshi did her Ph.D in English Poetry. She has two volumes of published poetry, 'Poetic Candour' and 'The Speaking Muse'. Her poetry was featured by 'Culturium' (March 18, 2019) on the occasion of Women's Day and Poetry Day. Her book 'Poetic Candour' features in their collection. A poetry judge and critic, her poems are published in many anthologies. She translated poems of Nirala for an International Journal. She published her poems in United by Ink, Spillwords, Confluence, Setu, The Bilingual Journal, The Madras Courier, MirrorSpeak, Duotrope Poetry Blog etc.

Arti Jain
A home for her children

She sheds her clothes slowly, methodically:
salwar, kameez and finally dupatta,
folds them neatly and puts them
on top of her black handbag.
Her pink bra,
she unclasps with care.
She's in no hurry.
They'll wait.

Lipstick red.
Two anklets twinkle.
Three rings on toes are silver.
Sindoor vermillion lies in the middle
parting her almost all black hair.
Hoops of gold dangle from drooping earlobes.
The pin in her nose sparkles a little
as she moves to face the others in the room
in her resplendent nakedness.

On the sofa, she sits
like Ma Saraswati.
One leg on the floor,
the other folded over
in a figure of four.
Her arms akimbo--
She's ready.

There she resides
in studio lights:
deep shadows create valleys where her anklets jingle
and settle in smudges in between hollows
of throat and blades of shoulders.

All of a sudden,
a beautiful woman.
No shame. No fear.
She looks up.

They start then
to capture her essence.
Pencils, charcoals, pens,
pauses, doubts, decisions fly
as time passes by.
She shifts, *please stay still,*
they tell her.

It's like sitting in meditation, she says afterward.
My legs go numb
and eyelids droop
but I love my job.
It wasn't always like this, you know.
I sat with all my clothes on
at first.

The session ends.
She goes over
to see
how they see her.
Each portrait is different,
every perspective differs.
Every stroke
an expression
of art copying life
in dots and lines.

I don't shy away from telling them
what works
what doesn't.
She says.
I know my body
better than anyone else can.

She smiles and carries on:
Why? Family and friends had asked me at first.
Why not? I said and told them:
this body will be earth when I die.
At least I can fulfill my dream this way
and build a house for my children someday.
My husband, he bought me an umbrella, you know
after my first day at work.
He gave it to me and simply said:
"This is for you,
so, you can be safe in the rains of Mumbai."

Arti Jain is a writer, poet, blogger, and photographer who lives in Doha, Qatar. Her idea of heaven includes chai, trees, trekking, and large doses of Sufi poetry. Maya Angelou's words, "There is no greater agony than bearing an untold story inside you." inspire her to write. Her work has appeared in Kindle India Magazine as well as in an anthology. Her blog is: artismoments.blogspot.com and her Instagram handle: @arti.a.jain

Arya
The Hoarfrost Splinters.

I had stepped out of the psychiatric hospital about 6 months ago.
Joyous and determined I was, on the way back home.
Albeit, after reaching home, very soon,
I began to witness prodding allusions and innuendos.
My language comprehension abilities augment,
there was continual whetting of distinct semantic sickles,
say sardonic humor and scathing remarks.
Here's what I wrote in my poetry journal, last night.

The Hoarfrost Splinters.

Conniving translucent Russet beads
mizzling steadily since a few months.
Are those euphemisms dripping
from the smothered sky?
Who craves to swoon interlaced
 in Amethyst and Amber.
However, now seems stranded
with stumbling-sapphire clouds
calming its shivers.
Today has again begun with shafts
from the lamenting Sun.
Coaxing me to thicken my tender heart walls.
They opine, I need to varnish those walls with
lacquer, scrounged from the depleting marrows in my bones.
For the patio that I am walking on
are bursting with deceitful gravels.
For the home-cooked morsels that I yearned to relish,
have become graphite lumps that strangle my gullet.
For my mother's arms, those relentless cuddles that would pacify,
are now the evasive crescent Moon-wings.
For even the tattered faith-quilts that try to nudge,
are ethers bobbing with hoarfrost splinters that devour.

Caveat.

He is the husband.
He walks up to her unfazed,
flings her as if a crumpled paper ball
is being thrown into a trash bin.
Unruffled is that wall,
which certainly has felt her skin and skull,
a few times already,
within the first week of the current month.
Every aspect of that home is complacent,
to her husband's routine.
The furniture, the window sills, the curtains, even the mother- in-
law...

In accordance, is the wife's undeterred obedience.
Her parents had married her off,
saying henceforth she is the husband's pride,
the torchbearer of Indian culture in his home.
She has been compliant till date to that caveat.
Her consciousness ironed each day, under that entrenched belief.
Dare it ever form any crease of rebellion!

Does anything ever simmer in that home?
Other than spicy lentils and husband's fists.
Hark! There's a call for the wife, from the kitchen.
The tea has spilled over the gas stove.

Memsaab.

Since her marriage,
Memsaab has been adorned in elan.
Of Ivory-radiance emanating sarees...
Of chokers gleaming with Emeralds and Opals...
Of porcelain etiquette and coy walks...

The whole town resonated in a calibrated tenor,
about her new-found panache persona.

However, her bedroom knows an array of truth...
Stark-naked truth of family legacy,
cloaked in burnished culture-poise, through the day.
Vehement truth of battered thighs,
stifled more beneath husband's lust- inflated lunges.
Plain truth of his, about to be interred conscience,
that he splays before her, nonchalantly.
While the vintage bedside lamp flickers, damask tapestries swing,
as if they are being tranquilized by the ghoul stillness nibbling that
room.

*Memsaab: In this context, Memsaab is a title for a woman who is the
wife of a Sahib-a man in a position of authority.*

*Jyoti Nair is quintessentially a learning and development professional,
she cherishes solitary mode of writing. Numerous articles and poems
penned by her, have been published in leading Indian tabloids, and
digital news media. She has won several accolades for her literary
pursuits, of-late the 'Sahitya Academy Award' for her contributions to the
literary world. She believes in incessantly whetting her writing skills,
traversing learning bends each day. Way forward, she aims to harness
the power of her pen, championing for inflammable social challenges
such as child abuse, mental health awareness, and women-centric issues.*

Dr Arya Gopi

Dr Arya Gopi is a bi-lingual poet who works in English and Malayalam with half a dozen published books including four Malayalam poetry collections. Her first English title Sob of Strings was published in 2011. A contributor to major journals, she has won several awards which includes the Kerala Sahitya Akademi Kanakasree Award. A Ph.D. holder in English literature, she teaches literature at Calicut University. https://en.wikipedia.org/wiki/Arya_Gopi

Avani Konduri
Outside

I Sweat, Sometimes
through the linen threads of the maroon mask,
the elastic stretched over my ears, breathing loudly and deeply
through the crevices of its threads.

I Suffocate, Sometimes
under the tyranny of the warm cloth, inhibited by the way it moves
in and out of my mouth as I try to speak,
stumbling along the uneven pavement, re-familiarizing myself with
a world I had long forgotten

I Am Scared, Sometimes
that as I stumble into the 'new world', I am forced to once again
remember what it feels like to have to be conscious of every part of
my body,
to walk on the streets in clothes that fit my body all too well,
unwanted eyes wandering over the way my jeans stretch across my
legs

I Feel Liberated, Sometimes
and under the sweat, grime, and acne that fester under the recesses
of this 'burden',
I walk with a spring in my step, somehow finding my freedom in the
fact that at least my face is still my own

I Am Sorry
that the very mask that hides, also makes me feel seen,
for it has taken me 25 years to feel at home with myself and I don't
want to feel like a stranger in my own body anymore

Avani Konduri is a Creative Learning and Organisational Development Consultant who has a great passion for mental health advocacy, psychology, mythology, and scented erasers. She lives in Bangalore with her family. https://www.linkedin.com/in/avani-konduri-42582https://www.linkedin.com/in/avani-konduri-42582516516

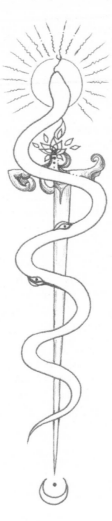

B. Geetha

Scribbles of a Madwoman

I am not well.
When you ask me, "How are you?"
I say, "I am fine."
"I am ready to take on the world."
But inside my shoe,
my blisters are rubbing against the sole.
As I boil the milk on the stove every morning,
the skin that forms on its surface reminds me of my wrinkled
fingers.
I draw a galaxy with my ladle keenly crafting a dosa,
where every milky pore is a glowing star.
If only somebody could acknowledge this creative act,
if only somebody could recognize
that our universe also lies in the kitchen
bound by gas, dust, and dark matter.

All my clocks have stopped functioning,
as I use the needles of time to sew my wounds gradually,
but the tiring monotony and endless repetition of my existence
have coiled me into running circular motions.
Cracking walnuts under my jaw, I swallow a lump every day
as he butchers my creativity.
The warmth in our relationship evaporating into thin air,
while the cold food lies on the table, stony and lifeless.
Do you know the difference between his favourite curry and my
          wounds?
He would never let the curry burn.

Every morning, I brush off his brittle hair and brittle ego under the
          carpet,
but the particles always get into my eyes.
I allow my tears to wash it out,
I do not rub my eyes hard enough,

as friction leads to painful scars.
As I look into his clear eyes,
I see a papier mâché female Frankenstein with pagan proportions,
conjoined in patches with paper and glue, not flesh and blood,
burnt body and watery eyes, dying and dead.
As I feverishly scoop out his prying gaze from my face,
I can sense his condescending curiosity,
the desire to pin me down in his semantic vocabulary
as a creation gone wrong, as an experiment gone awry,
as a woman gone hysterical.
As I run out of the room,
I realize the spider in the kitchen eavesdropping my muted
      mutterings.
It knows how the walls of the house and wrongs of the spouse are
      deceptively whitewashed
so that the hidden scratches and missing patches are smoothened
      without a trace.

They try to 'manage' my melancholic madness with tonic doses.
They think I speak to my own head and crawl into the corners of
      the bed,
Ah! The serotonin-induced happiness, a trap of orchestrated
      normalcy,
when there is none!
They control my mental mayhem
by pricking uncomfortable pins and needles all over my body,
but I try to bury them every time I nail a joke,
"What do you call a woman with a freewheeling spirit?"
"Names."
Here's another one,
"It is a joke about patriarchy, don't bother, you won't get it."
He says, "You are a kid stuck inside an adult's body."
That is why I could never under the difference between chivalry
      and chauvinism,
struggling with the spelling, trapped under his spell.
That is why when the conjugal rituals resonated,
"Put the ring on her left finger,"
I wondered if I had any right?

As I lie down on the bed in a pool of my own blood,
with every sneeze, I feel my uterus exacting revenge on me,
the clitoral tissues shrinking to the size of a dried raisin,
I experience a body in process, a body raging,
and I scream inside,
why do parents raise their sons and daughters in an unequal
fashion?
where a girl is raised to follow the rules, and a boy to create them,
where a woman is silenced because a man is 'speaking',
her speech a senseless babble, his voice the meaningful articulation
        of the pedagogue.
His ideas echoed philosophical incandescence,
and her thoughts were dismissed as dangerous scribbles of mind.
In (His)tory, she had hysteria,
and in (her)story, well, is the narrative even important?
I could not let the last words dissolve on my tongue.
Therefore, I write.
The handwriting scratches my pandemonium into a poem,
and the poem makes this imaginary pronoun a person.

B. Geetha is a Ph.D. candidate in the Department of Humanities and Social Sciences, IIT Bombay. She has completed her graduate and postgraduate studies in English Literature. She is a university gold medalist for her highest academic standing in M.A. English. She is also the winner of the Delhi Poetry Festival 2015. She has also been a part of the theatre group 'Expressions' in Jamia Millia Islamia and performed at various platforms like the National School of Drama and The Shakespeare Society of India. Currently, she is a part of the Fourth Wall, the dramatics society of IIT- Bombay.

Babitha Marina Justin
Wildflower Vulva

The men in khaki asked:
'Why now, why not then?'
The girl groaned
like furrowed earth,
her tears ploughed
through her ravines;

they wanted more.
'Describe his touch,'
they slurped.
'Did he elbow, finger, or palm you?'
'Did he err.... enter you?'
'Did he let you sleep?'
'Did he lift your sheet or skirt?'
'Did he err.... try to touch you there?'
(Did you enjoy his touch?
Why were you silent?)

'The process is long and
tedious madam.'
The doctor scribbled
a 15-page report,
her pen darkening
under her eyes.
Behind a screen
she checked her skin
for purple stains, prodding
her vagina, she sighed.
'Every woman is flower,
wild and vulnerable.'

She gave her
a file full vaginas drawn
in stealthy lines,
angular, frontal, and linear.
I looked away, the girl melted
like rancid ghee, her body
mapped as the vulvas
drawn from different ways.

She bowed her head,
plunged down the steps
of her esteem
she dragged deep down the
world wilted and wan:
like a wild-flower vulva.

Babitha Marina Justin is a writer, an artist and Associate Professor in English from Kerala, India. A Pushcart Prize nominee, 2018, her poems and short stories have appeared in international journals and anthologies by Penguin, Eclectica, Esthetic Apostle, The Paragon Press, Fulcrum, The Scriblerus, Trampset, Constellations, etc. She has published five books, including two collections of poems, Of Fireflies, Guns and the Hills (2015) and I Cook my Own Feast (2019).
Website: www.babithamarina.com.

Baisali Chatterjee Dutt
Deliverance

I understand your anger, Kali.

Tongue pouring blood
naked breasts roaring
hair wild with screams
and eyes the trifecta of fury —
earthquake
avalanche
tsunami.

I understand your anger.

For it crackles
like funeral pyres
burning in the bonfire of my blood;
it pours out of my multiple wounds
like acid;
it explodes in my head
like a snuff film.

Kali, I understand.

A young girl died today.
Yes. Another one.
A young girl
had her body
her tongue
and ultimately her life
ripped apart,
carved sliced pounded beaten slashed —
stolen.
Another one of the broken many.

But this is the part that I don't understand —

why this happened again
why this is happening still
why this could happen at all
why
and why
and why
and why
and why why why???

Why?

How could this happen on your watch, Kali?

Where were you
with your bloodied scythes
and beheaded demons,
your black hole mouth
ready to swallow all evil
into a never-ending abyss?

Too many places to be at once, Kali?
Another reason for your anger?

The demons are all around.
Wrapped in patriarchy.
Their names and penile appendages
their bulletproof vests.

Tell me, Kali,
is it time for us
to strip down
arm ourselves with rusted swords
smear ourselves with blood
and go crashing down the streets
in one collective rage?

Is it time for us
to deliver our own selves
from evil?

Is it time for us
to be You?

Rain Hailstones, Fire and Brimstone

This was supposed to be about
a girl;
her young body pulverised
like butchers meat
and barbecued
in a bizarre live show —
street theatre,
with the reviews
playing out in the papers
the next day.

This was supposed to be about
a young vet;
waylaid,
laid,
lit,
left behind.

This was supposed to be about
the nameless ones,
the faceless ones,
the missing ones,
the unreported ones.

This was supposed to be about
our rage;
the forest fires inside us,
the thick black clouds of smoke
billowing from us,
the earthquake trembling of us...

Instead

this about our shoulders
broken by the weight of the hate
that you carry in your bones;

this is about the ennui
that has set in
as we read
with expressionless eyes — yet again —
about another one of our tribe
done away with
in manners
medieval
and macabre;

this is about the dried up prayers
and tear ducts,
the impotent curses,
the meaningless curse words,
the unscreamed screams;

this is,
most of all,
like all things in this world,
about you.

Your hate.
Your hate.
Your hate.
Your hate

hate
hate
hate
hate
hate
hate
hate
hate.

And we're too tired
to ask 'Why?'
– again –
because it just doesn't fucking matter anymore.

Our bottomless bag of forgiveness
is finally empty.

Baisali Chatterjee Dutt, is a former columnist and agony aunt for 'Mother & Baby', one of India's leading parenting magazines. She has also compiled and edited two volumes of 'Chicken Soup for the Indian Soul' series, namely the ones "On Friendship" and "Brothers and Sisters". She has written "Sharbari Datta: The Design Diva", a biography on one of Cacutta's leading luminaries in the fashion world, published by Niyogi Books. Her poetry has been published in various anthologies and magazines, "Veils, Shackles and Halos", "For Rhinoceros in a Shrinking World", "Algebra of Owls", "Femina", "The Asian Age", "Panopoly", "Drabble" and Sahitya Akademi's "Modern English Poetry by Younger Indians". Currently she is the Spoken English and Drama teacher at Sri Sri Academy, Kolkata. Instagram @bchattdutt and @boioscope.

Barnali Ray Shukla
Anagram in Red

Running fingers through memories
eyelids heavy with yesterday

The wrap of the wall
against her bare shoulders
reminds, solitary
is a state of being

Togetherness a mirage,
it craves assurance
leaving nothing but a cloud
wafting over promises, fragile
like mornings that don't meet sunrise

Her gaze, today undone,
a storm which lost its way
in her mind's eye

She walks away naked, from
mortar and brick

She walks away from heirloom,
keys and *khandaan*

She walks towards the magic
of her wedding trousseau

A red Banarasi
woven with gold
worn one evening
to be unworn the next
tucked in folds of yesterday
She breaches
her arrest in white,
steps into red silk and gold
a pyre rages somewhere

She was no Sati or
Sita-in-the-making
she finds her voice today
Untie and **unite**
are but anagrams
It's where 'I' chose to be...

(Originally published in Apostrophe, RLFPA edition.)

Blue Sunrise

*Legend of Ahalya's beauty and unattainability challenged the divine and
evil alike. She was a loyal wife. Tricksters that some lords are, Indra with
the moon as his accomplice made a plan. He descended from the heavens,
let himself in her home, in the form of her husband, while her 'real'
husband was away.*

He leaves home before a blue sunrise
She drapes the indigo of a blue sunrise

Leaves rustle, wanton winds whisper
wayward heartbeats at a blue sunrise

Stealth of footsteps pause, swollen
dark clouds don't let in a blue sunrise

Moonlight combs jasmine darkness
One metamorphosis dares a blue sunrise

A halo flickers, douses light, smoky kohl
Untethered tresses over a blue sunrise

Audacity of thought probes her walls
She can't contain an inevitable blue sunrise

Disrobed desires devour myths of marriage
Breaking at the seams on one blue sunrise

Treachery of feelings now a burden of choice
Or was it chance that coloured a blue sunrise

Aftermath of fury, compelling a curse
Scorches the gift of that blue sunrise

The dew now gone dry at the fault lines
But regrets don't cave in her blue sunrise

Hardened by opinion, frozen in time
Ahalya is a rock through many a blue sunrise

She craves no deliverance, no pity
Her mind a mystery on that blue sunrise

Assertion was certain but was there violence
Insolence or pure defiance on that blue sunrise

Questions can't touch her silence,
no one but her knows the truth of her blue sunrise.

(Originally published in Apostrophe, RLFPA edition.)

Barnali Ray Shukla is an Indian writer, filmmaker, and poet. She has featured in anthologies in India, the USA, Hong Kong, Singapore, Australia, and the UK. Her maiden poetry collection is called Apostrophe (RLFPA 2016). In her cine life, Barnali has written and directed one full-length feature, two documentaries, two short films. She lives in Mumbai with her plants, books, and a husband.

Basudhara Roy
Rules for a Rape Republic

"Burning of women in India, most vividly of rape victims, is neither unprecedented nor inexplicable, and is an extension of the sociocultural habit of gender invisibilizing."
—*Kota Neelima & Tarangini Sriraman, Gender Invisibility and Women-burning; The New Indian Express, 26th January 2020*

When they come for you
know there is no way out and
that they will stop at nothing short
of digging in you a tunnel to
fathom their own murky darkness.

Don't scream. The chances are
that to a sadist's spine every scream
is wine. Blindfold yourself, open wide,
play dead. Jump up the moment
it's done. Gather your stuff. Leave.

Cease to think of your body as
copyrighted flesh. Understand it as
ground designed for plunder. Look at it
as a table where questions of caste, class,
language, religion, even education

must be decisively settled through
excavation. It isn't about desire, clothes,
confidence, recklessness, lack of wisdom,
or even about lust for that matter. It's
simply about habit, their need to assert.

Ignore the intrusion as one ignores
flies. Don't talk to the papers. Walk,
keep walking towards the sun. Remember
honour doesn't blossom between thighs; it
cannot be nurtured or plucked overnight.

Breathe deep, thaw. Rejoice there are no
limbs severed; no acid on your face, no
iron thrust anywhere deep. Rejoice you live.
If, however, they've already set you on fire,
that part's going to be a trifle problematic.

The ruins won't speak, you see. It will be
difficult to conjure from ashes the story of
gags, rips, mauls, thrusts; to discover trails
of blood-semen branded on thighs. On the
brighter side, your clothes will retain dignity

in death. Burnt to cinder, they will be free from
scrutiny of form, length, texture, colour; will spare
your character of assault. Your invasion coffined
in you, you will live forever chaste in memories.
Yet, after every cremation will haunt a disquiet.

The Right Kind of Woman

The right kind of woman will
inspire affection, regard, trust.
Not promiscuity, never lust.

Bred by a mother equally right
she knows to avert her eyes to
innuendoes, meaningful smiles.

In crowded buses, shops, streets,
she knows, bud-like, to shut tight,
relinquish space, circumscribe limbs.

Above all, she knows the prudence
of holding her tongue, of choosing
silence's worth over wordy rebellion.

Schooled to surrender in unprepared
rooms in the dark, she knows, unasked,
to feign desire, moan, stifle, sigh on cue.

Once on her undramatic forehead, she
had a third eye to emit fire, take sides,
rake storms. Last night, its lid rusted

with disuse, fell out and the right kind
of woman laughed herself to death,
for all that she had left undone, unsaid.

Off/Duty

We trade in aches,
in missed words,
misplaced affections,
squandered moments.

We spill mirth sometimes
when our cups are generously filled,
only to rue, to rush, to mop
and regret what we dropped, lost.

Inducted into waiting,
we know to wait for rice,
milk, tea leaves to come to boil;
for husbands and children to return;
for henna, papad to dry in the sun.
We wait for seasons to pass,
for children to be born,
and when they are grown and gone,

for reasons to bring their mothballed
childhood out of boxes and albums.
We lie awake at nights with bated breath
listening to the footfalls of death

benedictively passing us by, as
mothers-in-law lie sick, answering
voices of their own, as eclipses
threaten the awaited unborn.

We wait for dawns to break,
for fog to lift, for our elderly
to part chapped lips and place
morsels on drug-numbed tongues,

excavating buried memories
of flavours, touch, promises, song.
We anoint petals with turmeric,
vermillion, coconut water;

pray for domestic prosperity,
for blue skies, stocked granaries,
loyal husbands, faithful progeny,
and a pinch of peace.

We will leave all this behind
someday, break free of tradition,
of want, of love, sprout third eyes
like danger on foreheads,

untie unwashed hair and step out,
rejoicing in the musk of our sweat,
in the lust of our breath, knowing
no conches can ever call us back.

Basudhara Roy teaches English at Karim City College, Jamshedpur, India. Her areas of interest are postmodern criticism, gender studies, and diaspora women's writing. She is the author of two books, Migrations of Hope (New Delhi: Atlantic Publishers, 2019) and a collection of poems, Moon in my Teacup (Kolkata: Writer's Workshop, 2019). Her second poetry collection, Stitching a Home, is forthcoming in 2021.

Bijoyini Das

Kubuja*

Hasn't the *Konark* of my words
Ever rippled the calm waters of someone's mind?
Not filled it with a magical feeling,
Or magnificent utterance
Full of surprise and excitement?

Hasn't the splendor of my thought
Planted a sapling in some soil
Fertile with an affectionate heart?
Hasn't the infant of my sympathy
Placed her feet
On the arid sands of unrelieved sorrow?

I always forget the mathematics
Of loss and gain
A foolish pupil in the village school,
Though I bleed
At the cane strokes of the teacher,
Still I fail to grasp the arithmetic of worldliness.

I have never been miserly
About sharing the treasure of my experience
With the prince as well as with the pauper.
I have painted pictures
Of the world's sorrow, misery, love, and betrayal
Like the golden footsteps of the *Goddess Lakshmi*
On the mud walls of my mind, wiped clean.

Still, the world hasn't understood me
Like a worm-eaten book, unread
I still lie in some corner of the house;
Or else, I am an oyster
A pearl within its womb

Lying on a desolate seashore
Measuring the distance from sunrise to sunset
The distance from the cradle to the burning ghat
The distance from the temple of faith
To the grave of treachery.

The fresh flower garland withers in the evening,
The morning's pestled sandalwood paste dries up in the evening,
Still, I go on stringing garlands and pestling sandalwood
Every morning,
The anticipation of someone's coming
Goes on cooing like the pigeons
In the temple courtyards of my mind.

I feel as if there's someone all my own
In some corners of the earth.
He will come one day.
Will take away my burdens, free me
From the dark shadows of my nightmares
The agony of sleepless nights
The pale corpses of my hopes
And the corpse of brooding moments.

He will touch my motionless hands
With the warmth of countless promises.
Bent beneath the weight of
Misery, sorrow, sin
My personality will stand up straight with pride
Garland the sun
And decorate the moon with sandal-paste
Will seek her own identity.
Surely there is someone
Who is mine and mine alone!

(*Kubuja – The hunchbacked woman who turned into a beauty at Lord
Krishna's touch.)

(Translation from the Odia poem "Kubuja" by Dr. J.P. Das, Sulekha
Samantaray, and Arlene Zide. The English translation has been
published in "Under a silent Sun" —an anthology of Odia women poets.)

Bijoyini Das is a popular and respected Odia* novelist, poetess and short story writer. She has over 30 published books to her credit, not counting the numerous short stories, articles and poems which get regularly published in the State's leading magazines and newspapers. She is the recipient of numerous awards including the prestigious Sahitya Akademi award in 1991 for her novel "Debdasi". She is a social activist and advocate of women's rights in the State.

Bina Sarkar Ellias

The Book of Life

for Gauri Lankesh, Malleshappa Kalburgi, Govind Pansare and Narendra Dhabolkar

one bullet?
two, three, four bullets?
they claimed her
one or four.
they claimed her
with hate.
shot her into
a forever eclipse.
her bloodstains
the conscience
of they who seek justice
her blood flows into
the stilled veins
of brave-hearts
who, like her
had reason... to reason.
they are all gone
and there will be more...
the river of blood
will flow forever
and the demons will sail
flying their flag of venom
fuelled by chauvinism
of race, religion,
power, territorial jingoism.
this is our history
and the educated
do not learn.
and THEY know that
the book of life
has many pages...
that you turn a page
and move on.

there will be
more dissenters to kill
more pages to turn
while the book of life
sits on our shelf
like a phantom
as voices are erased
one voice at a time.
one bullet?
two, three, four bullets?
Do you hear a satanic laugh?

#MeToo

It crackled
in the dark of night~
a sonic spear
that struck open
her voice locked
in the stealth
of time.

it crackled
in the still of night~
this voice
that rose from
the grave of her guts
that swam through
her anxious veins
bathed in blood
and pain that stained
the ocean
of time.

it crackled
in the womb of night~
this voice

that rose from
the grime
of her shattered mind
and claimed its space
in the ruptures
of time.

The House She Never Visits
—for women in Kashmir

the house
she never visits
is in her heart.
locked through
thirty years
when they came
to claim the land
that once was
jannat... paradise.
they came
and colonised
with the arrogance
of guns
built barracks of fear
erased the sun
nailed the youth
invaded bodies;
bodies of girls
and women whose
fragile lives
are since locked
in that sunless house
within their hearts.

her eyes are dry
her tears are ice
the house
she never visits

is within her heart
a tomb
of mute rage.

Bina Sarkar Ellias is poet, founder, editor, designer and publisher of International Gallerie, an award-winning publication since 1997. Besides, she is a fiction writer and art curator in India and overseas. Her books of poems include "The Room", "Fuse" (which has been taught at the Towson University, Maryland, USA), and "When Seeing Is Believing". Her forthcoming collection of poems will be launched in December 2020. Her poems have been translated into French, Spanish, Greek Chinese, Arabic and Urdu, She received a Fellowship from the Asia Leadership Fellow Program 2007, towards the project, Unity in Diversity, the Times Group Yami Women Achievers' award, 2008, and the FICCI/FLO 2013 award for excellence in her work.

Chaitali Bhattacharjee
A Villanelle for Fallen Daisy

What hides that lies within?
A house of glass shards and clay,
We are girls wrapped in skin.

When do you think the strip begin
through wanton walls and streets stray,
What hides that lies within!

Our stairs reek like an empty bin,
Every pick and pull to keep up with the pay,
We are girls wrapped in skin.

They hunger and crave for white of virgin;
In the city of evil, we touch death every day,
What hides must lie within.

Our silk and soil now shrunk paper-thin
with chipped mask and wasted fancy play,
We are girls wrapped in skin.

We are just who we are, not pretending
With our truth wearing the smirk gray,
What hides that lies within.
We are girls wrapped in skin.

Euphemism

At 17, she got married. Not by her choice but by her fate.
Father said if you keep your gent happy, we will be happy too. What
about her!
So, what about her?

Do dig traps to bait her passions.
Douse the fire in her belly with your corny greasy rules of creed.
Like the warm kinder Zephyr of springtime,
Blow winds to her
in the garb of redeeming kisses and stifling overprotective heists.
Plundering her deeper stabbing hunger to aspire or seek.
Hazy enough now for her to struggle to even stutter her needs.

Equate the length of her skirts to the minuscule of your psyche.
Please with good humour I plead,
You must marginalise her voice or air to prove you are virile.
Then you tell me, what about her?
 I will say,
If she raises a voice you may call her a propagandist.
If she didn't, blame her for acting as one of those beaten-down-
preyed-upon-victims.

"To live a life" in verbatim
What a big scam she asked for!
A life which started just like yours
With one telltale thump of pump,
gushing out from a smooth tube in the womb to by now
billions of beats. Somehow somewhere being encroached,
Led astray, duly trampled and breached.

Yet a tiny flicker
Conspicuously persisting
Like a candle in the wind.
Reflecting the glimpse of her soul

In the shadow of the flamed out vapored paraffin.
Seen by few, maybe touched by one.
And felt by none.

But she can relight her candle with its smoke trail with one
incredible fire trick.
As the trail of smoke released by the smoldering wick still holds
a bit of wax that hasn't been fully seared.
The verdict is erroneous anticipative though.
Her tryst with kismet always ends
Between the pearly ovals mounting from her ribs
And the girdle smothering her triangle of abyss.

Chaitali Bhattacharjee is a content editor and columnist. She occasionally conducts creative writing workshops and does poetry reading for her community kids, something which gives comfort to her fidgety heart. Her works are published in varied publications such as TOI, Indian Express, Huffingtonpost India, Soulspot, Oddity, Indiblogger, Narrow Road journal, and is part of two international multilingual anthologies of poems. The stimulants to her writings are race, equality, gender, empathy, connections, life in itself; which flock together hoping to find a voice not always conclusive, but mostly inquisitive.

Chaitali Sengupta
Red light

Yesterday's silence
spread luxuriously
on the sofa.
Living words
rustle on muted pages.
Precious moments
hook in the folds
of the cushion.
Pleasures of night
brim over
from the hands of the clock.
Whispering breaths
trace the fall of stars.
Shadows lengthen and shrink
while we wait...
to restore the fault lines of our lives...

we, the modern Madonna's
of the 'oldest profession'
like the ghosts
in red light
stitch our barbed skins
through our torn souls.

The blood-red of birth

You're inside me.
Floating, in amniotic fluid,
a dream,
attached umbilically..
to the fathomless fortress within.
A radiant heart,
A sparkling dawn
A miracle nourished
and cared upon.
Womb-warm, sequestered,
you grew, like the pulse of God;
Forging a bond, unknown
that very soon
your life will come undone.
For you, little one,
you're a girl
and you needed to
stay unborn.

Oh, the blessed spark of the Goddess
force- flushed under my thighs...
you were just a memory then,
a tear pooling in my eyes...

Emptiness comes crashing
on my blackened earth,
the womb remembers forever,
the blood red of birth.

In the womb of past

Would you allow me to pen your tales?
A tribute, maybe
With the ink of reason
echoing your thoughts...
in whispered words
through the mists of time?

A history of your trials,
since time immemorial...

of you, Draupadi, your flowing mane,
Untamed, your hair, blood-red,
twisted in the hands of tyranny
the cause of a thousand pains?
Of you Sita, your tears
a pitter- patter
on the arid desert of customs;
pedestalized, docile
proving your chastity,
walking through fire,
divinely ordained.

Of you Ahilya, your swirling curse,
Your stoned image... voiceless
a victim of patriarchy
Abandoned, mute,
waiting to be redeemed,
by the brush of a man-god's feet...

Or, of you Ganga, the thundering river of rebirth,
your mighty torrents waltzing
upon the breast of earth;
You, an extension of the Divine,
a captive in Shiva's hair,
how your arrogance and speed, trapped
between heaven and earth.

I flip through your minds,
Caressing your unspoken words
That bends time, like the spine.
Your follies and flaws,
Your rebellion and surrender.
Braid into our psyche,
Course through our veins.

In the womb of our past,
the present lives on.

Chaitali Sengupta is a published writer, translator, journalist from the Netherlands. She is involved in various literary & journalistic writing - translation projects for a Dutch newspaper and online platforms in the Netherlands. Her works have been extensively published in many Indian literary platforms like Muse India, Indian periodical, Borderless Journal, Setu Bilingual, The Asian Age. Her recently translated work "Quiet Whispers of our Heart" (Orange Publishers, 2020) received good reviews and was launched at the International Book Fair, Kolkata, India.

Chanchal Sarin
Goddess Durga

You are my creations
You are my reflections
The Goddess *Durga,*
The *Shakti,* said to humans

My nine images
My incarnations
Save you from all your pains
you meet within life's terrain

I am *Shailaputri,*
The embodiment of the collective powers of Brahma, Vishnu, and
Mahesh

I am the *Brahmacharini*
The blissful
I endow happiness, peace, prosperity, and grace
The way to emancipation and *moksh* sake

I am *Chandraghanta*
The symbol of bravery
The beauty and the grace
I bestow peace and tranquility on your race

I am *Kushmunda*
The creator of the universe and prosperity

I am *Skandmata*
The mother of Skanda and Kartikeya
The protector against demons

I am *Katyayni*
Born to great sage Kata
I exhibit immense courage

I am *Kaalratri*
With dark complexion, disheveled hair and fearless posture
The most fierce form of Durga
Dressed in white
Representing peace and prayer

I am *Maha Gauri*
I bestow intelligence on human beings
Saraswati is my daughter
I am *Sidhidatri*
I have supernatural healing powers
I bestow on humans
A blissful state of mind
Like the clear sky in the night

I am *Saraswati*
The daughter of *Maha Gauri*
The incarnation of wisdom
The personification of all knowledge
Consort of creator *Brahma*
Brahma generates me
I possess water

I am writhing in pains
The pains of childbirth
When humans abort humanity
For worldly gains
Dance with demons
On crude and harsh music
Causing ears in severe pains

I am the river of consciousness
that enlivens creations
I resurrect all forms of *Durga*
with devotion

I am hope that kills the devil
I resurrect my existence in you
When you, the humans,
Listen to your inner voice
The voice of silence

In my resurrection in you
A paradise is created on earth

The nine avatars of *Durga*
Dance on serene music
A divine music
It is the victory of good over evil
The supremacy of spirit
Over the muscle power of demons
The blessed moments

Dr Chanchal Sarin, Ph.D. in Genetics retired as Associate Professor from University of Delhi, India. She has authored seven books on Genetics and Biology besides several articles on research and popular science. She is the co-author of Anthology of poems "In All the Spaces: Diverse voices in Global Women's Poetry" (2020). Chanchal had been actively involved in scientific and welfare organisations for promoting welfare of women and children. She was the Convener of the Women and Association Science cell of Indian Science Congress (ISCA).

Dr. Chayanika Saikia
Joba- The Tea Garden Girl

Sun rises from her *sindoori bindi* and droplets of dew
wake up at the tinkle of her silvery anklets. Scent of her
hair oil floats in the morning breeze and the narrow road,
as familiar as the border of her nylon *saree*, carries her
to the tea-garden. Her vacant eyes rightly match the
utter numbness worn by her face. The girls who pluck
tea-buds, she is one of them. Her name is Joba,
the hibiscus, a name that used to compliment her once,
now seems to be incoherent to her own existence.

Joba walks down with her little girl Chandni.
They walk past the village, the woods, and the Sahab's
bungalow. She walks past that pair of eyes looking at her and
Chandni from there, the pair of eyes which can alter hearts
or someone's life to the core.

It was the night of the full-moon, night of the *Karam Puja*
Night of her maiden heart dancing to the beat of *Jhumur*.
She, as fresh as the flower tucked to her hair bun.
She, as red as the night warm, with ritual fire, heavy with *haria*.
Sahab's eyes were all upon her, so, as to his desire.
She intoxicated in a dream as sinful as the night itself.

The full-moon disappeared, but a little moon-light was
absorbed by her as the souvenir of that Autumn night.
Her father was quick to give her hand to a man in exchange
for 5 ducks, 10 bags of rice, and a few bottles of *haria*.
After all, he needs to feed his prestige.

The man filled her forehead with *sindoor* and she emptied
her heart. Her fingers remained lost searching for fresh tea buds
and heart remained caged in those pair of eyes in the bungalow.
She paled in winter morning, walked past the Sahab's bungalow.

She ripened as the Spring's wild fruit, walked past the Sahab's glances over her belly. And in a full moon night, her vacant eyes sparkled with a little moon of her own, her Chandni, the moon-lit girl appeared in her sky like a new bud of the tea,
to brew the only essence of her life.

P.S.
Chandni walks past the Sahab's bungalow daily with her mother. Sometimes she catches a glance of Sahab playing with his daughter. Chandni's eyes beam with excitement to see the beautiful doll in the hands of his daughter, she doesn't notice Sahab's eyes get moist by looking at her face.

Joba and her girl walk towards their distant hut.
Sun prepares to set into her bamboo **tukdi** filled with tea buds.
Their faces chase the dusk.

*(**Karam Puja** = a harvest festival celebrated in few Indian states especially by tea-garden workers; **Jhumur** = folk dance and song performed on the occasion of karam festival ; **Haria** = An ethnic tribal rice **beer** or alcoholic drink popular among tea garden worker community; **tukdi** = busket)*

Dr. Chayanika Saikia is a poet by heart & a Geoscientist by profession. She lives with her family in Noida. Poetry is the prescribed tonic for her heart and an 'after-dinner' ritual. Her recent works have been published in New York Parrot (Aug' 2020), Indian Periodical (Sep' 20), in anthology like "Ismat" (2nd edition), 'Antargata' (upcoming) by Bangalore Poetry Circle, etc.
https://www.facebook.com/DrChayanikaSaikia/
Hash-tag: #cherishablesbychayanika
Instagram: cherishables_by_chayanika

Deepa Gopal
Kali

She rose among the grey dust
Dark and red, her pulse the sound of the atmosphere
The rhythm beating with the rest
Warm darkness spread across the plain
Red flowed merging with the grey
Life simmered in dust of gold
All ornate with skulls around her throbbing neck
Blood dripped from various forms
Her eyes deep set, ensuing a vision
She's not demure and obedient
She's daunting, not dainty
Erotic and raw, a killer of deep-set fears
She's the child of nature – wild and ferocious
She's unique and pulsating with life
She holds no qualms for being relentless
She's benevolence and boundless freedom
She's feminine power, the quintessential core
Her femininity, unabashed and untamed
She's dark, she's death, she's **Kali** – for god's sake!
She is no female subdued in spirit.

Untamed (inspired by the nude of Sylvie Guillot)

Born in India and currently residing in Dubai, Deepa Gopal is a visual artist-art blogger. Most of her paintings are coupled with her own Haiku/micro poems as titles. Author of the blog, Hues n Shades, she has done her Masters in English Language and Literature. Her works are often "mindscapes", introspecting the emotional and psychological states along with the physical one and its impact. She likes playing with dreams, myths, and visions. Her poems have been published in three anthologies – "Whispering Poiesis" (2018) "Beyond Words" (2020) and "String of Hearts" (upcoming) respectively.
Blog: https://deepazworld.blogspot.com/
Instagram: @dee.huesnshades

Deepali Parmar
Living in Translation – free(to)verse

How does it feel, girl
to be flipped around
like a page and read without
knowledge of your language - which seeks lay spaces and is
offered a line ruled with *su sanskar* – (good inherent manners)

First born in a Gujju* family
then told to be womxn enough, cook *dal, sweeten it,*
bring it to boil and temper it
with black mustard seeds, green chilies
and asafetida - Done?
Learnt to be womxn? Now claim its peak of possibility?
Dare to.

Kem Cho is 'how are you?'
Don't answer literally – stupid girl.
Literal translations are week at the knees -
will knock you over with a hammer from his "tool" kit.
Being knocked over should now
come naturally.
Continue.

Can't you bend enough to touch
each big toe of *dadaji* and take blessings properly?
What a pathetic bearer of malady.
Pappa grows his eyes bigger
explaining the meaning of "proper" poetically
– help me construct one more
verse for this poem sits un-translatable now.

Sitting on the *umbra* will bring bad luck.
This threshold you cross never to re-turn.
The day we marry you and off you go go go...
Your life begins when you husband a
boy – cling to him suitably.
Try to turn your page to the light of domesticity.
Time to forget about your degree *(which you wished you had but
we made sure you never could).*

You see, vessels have enough space to
keep you occupied all day and if not –
have babies.

*My mother seemed to always say, "Speak in a way, you could be read."
Childhood neglect, abuse and the challenges that naturally followed, has
always been an inspiration to study & alter the narrative that we, as
humanity collectively create, practice & pass it to our children.*

*Deepali Parmar, 48, Founder, Director - Live More Initiatives. Altering
the Human Experience with Presence & Creativity. Deepali is a Creatif &
unschooler working as an artist, poet, thespian, story-teller and
creative educationist. Her art, writing, plays & educational models have
been appreciated, published, awarded and curated well enough. She lives
an empowered life with her young child and tribe of Creatifs &
Unschoolers in India. Presently she curates The Artist Within Journeys to
cultivate more Presence Creatively & Thrive right where you are.
Deepali is accessible on FB & Instagram.
You can write to her at deepalistable@gmail.com*

Kali Kalyani – Balance your Forces

Deepali Parmar

Devika Mathur
Candles that die out soon

There are things that happen here silently.
Almost like a death slowly happening and residing in your stomach
with a mesh of despair on face,
with patriarchy still sitting atop
hands wrapped in the moist oceans.
A mother,
a daughter,
 a sister
raped almost every second in India,
                    I know of a lady at home too,
The one with *'chameli'* flowers on her bun,
Mopping mosaic floors,
hands covered in floral *mehndi*,
patterns directing towards her visceral dreams.
                    And a lady who sits in the verandah,
a soft glow in her eye about something she desires for
a mustard crepe dress,
a daughter not killed,
 grandson, granddaughters, valiant,
As I speak this poem,
a girl gets raped somewhere
with a shade of dead hibiscus pressed in her womb.
Hibiscus- a dainty flower offered to goddess 'Kali'
murals of loss plastered on cheeks,
As I speak this poem,
a lantern is dimmed in one of the nearby villages,
a ghost is awakened,
to loathe
to sink and rise,
to rise and sink
to mollify over the detachments occurred.

The sky must weep,
the ceilings should crack,
there...as I speak of this poem
the fingers become almost boneless now.
Petrified,
So small.
A part that lingers with the moon-shaped women of my country.

Seasons of Sin

Quiet now,
People do not speak of "periods" here.
We worship deities, sayings that are unstained,
We do not utter words related to formation of a newborn,
The act is a sin.
Quiet now,
The bosoms are to be covered
with a dainty white thread,
a thread if loose,
becomes a home to predators.
Quiet now,
A moral speaks highly of your poise
of your thin-skinned chin,
of bones and fragile flesh.
A moral as crisp as sun-flowers
Things are stagnating here,
in our homes of desiccated faces
where leaves refuse to fall from the *Ashok* tree,
tendon, ligament, marrow: now akin to this monastery of stale air
of losses of joined blood,
a duller, vicious loop of swollen eyes
that hides beneath the surface of each Indian soil.

Quiet now,
do not speak of a wilting flower,
of cracks upon throat,
a bud wilting.
Hush now,
do not speak of the black widow now.
I have overgrown an extra pair of hands now,
to defy the abhorrence of your soul.
  a mirage of a bee absorbing the walls,
  absorbing the deluge of life.

Devika Mathur resides in India and is a published poet, writer. Her works have been published or are upcoming in Madras Courier, Modern Literature, Two Drops Of Ink, Dying Dahlia Review, Pif Magazine, Spillwords, Duane's Poetree, Piker Press, Mojave heart review, Whisper and the Roar amongst various others. She is the founder of the surreal poetry website "Olive skins" and writes for My Valiant Soul (https://myvaliantsoulsblog.wordpress.com/). She recently published her poetry collection "Crimson Skins", which talks about all the peculiar emotions we go through. Five (5) of her poems were also recently published in Sunday Mornings River anthology. insta- @my.valiant.soul

Emily Thomas
Prostitute

1, 2, 3
She counts
The greasy, folded notes registering the color
not bothering with the number printed on the legal tender,
a barter
for her services,
The currency don't matter,
It doesn't belong to her
She has to hand it over
To the man sitting downstairs in the corner
His pouch bulging around his
Waist

Gulping down another can of beer

4, 5, 6
The hands of the clock swipes replacing hour after hour
She stares at the dusty timekeeper high up on the wall, transfixed,
ready to numb herself staring at the face that watches her,
silently,
as it shares the sights of the dirty deeds and her sins,
The man removes his clothes, and he starts to lay his hands in her,

7, 8, 9
She recalls,
The ages of her daughters
The faces and soft touches
Of the children she bore,
Pushed hard and nearly broke her back-giving birth to them,
in a dingy room at the hands of a rather questionable doctor
And then in a painful act no mother should endure,
she has to hand them over to be looked after by someone other

Because
Society dictates
a prostitute doesn't make a fit mother.

She can't help to wonder if they are thinking of her
Asking for her,
Yearning for her,
Praying
That the ignorance of their childhood
Manifests into good things
That their lives turn out better
That they may never see
May never live life through the eyes of their mother
It is why she must in agonizing silence suffer

10, 11, 12,
Times he has spit on her
His hands, tugging and pulling, at the parts of her body imagining
himself Pete "Maverick" Mitchell and she the F-14 Tomcat.
Boy is he going to ride her.

He positions himself to penetrate her,
Spreading her legs
He climbs on top of her
He smells of cigarettes and cheap liquor
A perfume of the only scent she knows and for the longest of
time can remember

As he goes In and out of her,
She is thankful he is young
At least the youth in him will bring his climax a lot sooner,
And then this job will be over
And she can take a long deep drag of her contraband cigarette,
Sip from her unwashed glass of water,
Sitting on the dusty counter,
Waiting for her next customer.

Tapi ingat oh sayang,
Kesucianku segabai seorang bonda
Tidak akan ghaib begitu saje,
Ketulinan kewanitaanku takkan dicemari seperti air didalam baldi
yang digunakan untuk membasuh kain kotormu

Aku bukan hamba mu
Badan aku bukan dicipta
Untuk Di jahanamkan didalam mindamu
Balang diantara kakiku
Bukan sebarangan alatan untuk diroyakan,
Dikoyakan semata mata untuk nafsumu
Akulah ibu pertiwi, kakak
Akulah insan, yang masih sayang Dan loyalist terhadapmu,

Aku takkan mengizinkan racun Di Dalam hatiku bisa
mengkoruspikan badanmu

Kerana aku bukan malah
Kekasihmu untuk digunakan semata mata didalam keghairan
pasrah untuk dibeli macam rokok batang Di kedai anneh, untuk
dihisap Dan dibuang begitu saja.
Satu, Dua, tiga Empat Lima
Lima minit untuk habiskan sebatang rokok
Lima minit untuk dicabuli
Kerana aku perlukan duitmu
Dan engkau mahukan kewanitaanku
Bila selesai tugas , engkau masih maverick
Dan aku masih seorang prostitute.

(Translation from Malay to English)

But remember
Oh, my dear
The promises of my motherhood
Doesn't just magically disappear into thin air
The sanctity of my Womanhood
Cannot be soiled like the dirty clothes soaked in a pail of tainted water
Of which you use to wash away your sins,

I am Eve,
Who was made to walk beside you
Never a slave
I am Lilith,
Born of this earth,
Mother of your sons,
But you vilified me and condemned me in your mind
Because of the void in between my legs,
The space in between my legs
Is a sacred place,
Not a feeble toy to be torn apart, defiled
Only to feed your cravings and lust

I am the divine mother of the earth
I am your sister borne from the same womb as you
I am the woman who will hold you, protect you and
I am loyal
To you
I will never allow the pain and torture
Inflicted upon me
To creep up into my heart,
The poison shoved down my throat
Will never manifest and infect your flesh
For this is my make

For I am not just your lover
To be used in the throngs of passion
Only to be thrown away
Flicked away,
Like a cigarette burnt to the butt

One , two, three, four , five
Five minutes to smoke that cigarette,
Five minutes to be violated,
Because I need your money,
And you want my femininity,
And when the deed is done,
You're still the ace maverick
And
I am Still a Prostitute.

Emily Thomas is a professional clown, spoken word poet, and speech and drama educator. Wisping around like a puff of purple bohemian smoke, jumping on every box, screaming into the microphone hoping you would join her in her quest to make the world a better place. One of the poets featured in Tongue Tied 2, a spoken word cabaret, and Malaysian poetry slam and events curator, Emily writes about topics that are hard to swallow but are the necessary truth.

Ermelinda Makkimane

Mangifera Indecorum
or
How to eat a mango

Ignore the cries of your kids
their persistent demands
Block out all else
Let them choose one if they wish
Your task is set before you
Select one that is soft, a softness
that resists yet responds to the touch.
Here, softness indicates mellow fruitfulness.
Wash with love and care.
Resist the urge to share
The reward is yours
and yours alone
Cut the teeniest bit at the top to
remove the sticky sap. You can
do this with your teeth but must spit
out that portion quickly and since
spitting is not recommended in
these times of corona, just
stick to cutting.
Don't capitulate to decorum
Throw all caution to the winds
Don't slice if you are a wanton hedonist.
Close your eyes and concentrate
This is pure meditation
Draw your mouth closer to the juice
dribbling at the cut. If it's oozing
more than dribbling (and it
almost usually is), sigh, lick up the
escaping drops.

Still yourself
Submerge yourself
It's time to be delighted
When you're satisfied that no
more juice is escaping, cover
the cut part entirely with
your mouth like you're doing CPR,
applying only slight pressure with your
teeth. Be prepared for the flood
of insane goodness that threatens to
submerge your senses.
Forget now the
icky, itchy routine of your day
Once you've got hold of some
semblance of decorum, gently apply
dental pressure to skin making
cuts on the upper body of the fruit.
This is your time of reckoning
All for self
Peel off the skin and keep on a
plate nearby to clean off any lingering
flesh. But that's for later. For now, dig
deeper into the flesh with your teeth.
Ignore the juices flowing away
freely or, if you must, lick your hands
before you roll the thick pulp you've
bitten off in your mouth. Let your
tongue judge its size and weight.
Chew less, slurp more.
Forget the cranky boss
The nosy co-worker too
Forget the grief that
lechy co-passenger gave you
Forgive or don't
For now, just forget

Then dive in again and again till the
mango is quite nude, simply ravished
by your teeth and tongue.
> *Ignore the spousal needs for now*
> *The creaky wrecky bed*
> *Dive in again*
> *Do concentrate*
> *Such is the path you tread*

There it lies, the seed still not bare
though. Go to it with your fingers
holding the edges of the rock hard pit,
chew on and keep moving to
sweeter areas of the piece round
and round till you feel sated.
> *Feel yourself grow at ease*
> *The throbbing pain release*
> *The chores can be divided*
> *No supermom we need*

If your eyes had closed of their
own volition by this time now's
the time to open them to the
world at large and take stock.
Also, there's some unfinished
business in the plate of drippings
on your lap.
> *Emerge from this you time*
> *Or linger still*

After all is finished, just sit back and
accept what you've done.
> *You've been loving*
> *yourself baby*
> *Go, girl*

There, you've just finished eating a mango.

a piece of blue

that's all i can see
lying flat below you
past the flying curtains
peeks a piece of blue

it's still there
when i lean out the window
blue-eyed amazed to see me
as i am on spotting it

the curtain stands stiff now
no play in the breeze
to hint a flicker
my piece of blue

is waiting
aching to see me too
but i'm too weak
to raise a finger

after the battering
so we cry together
blue is now bruised black
and i am black and blue

Gender Parity

I stare at the computer screen
all bleary-eyed.
My deadline looms
yet I have nothing to say.
Why do words have such value,
I wonder.

A single article on gender parity
is all I have to submit
yet the words don't flow out of me.
Wasn't I the best student in college?
Best at writing,
best at debate.
Always ready with a witty repartee.
And now, I feel all tongue-tied.
Why did I agree to do this article?
'Waaa... waaaaah..' the baby wails in her crib.
I look to where my husband is...
Will he attend to the baby?
But he does not seem to have heard.
He is furiously typing on his laptop.
I attempt to rise, the pain in my back
limiting my movement.
Suddenly my husband has jumped up
and is already walking the baby.
He puts her back into her crib
and I find my writer's block lift.
I say a silent prayer of thanks to the Almighty
and put down my thoughts on gender parity.

Ermelinda Makkimane loves thinking about poetry and sometimes she writes down those words. Her work has been published online and has appeared in anthologies. She has recently published her debut book "Her Story - A Womanist Perspective on Mary." Ms. Makkimane is currently working on her second book in the "Her Story" series.

Gayatri Lakhiani Chawla

Bondage

Arranged marriage is like buying a crate of mangoes
They stare at your body from head to toe

      Touching the soft supple skin of the mango
They look at your dark complexion, disappointed
       Shoving the green mangoes away for the sunshine yellow
ones
They look at your breasts, a sign of fertility
      Inspecting which ones are bigger and juicier
They gauge your height, your weight, the size of your vagina
      Holding the mango erect and examining it visually
and then
      How much?

('Bondage' is from my book of poems 'The Empress').

Arms and the Woman

He thinks she doesn't know of his animality
How he pilfers, a lump of clay in the dark
from the garden outside her house.
Every year tiptoed, head covered
his hands move like a raccoon
digging the auspicious clay.
On a full moon day
The air smells of the fresh rainwater
the night is a gypsy dancing queen
melting in the arms of her lovers.

She adorns her golden anklets, her neckpieces
her coiled hair braided neatly to one side,
lips smeared with a honey balm.

She wears her underwings of grace
standing majestically, a mace in one hand
Devi

*('Arms and the Woman' was first published in WE Scream by Rhythm
Divine Poets).*

Concealer

She glances at her exquisite gold watch
it's way past supper time
The LCD is blaring away like a
loquacious loudspeaker in a railway station
The fancy woman on T.V. in her fancy pants
opens her glossy seductive mouth
The screen is a battlefield of estrogen
hormones are pacing up and down
flying high like a fish-tailed kite,
behind the hijaab she's breaking into a sweat
droplets of shimmering diamonds collect on her brow.
Her twenty-four karat necklace
looks like a double tier choker
choking her with its ugly social stigma
she's a fish out of water
Her throat is dry, dry like the land she lives in
the winds are blowing in all the wrong directions
The fancy woman in her fancy pants
is selling a new fairness product
It's a one-way ticket to flawless skin
The commercial goes;
'Buy now and say good-bye to marks and dark circles'

She thinks from behind the hijaab
'Will it conceal last night's bloody scars?'

('Concealer' was first published in 'The Woman Inc' 2016 and my book 'Invisible Eye').

Gayatri Lakhiani Chawla is a poet, translator, and French teacher. Her poems have been featured in 'Modern English Poetry by Younger Indians' (Sahitya Akademi) and Red River Book of Haibun.She is Winner II of the US National Poetry Contest by Ræd Leaf Foundation for Poetry & Allied Arts 2018. She is the author of 'Invisible Eye' and 'The Empress'. Her poem won a special mention award in the Architectural Poetry Annual Competition 2020.

Gayatri Majumdar
I am that old woman now

I am that old woman now
talking to palms, roses, thorny bushes;

Walking slow with varicose veins bulging –
still feeding cats.

I stumble here, I thought on time,
but the clock struck gentle

turning my face pale,
lipstick smudging coffee mugs of leftover desires;
the air rent with sparrow rain-songs and familiar
beat of metal music.

I create this whole edifice
just in case I forget my name,
or the various shades of colorless-ness, not white.
I return to unearth the long dead.

I am that woman with her back bent,
her remarkably beautiful face duned
always busy leaving buff pages of fiction
and *alaaps** of *sarangis* and *santoors*^.
Abandon me now, let go final
vestiges of the fire that consumes –
there is nowhere else left to leave.

The sky overcast,
the sea dances bearing possibilities of this hour;
the woman now cycles to sea
listening for distant trawlers and gull cries
beginning to relive the myths
of a place, she once called home.

(*alaap: A long tonal melody / ^sarangis and santoors: String instruments)

Gayatri Majumdar is editor, founder-publisher of the critically acclaimed Indian literary journal, The Brown Critique. Gayatri's books include A Song for Bela (a novel, 2017), poetry collections Shout (2000) and I Know You Are Here (2019). Her third volume of poems and a non-fiction book titled The Lotus of the Heart will be published in 2021. Gayatri curates poetry/music festivals in Pondicherry and in Ramgarh in the Himalayas.
https://www.facebook.com/gayatri.majumdar.5/
https://www.facebook.com/groups/browncritique/
https://www.linkedin.com/in/gayatrimajumdar/

Geetha Nair G.

Pind Daan *

Her wet palms strike each other.

The sky darkens at the sound.

Pinions beat, air whirrs,
The cocky ones arrive;
Wheeling lower, lower
Above the hunting ground.

Wings spread, they glide to land –
Grey, black, grey-black,
Young, old, middling –
Egos engorged like their rotund bodies.

She throws them words to feed on;
They peck and gulp,
Then hop towards her nubile figure

In vain she scans the sky
To glimpse the gift of him
Returning strong
 from the empty blue.

Then, grown red-tongued, ten-armed,
She whirls,
Her gleaming weapon
Drawing flame...

The cry of birds rends the captive air.

* Pind Daan is a Hindu ritual for the dead. After prayers, cooked rice is offered to crows by close relatives of the dead person. The birds are alerted by clapping wet hands.

Geetha Nair G. is an award-winning author of two collections of poetry - - Shored Fragments and Drawing Flame. Her work has been reviewed favourably in The Journal of the Poetry Society (India) and other notable literary periodicals. Her most recent publication is a collection of short stories titled Wine, Woman and Wrong. Geetha Nair is a former Associate Professor of English, All Saints' College, Thiruvananthapuram, Kerala.

Geetika Kohli Amla
Prayer Wheel

A prayer wheel, I had been set into motion –
my body branded with mantras, I conformed to the axis
of a man's needs.

Gambled thus, every emotion, each little fancy of his
added character to the catastrophe – mass to the explosion,
this man's needs.

And spinning, thinning the gravity of love,
I lost the invisible anchor, an old boulder –
life beckoned me outside of the whirlpool.

And now, when he holds me by the waist,
I do not play a tool.

I look beyond the golden shoulder.

Who Were the Men?

Who were the men who planted her voice
across their vast, brown, barren stories?

Scarlet, emerald and ink, her whispers –
smeared around the edges of nothing.

They told her that she'd been only a drum
they beat to feel the blood in their veins.

Who were the men who lit walls with her eyes,
and saw their houses come into being?

They bejeweled themselves wearing her hands –
who were the men who'd needed all the sheen?

She dwelled a persistent hum in their heads –
they belittled her, a God in their hymns.

Geetika Kohli Amla is a multilingual writer, activist, and entrepreneur from Jammu and Kashmir. She has authored six books of poetry in English including The Lost Sonnet and Other Poems, Yonder, Nothingness at Boiling Point, Lucid Blood, Crooked Hyphens and Rooms That Occupy Us. At present, Geetika is leading Hymns and Harmony, an international poetry movement for peace-building in Jammu, Kashmir and Ladakh.

Ghazal Khanna
Bitch Face

my tongue bleeds blue
on yellowed pages
my hair painted pink
dog-eared at edges

my brown eyes don't
waiver while talking
my green bra strap left
on my shoulder hanging

my lips dyed red
hurt to smile so I don't
and they call it
a Woman's Dissent

My Mother, a badass

Nani tells me
that teenage maa
was a badass
with stories of her
dancing in the rain
unabashedly
without a care in this world
Nani tells me these stories of maa
thrashing bad men for their doings
It's hard to picture but I try
She catcalling Patriarchy on the roads
She pulling Patriarchy by ponytail
She pinching Patriarchy on the skin

My mother, a badass
The woman that I only see
between her household chores
The woman who fumbles
through sentences while talking
She has now developed a stutter
her words only come out in intervals
while the men call her unreadable
Her dishes carrying the
aroma of her buried feelings
while she lives between
the whistles of the cooker
spending a lifetime in the kitchen
the only space in our big house
that is hers, truly hers
The woman who could be
a painter, a poet, a psychologist
but never had a space of her own
to think, contemplate and just exist
confined in a house to feed
a mouthful of mouths
My Mother who now cribs the rain
because rain means
doing the laundry again
She takes pride in the jewelry
that left purple marks on her skin
Nani must have told her
"Diamonds are a woman's best friend"
so many times that she started to believe it
My Mother who wears her feminism
under layers of shame
and hides her revolution
like the slippers under her saree
My Mother is not a rebel anymore
and looking at her

I wonder
how rebellion dies
a slow death
in the womb
of a
Woman

Ghazal Khanna is a confessional poet, writer, feminist activist, and educator. She first got published at the age of 12 in a local magazine. Her work has made its way to various platforms like She The People, Zoom TV, Women's Web, Times Now, UNREAD 2020, Verses of Silence Literary magazine, Buddy Bits, Kommune, Habitat Studios, Poems India amongst others. Her poems have been nominated for The Orange Flower Festival for the best poetry on social issues. She lets her words do the talking as they speak volumes about her lived experience as a queer brown woman.

Hema Ravi

Life of a Crematorium Worker

From dawn to dusk, tryst with death on all days
Breaking stereotypes to do such jobs
Arranging pyres for a proper blaze
Dealing with corpses amidst human sobs
Their youth and peace many a time it robs
Generation after other engaged
Even if the stomach growls and head throbs
With ghostly calm, they toil, never outraged
When untimely deaths bring along people enraged.

Day after day as the huge fires rage
Even when their progenies' future stare
Inhaling smoke as they stoke for their wage
Infections and ailments are theirs to bear
It's a man's locale, they've managed to dare
Their abode sooty, dark, and ramshackle
They have stood their ground amidst all the scare
Social stigmas managed to tackle
I salute the women who've broken such shackle(s).

(After reading an article about the plight of women working in the crematorium. (First Published in Setu Bilingual English for Best of Women Poetry 2020)

TIGER WIDOW*

She leads a life of shame day after day
Ostracized by the members of the town
Pitiable existence, what to say?
Sans partner, in utter poverty drown(ed)
Friends until the previous day now let down
In superstitions they lie submersed
Witch! Tiger Widow! Depressing comedown!
They consider her unlucky, accursed.

Out one day, her man met Death on the way
Left with no choice as drought brought the clampdown
Waded far through the mangroves, lost his sway
Searching for honey, far from his hometown
To fetch his fortunes, avoid a crackdown
Took the road not taken, unaware, unversed.
Encountered a man-eater at sundown.
They consider her unlucky, accursed!

Camouflaged, motionless the feline lay
till it spotted the man going downtown
A sudden mist appeared, then all turned grey
Up to the waterway, it soon dragged down
Screams grew louder, then a sudden die-down
Gratifying days of hunger and thirst
While bloodied water flowed past woods, deep-down
They consider her unlucky, accursed.

With taunts, they flay, even as they turn down
Such a life in century twenty-first
She moves on with life zombie-like, cast down
They consider her unlucky, accursed!

*(*This poem was written to bring out the plight of the widows of rural
Bangladesh who face abandonment after their husbands are killed
by tigers. They are often viewed as the cause of their partner's ill-fate....
In response to a newspaper article)*

*Hema Ravi is a poet, author, reviewer, and editor (Efflorescence), her
writings have been featured in several online and international
print journals, and won prizes too. She has authored 'Everyday English,'
'Write Right Handwriting Series 1,2,3,' and is co-author of 'Sing Along
Indian Rhymes' and 'Everyday Hindi.' In July 2020, she organized an
international poetry webinar "Connecting Across Borders." She is a
freelancer for IELTS & Communicative English.*

Himangi Nair
light & dark

it's dark in here since they blocked the keyhole
we had for a window

the water seeps in
from the low ceiling;
the chairs we were tied to
can't hold us anymore

paper ball after paper ball, I try to pen down
these feelings and thoughts,
though guilt isn't one of them.
I'm clueless as to why you often beat yourself up,
perhaps hoping you could morph into one of them.

our cellmates are kind, so they help us out too
one helped me write this to you
and of course, I'm scared, I'm anxious, but the truth

is we can't get out of this cell. Not anytime soon.

and when every night you cry in my arms,
and I kiss you all over, try and sing to calm you down

and you look at me, helpless, red,
asking me, "what is it that we did?"

and every night, in a trembly whisper,
I tell you,
"we love".

(although we love no differently)

I have all the light I need:
you're here, stuck with me.

For epochs and a fortnight

I wish this could be happier.
And I so wish this could be just us.
Just us.

Not mother after mother, her womanhood up in hair buns tied,
worried about her daughters, drowning in tears,
(meet no one's eye)
both tired, fighting
for epochs and a fortnight.

Not dozens of women, together in hiding
Plotting and planning,
Like misunderstood villains not immune to dying
(pretend that you're crying)

Not decades of torture and millennia of whipping
Bodies upon bodies, see
The red silence is still dripping;
Oozing out of humanity this woman is bringing
(remember to walk quietly)

I'd do anything to make this happier
Like glorify death, reduced to household blues
But we're stuck here for what feels like forever
(make sure to not leave behind any clues)

I just got a message; freedom was the messenger

I just wish we could be happier

I just wish now could be safer.

Himangi Nair is a poet, blogger, and aspiring writer. She is a student, 16, and an avid reader. She strongly believes in love, equality, and feminism. She is greatly inspired by nature, and her favourite authors include Elif Shafak, JK Rowling, and Chitra Banerjee Divakaruni. Himangi is a fierce advocate on the need for self-love and body positivity.
Instagram: @himangiinair Facebook: @Himangi Nair

Ilakkiya
When A Woman Falls Sick

When a woman falls sick,
Nothing changes at home,
Or everything does.

She might drag her feet still
From room to room
Picking up,
Setting down,
Straightening up,
Sweeping away -
A ghost of her regular self
Muttering and sighing her way
Through migraines, fevers and aches,
Tackling chores
That won't do themselves.

Or she might stay in bed
Muttering and sighing her way
Through the cacophony
Of strange hands
Navigating their way through
The uncertain terrain
Of pots, pans and detergents
Searching,
Dropping,
Clanging,
Spilling –
Socially sanctioned naivety
Blended with a touch of resentment, perhaps?

When a woman falls sick,
Nothing changes at home
Or everything does
But the sighs remain either way.

Ilakkiya hails from Kerala but has been residing in Tamil Nadu and Puducherry for over a decade. An accidental doctor with a specialist degree in public health, her true passion lies in the intricacies of languages. She loves pretending to be a polyglot, lecturing people on feminism, delighting in useless trivia and generally floating through life. More of her work may be found at her blog, Serendipitous Rambling, on WordPress.

Irtika Kazi
War

Walking down the promenades of my girlhood,
A war-torn republic
I reconnoiter and examine
Ways to –
Hammer nails back into scotched parapets,
Broken jaws, severed heads,
Shamefaced cobwebs,
Moth-eaten breads

All that needs to be cleansed.

Someone needs to wash away
Streets that once flattered my vanity,
   Now,
Pocked with doubt

 Parklands that only felt the touch of falling petals,
   Now,
Refuse
To be touched.

The sinews of my nation,
                    Burning.

Without a cape, I am dust

Outside, the November night is cold and dark
Alexander the Great's death is still an unsolved mystery
In my mind, I am a warrior taking on
Paradeisos, where
The sky is just a crater of wine.
Without a cape, I am dust.
A conduit of misery—
For now, I must settle with a saree,
Brine fish as an afterthought.
In my mind, I am a noblewoman with a sleek hair updo
Making peace with a blink of my eye.
For now, I must sit with a tucked-in *palloo* over my head observing,
The marriage of ants.
In my mind, I soar like a long-winged bird
For now, I am a woman.
Trying to exist in two worlds is like
A conflict between head and heart—

You belong to none.

Twenty-six

I was only two when
Mother decked me up like a bride
With her red *zardozi* scarf,
Its tassels golden and shimmery propping up
Myriads of suns along its border.
More than rotating blades of a fan on the roof,
I stared at the blank faces of brides &
Their innocuous smiles from behind the wall of chagrin.
What did it mean knowing—
The idea of marriage to me was as futile as placing
A scarecrow in the middle of busy streets.
I fed time with my hands and reposed
In seashells.

Trees—
Their leaves shedding valor, could
Never tell, of

Drooping stars and magic.

Irtika Kazi is a poet from Pune, India. She has been published in YuGen literary magazine, The Metaworker: an online literary magazine for millennials, Brown Girl magazine of Texas, Spillwords press, Fragrance of Asia, Contemporary Literary Review India, The Literary Hatchet, Peacock Journal, Madras Courier, Savant Poetry Anthology, Sahyadri Echoes, Indian Ruminations, Few of her poems have been selected for publishing in the Indian Literature journal of Sahitya Akademi.
Instagram – @duchessonthewall   Facebook - /irtika.kazi

Ishita Singh
Breathe

The restlessness within writhes violently,
asks me why these fingers are stagnant,
"why do you not bloom lotus flowers"
and I mould the earth in my hands where I lay,
pull out grass and hair by the fistfuls,
wreathe something concrete out of thorns
that I can hold between my teeth and I
breathe,
it takes vehemence sometimes,
heavier in moments I cannot be unkind

and I know existence is enough
and I know I do not have to shrapnel my heart over stone every
moment for it to beat

I know, I do

but I cannot stop clutching the nearest life raft, bruised from the
world,
building imaginary outs, always unable to leave.

I reach out for your hands,
and this isn't saving each other
or redemption for makeshift sins we are supposed to carry
or home.
It is far far away, I tell myself instead.

I open my eyes and it is us,
our bangles crashing against each other
on the shores we washed away on.

I am so tired of my love being an act of revolution

and I know it always has been a fight,
and I know our fingers entwined is not what the violence seeks
and I know this soft, warm love is mutiny.
I do. I do.

I am simply tired of every bit of my existence being insurgence,
tearing apart to hold my hair by the fistfuls
as the restless breathes,
"why do you not let go"
and with our fingers interwoven into each other,
I look at you through the gaps.

This is just breathing, existing, soft acts of nothing on a summer far
far away
where kissing you is only kissing you
and not criminal,
I hold our hands up, fingers laced, look into the sun
I have woven another moment. I breathe.
I cannot let go. I never really had a choice.

Ishita pens poems at the edge of this kingdom, sword in hand, fingers clammy with warmth for two little kittens dressed in dragon scales and the trace of a golden pup panting because morning walks are hard with arthritis in the bones but it is harder still not to love. She writes poetry for the sake of stories she needs to tell but doesn't know how.

Jael Varma
Asifa Bano – a chirping bird who ran like a deer

She woke up "that" day to
wear the same old
faded purple frock, drank her porridge!
She galloped out of her
house with speeding
light, around the corner
she saw her mother
smiling at her.
The last time she would look at her mother.

The same old streets,
those maple trees, same shops,
she knew the landscape inch by
inch. She loved horses!
She ran towards it, to
caress them, love them,
talk to them, play with
them. What a wonderful world,
she smiled, looked at the sun squinting.

Next thing she remembered
was excruciating pain between
her legs. Slitting her apart.
She screamed but no voice
came out, she wanted to cuddle
her mother, wanted her horses,
wanted to hold her
father's little finger.
She wanted her favourite doll.

Blood dripping from her vagina,
mouth, bruises on yet to
be formed breasts. She heard
men laughing, cursing her tiny
body, same men who went
home to play father to their
8-year-old daughters.
When the last man shoved his penis inside, her
gut opened, ripping her insides.

That innocent child who
could have been "your child"
died a million deaths every
second until they killed her one last time.
The day Christ, Mohammed, Shiva
renounced their faith and killed
themselves in shame.
Only Devi sat there all stoic with
blood dripping from her vagina and eyes.

They didn't rape a child. They
raped a deity inside her own abode.

Jael Varma is based out of Bangalore, India. Holding a Masters in Mass Communication, she started writing young, and has published the poetry collection, Living on the Edge in India and is a part of poetry Anthology, Women of Eve's Garden in USA which was accepted by the Library of Congress. She runs a charitable trust for cancer patients in her Mother's Memory. She is certified in counseling psychology and works to create awareness about Mental Health. She aspires to be a voice to the voiceless.

Jaya Avendel
Queens of the Night

These women
Rise from bed
Holding diaphanous cloth to
Their carved breasts
Trail across the marble floor
Swaying to mute music.

Their fifth cousins
Twice removed
Now husbands
Will not wake
Drugged by flowering lust and its red rewards
Buried deep in cushions and sheets
Too light for comfort.

These women
Walk to the nearest window
Welcome moonlight
As the purest cleanser
For their disguised faces.

These women
Stand naked
Eyes closed in the window glass
Linking soul hands with their sisters
Framed somewhere in their own windows
Miles apart yet side by side
Alone and never alone.

These women
Let their skirt hems grow shorter
Quarter-inch by quarter inch
Sewn down firmly with threads
Spooled from the past.

These women
Tie the night around themselves
Knot it with dawn
Take mist for their hair
Disregard sleep to prepare
Their bodies for painting
Let the men in bed
Awaken to Lakshmi
Wonder that she never rumples.

Pathfinder

This is the way it was
This is the way it is
This is the way it shall be.

One step
One refusal to be blind

You are falsely entitled by
Outsiders

People who
Think of themselves as
The progress of man
Those who do not know
The dead origins of
Our traditions.

This is the way it was
This is the way it is
This is the way it shall be.

If you are
Change
We do not know you
Though we have touched you
Since birth
Carried you through love
Led you along our paths so
You can walk where we
Leave off.

This is the way it was
This is the way it is
This is the way it shall be.

"This is not the way it will be."

Arranged Marriage

Beneath a mudslide
Lies my heart
Buried because you dislodged
The wrong rock on the
Search for my soul.

In your hand
As rough as the settling dust
The shovel is bent
Like the lines of your palm.

You dig for the rose
Between my teeth
And the diamonds that are my eyes and
Find scattered petals and
An oval of coal.

You weep for your child bride
With a laugh like the sunrise
But I die happy
Crushing your ring between two fingers
Until the jewel pops off and rolls
With your head
Down the slope into the river
Where I plan to take the midnight boat
And sail with the moon.

(First Published in Free Verse Revolution)

Jaya Avendel is a blue-eyed mountain girl of Indian descent living in the Blue Ridge Mountains of Virginia. She writes family, fantasy, and poetry and can be found on Twitter as @AvendelJaya.

Jhilmil Breckenridge
reclamation song

Too black. Too white. Too straight. Too gay.
Too Hindu. Too middle class. Too thin.
Too fat. Too loud. Too quiet.

Language assaults my body. I bleed
rivers, wading through my own blood.
I cry; my single cry echoes the cries

of a hundred sisters, huddled, waiting.
My cry, the echo of every woman shamed.
My cry, the memory of every girl child killed.

And still, they speak.
Too trans. Too sexual. Too frigid.
Too much. Too little. Too.

Language, a hammer beating nails
into my body. My body, home,
to carpenters, plumbers doing DIY.

As the echoes get louder, my blood roars.
I hear the *dholak*, smell the fire,
see vermilion on her brow, hints of *mogra*

braided through her hair
Too sexy. Too fat. Too loud.
And my hips dance as I laugh.

My body reclaims my ancestors,
hears only *dholak* beats;
the scent of *mogra* everywhere.

And I am home. I am finally home.

Gateway to pleasure

My body is a broken gateway —

Gateways to pleasure
Gateways to a home
Gateways to security

How many visitors can it allow
before it begins to crack?
My body is your home, you said

Bloated from your presence, I swallowed
screams — marital rape
as commonplace as salt

How do you make a home
amid blood and placentas,
sindoor and *shehnai*?

Day after day, I decorated your home —
alta on my feet, henna on my hands.
Night after night, your hands,

a hammer on its locks
My body is a broken gateway
My body is a broken gateway

India
(after Fatimah Asghar)

India, am I not your child?
Brown, raised on your land —
saffron, basmati, mustard fields

My mouth teeming with pins
and a hundred silences,
tongue bloated

with pesticide
creeping into the loams
surrounding the holy Ganga

India, didn't you raise me to be free
and then tell me to be silent:
Women don't speak, women don't question

Wasn't it you who moulded men
who undress me with their eyes
and go on rape parties?

India, don't you make me
an orphan every day
when you make me

question my roots and watch me
burn down my house
again and again?

India, didn't you turn your back on me,
asking me to use fairness creams,
to drink Ayurvedic slimming tea?

India, am I not your child?
Who do I call Mother,
if not for you?

(All poems previously published in Reclamation Song by Jhilmil Breckenridge, first in India through Red River Press 2018 and then in the UK through Verve Poetry Press 2019.)

Jhilmil Breckenridge is a poet, writer, and activist and is the founder of Bhor Foundation, an Indian charity, active in mental health advocacy. She advocates Poetry as Therapy and is working, both in the UK and India, taking this into prisons and mental health institutions. She has recently co-edited a collection of essays on mental health and this was published as Side Effects of Living (Women Unlimited and Speaking Tiger, 2019).
Twitter @jhilmilspirit Instagram: jhilmilbreckenridge
Facebook: jhilmil.breckenridge

Jyoti Kanetkar
The Winner

Days have merged into years
And decades since my birth.
Yet inside the greying façade
Gambols a child that compels
Climbing mountains of adversity
Tirelessly till I behold the
Sunlit meadows high above.

Slowly but surely the mists
Lift as the journey is completed
From victimhood to sure-footed
Womanhood and its anointed
Destiny of victory over
Unimaginable, hard-fought,
Bloody battles, to reclaim
What was always ours:
Honour, equality, love
And freedom.

Jyoti Kanetkar is an international and national award-winning writer and poet, both in English and Marathi. Her poems, stories, essays and articles have appeared in the US, UK, Canada and India. Her published stories and poems have appeared in the Destine Literare Magazine, Canada and InnerChildPress. She has contributed to the literature art and culture journal 'Setu'. Her published material includes four short story collections and two collections of poetry.

K. Srilata
Learn From Me How to Make Pickles

And since he is a Bombay man with an avakkai heart,
mother-in-law stands on creaking knees and says,
the hope still alive in her eyes,
"Do you want me to teach you how to make them?
Mango pickles of various sorts: avakkai, maagai …
Let me show you how to pluck the mangoes
before they fall in summer,
the shapes and sizes in which to slice them,
and just how to subdue them –
in what spicy, salty, oil-pools.
It isn't hard.
Woman, you who sit at your desk all day long
and read and write. I have caught you often
staring out the window.
Learn from me how to make pickles,
and sashay, without a stumble, into my son's heart.
Wrap your fingers around kitchen-knives, not pens.
Books aren't bad, I know,
and there's nothing the matter with pretty views,
but they are nowhere close to pickles
when it comes to certain things. I should know.
I have lived on this earth longer than you
and have three grown children all raised on pickles.
But first things first: the chili should always be a bright Guntur
red."

(From The Unmistakable Presence of Absent Humans. Mumbai:
Poetrywala: 2019)

A Woman of Letters

Some days what I want to be is a woman of letters,
to retire to my study and be
solitary.
I can see it all:
that desk - neat, rectangular, coffee brown,
its drawers seductive and deep,
holding secrets from another age,
on it some paper, a pen, and an ink well,
and a bookcase filled with every kind of book -
Austen definitely and Dickinson and Chugthtai...

No adolescent daughters abandoning dresses in contemptuous
heaps.
No grubby sons, their dirty socks like bombs under my books.
No spouses, no mothers, nor mothers-in-law
with their urgent thoughts.
Sometimes all I want to be is a woman of letters.
Between chores, the very idea makes me weep.

Boxes Have That Effect

All evening, I have been considering boxes.
Hand-crafted ones, compelling and impractical,
the sort that jam easily.
I drop my earrings into one of them,
its blue-bird shimmer
gone before you know it.

I have lived in them all my life,
boxes in which I have become,
with a dangerous degree of precision,
this, that, the other, or etcetera.
I have noted the contents of their insides,
Not bad boxes to be in and yet,
I have clawed at their lids
like some death-row prisoner.

A Professor of English at IIT Madras, K. Srilata was a writer in residence at the University of Stirling, Scotland, Yeonhui Art Space, Seoul, and Sangam house. She has five collections of poetry, the latest of which, The Unmistakable Presence of Absent Humans, was published by Poetrywala in 2019. Srilata has a novel titled Table for Four (Penguin, India) and is co-editor of the anthology Rapids of a Great River: The Penguin Book of Tamil Poetry.

Kaikasi V.S.
A Natural Death

The night train ran past a listless female body
A scattered ensemble of entrails remains
The tracks reek of a pungent disdain
Parts carried away to distant lands by the benevolent Jammu-Tawi
To be a speck in the multitude of tales that are smothered on its way
She who has not stepped out of her hometown
Now has the privilege of peregrinating the nation
Raped, some say
Honour killing, perhaps
Torn apart by remorse, probably
Accident, no way
Bored with life, sure
Speculations galore hushes unleashed
Whimpers, flash cries, flood of narratives
Low cost
High decibel Speculative Cacophony
A set of dishevelled stories hover around
An apology of a blood-soaked body
A silent reminder of a momentous night
The carrions seem disappointed
So are the vultures who left the scene
In search of a body with the internal organs intact
A team was formed to reconstruct her past
On a table where scraped up pieces strive hard to create the story
Carving patches of edgy mysteries
Into a vast piece of being
Raven hair and sullen eyes
Sultry palms, cracked up heels
Impoverished intestines and dried up food pipe
Caved in insides like dark chambers within the craggy terrain
Icicles laden cavities of abandonment
'Death due to natural causes', they conclude
The front-page story slowly crawls up to the corners
And neatly fade away from the collective memory
Yet, the hounds near the tracks have never visited the spot again.

Why are Cyclones Named After Women?

Why are cyclones named after women?
Not all, but a majority of them sounds feminine
Violent as it unleashes its fury
And brings down structures of glory, feud, and blood
In a matter of seconds
Disrupting boundaries
Challenging the forecasts
Mocking at man-made wonders
Disregarding entreaties
Makes a cursory glance at boards that say 'No man's land'
What makes them name these cyclones after women?
Who makes an ally with the subtle rains and breezy winds?
Feed them with tales of suffering and injustice
Trigger their passions, instill in them the madness
Ensuring a triple alliance
The rivers, mountains and the earth are mere accomplices
To dismantle the cartographical signatures of man
The last time they named one as 'Shakthi', the all-powerful
'Kali', they name her as an appeasement strategy
"Have mercy, they cringe and plead
Yet she notices beneath their blotchy eyes
Seeds of revenge when everything gets subsided
She has seen a helpless soul crushed under his feet, a severed
foetus, a dismembered soul
Still I wonder
Which sagacious souls name these cyclones after women?

Kaikasi: A Lamp Abandoned in the Forest

aha! There you are reading again-
Oh! This is that inauspicious time of the year
The lamp is lit; the dust has settled
Sacred mantras from the temple fill the air
Are you reading or simply chanting?
Verses from the Adikavya.
Good! A pathway to the elusive heaven
Do you know that this was written by a thief!
Transformed for the better
One who was flickering amidst duty, faith, and penalty
So you believe everything written as a shloka?
Where are our voices?
My voice?
My clan— the mighty demonic abode
Emotionally blackmailed by the father Sumali
"Kaikasi, my child, the future of our Rakshasa tribe is in your
hands"
My wide-eyed innocence urged him to proceed
"Marry Sage Visravas "
"Your children alone can save us "
I have not heard of women empowerment
Neither have I received a lecture on gender equality
Not heard terms like patriarchy —
I loved my father
The faint smell of 'chamatha'
Failed to ignite my passion yet—
The clarion call of 'puthridharma' beckoned me
Caught in the snare of my charm
Lay the penance of Sage Visravas
Dedicated his wisdom in return to my passion
Like an ivy crushed by a mighty oak
The weight of his penance upon my frail self
A heap suffocated by an alien Aryan ethos
Motherhood in shackles
Three times it deified tradition

The fourth was incomprehensible
Condemned by the world as the mother—
The mother of Ravana
All this for you, O dear father
I live on like a lamp abandoned in the forest
Waiting to be filled with silence
Don't close your book
Give me a better story

Ms. Kaikasi V.S. is presently working as Asst. Professor of English, University College, Thiruvananthapuram. She has published a number of articles in the field of literature, sociology, and film studies. Her area of research is Indian Mythology and she is equally interested in translating literary works in her mother tongue to English. She is also an accomplished creative writer and bi-lingual translator whose poems have appeared in several national and international anthologies including 'The Poetry of Flowers' and 'Mytho Madan'. She has also contributed to 'Indian Literature', the bi-monthly journal published by Sahithya Akademi.

Kalpna Singh-Chitnis

The Salt of a Woman

Here she goes down, again
like a tree. Bark naked.
Her flowers stolen, fruits eaten,
tongue clipped, and vagina axed.

From every stem of her body oozes
the salt of a woman, and her tears
like the ancient rivers of her land.

Her story is much older than her civilization
invaded and plundered, conquered and gifted,
questioned and blamed, dismissed and shamed,
over and over and over again.

Mirror

They would call her Kali,
tease her with a Bollywood song
"See the raven fly like a swan."

Playing hopscotch in the street,
she would run at once inside her house.
She hated the song. The bully kids!

She would lock herself in her room
and look at her face in the mirror
piercing gaze in her olive skin.

Her lips were lilac.
There was a fire glowing in her brown eyes
like the gold filaments of violets.

She was beautiful. Mirrors don't lie.
She made all the mirrors, her friend.
But the story didn't end.

Kali

She was made with kohl of endless nights,
with darkness, before the light appeared in the universe
sparkling her eyes to begin the creation.

She is the consort of the Shiva,
the eternal mother, wrathful and merciful.
Her eyes are intoxicating, and teeth a string of white pearls.

On her protruding tongue, the forces of
creation and devastation dance eternally.
She is tumultuous like a sea, unfathomable.

In her essence, she is elegant.
In her appearance, she is dark and ferocious.
How she alighted on the earth, and why,

there are many legends to tell,
but the truth is one - She was always there.
She is the *Kala*, the time,

the past, present, and future unmanifested.
Transcendent, she has existed,
beyond the limits of our five senses.

With her sword and sickle, trident, and skull-cup,
she appears on the battlefields. She drinks from her cup,
the blood of the beasts, preventing them from cloning.

In her madness, she is sane.
In her darkness, she is light.
She isn't a myth. She is the crux of the universe.

She is the earth, wind, fire, water, and sky.
She is the darkest shade of the eternal flame,
which devours the darkness itself.

Kalpna Singh-Chitnis is an Indian American poet, writer, and Editor-in-Chief of Life and Legends. Her works have appeared in notable journals like World Literature Today, California Quarterly, Indian Literature, Pirene's Fountain, and others. Her poetry books have won multiple awards, and her poems have been translated into many languages. Her latest poetry collection Bare Soul was awarded the 2017 Naji Naaman Literary Prize for creativity. Her poems and translations are anthologized worldwide. Website: www.kalpnasinghchitnis.com https://www.instagram.com/kalpnasinghchitnis www.facebook.com/KalpnaSinghChitnisOfficialPage

Kalyani Bindu
This is how I knew

This is how I knew:
You *even* subverted my mornings.

Morning air cracked in shy slivers
from the pith of your nose
legs opened triangular bird mouths
spewing clairvoyant basilisk lizards
walking in hot algae-ridden pee
finding waterways for veins in fiery calm
to read mishaps like seers in bugs
flipping in the gravel and bone of my eyes.

You dawned on me like an impostor of my morning.

This is how I really knew:
a sentinel shadow of a *"coo"*
drumming under your breath—
a skeletal vestige of a fatal hoot
from your nocturnal haunt.

Now you know.

(Published in Asian Signature and Active Muse)

Cartography of a time

Shoulders grow mounts and valleys, hold pools of afternoon
      sweat—
fluidic mementos of a day that rose and fell from the hills to the
      zenith
of your crimson bloated eyes, the fever of your focus — a collateral
      damage
(of) the fragmentation of your biodiversity — of appearances and
      reappearances
of a muse, teeming (in retrospect) with dogs, cicadas, snakes,
      purple flowers
bitten and stomped. But, most of all, the dirt on your hairy legs
      fusing
into a developing hurricane on weekends, the meticulously skinned
      and deboned
flesh fillet on my thigh becoming a stand-in for a neat landscape.
      Clean and bloody.
With gravel in my mouth, I recollect you in a disembodied voice.

*Kalyani Bindu is an Indian writer and researcher, and author of Two
Moviegoers. Her poems and essays have appeared in Better than
Starbucks, Ethos Literary Journal, New Asian Writing, Variant
Literature Journal, Madras Courier, Muse India, Modern Literature, the
Indian Express and others.*

Kamayani Vashisht
Recipe for Ladyfinger Pickle

You will need to hunt for the finger
That has learnt to explore herself
Not slender, not manicured, not gloved
Maybe one that has stood up
In the face of challenges and denials.

A bottle of oil
From the deepest crevasses of desire
Collected from the press, drop by drop
Each time the finger has found home
And home has found her.

Some salt from the sweat and tears
That have found way
Through the network of lines on her face
That deepened and widened
With each passing life she let go.

Some vinegar she has fermented
In the casks of sweet nothings gone sour
And in the bottles that stored her dreams
Before they became rancid
And smelt of putrid possibilities.

Condiments she has collected
Over years of delicious encounters
That tantalized her taste buds
In the most vibrant gardens
Of love, of joy, of hate, of anger.

Assemble the ingredients at room temperature
And let the jar bask in the sun
For a lifetime.

NOTE: DO NOT SERVE TO PIGS
They don't relish pickled lady fingers.

Born to the Mountains

We're born to the mountains
Where landslides are the norm
Where clouds like to burst
And sweep away hamlets
We're born in ravines
That connect to the other side
With bamboo and rope swings
Woven with faith in each leap

Dear girl, we cannot wear slippers
Made of glass and dreams
Or gowns that sweep
Carpeted banquet halls
We cannot wear our hair
Like the beauties in ivory towers
We must not wait for carriages
Driven by charming prospects
Or seek candy and chocolate
On walls plastered with gems.

We are born to the mountains
Where landslides are the norm.
Go shop for a pair of reed slippers
Some sheepskin to keep you warm
Firewood, wild-berries, and honey
A knife, a flint-stone and a pot
To cook your broth atop the crag

Displaced from its hook
Go sleep in the cave with the wolves
And illuminate your heart with your pain
Eat nettle for dinner and
Drink deep on dew
Write your story in blood
And blow it to the wind
Set out alone for picnics
By the stream or on the moon
Dance with your shadow
To the hum of the universe
We're born to the mountains
Mountain spirits we must be.

And
don't forget to shave your head
Hair is entanglement!

Kamayani (Bisht) Vashisht teaches English at a Government College in Shimla, Himachal Pradesh. She has recently discovered poetry as a friend who delivers her aborted experiences. Her area of interest has been a feminist understanding of fantasy, especially in fairy tales. She has two published books: Dioramas of Girlhood, 2016, The Witch must Die and Other Poems (Poetry), 2019.

Kanchan Rathna
Dustasamhartri- the destroyer of all evil

Kanchan Rathna is a Visual artist based in Bangalore, India. The 'Kali Project' is very close to her heart as it is the perfect platform for the expression of anger, frustration & extreme sadness over the most gruesome crimes against women in Indian society & the world over. Her artwork is particularly in reaction to the most horrifying recent rape case in Hathras, a small town in the state of Uttar Pradesh in India. Hence, she has named her art work 'Dustasamhartri- the destroyer of all evil' to bring out the fact that the 'Kali' resides in each of us mortal women & she will be aroused each time women are faced with injustices, atrocities & crime!

Kashiana Singh
The Goddess Fallacy

My goddess is Ananda
She quickens into her
Shakti, into her bhakti
She writes her ghazals
Into her dohas, and she
Sings with abandon, her
Voice a seductive flute
Floating into the minds
      of lame Gods, her
      ecstasy now haunting
Burning into them, vibrance
Scattering all across her
Lakshman Rekha's—
Is a ripe cedar fragrance
of wild desires.
She is chorus
Echoing into his cliffs
Gods and
      His kingdoms
      consumed, she
Brings the dimming Surya
To his feet, as her currents
Thrust through his fire, in
a daze, she shifts her gaze
Into the quicksand of her
Ganga, impure she invites
The rainbow devas, cradles
Rudra's flickering desire
Into her floating waves
Her hair asway
      tossing drunkenly a
Volcano of untruths
Her bosom rising
      and falling
quaking
awakening

earth swerving
to a heaving goddess, as
She soothes the lisping
Sages who simper chants
      into her heaving embrace
      slaves
to their own vapors, they
dwell in colors of pretense
She a goddess
A ripe pomegranate chanting
She a goddess
A tandav inside her wombs
She a goddess
A lava spouting in her sky
She a goddess
A verse crumbling in hiccups
His egos grudgingly in awe
Of her lusting goddess forms
Of her Ganga, Parvati, her Devi
her Sita's, her Andal's, now her
dancing Apsara, a Meera anew
Under the squinting sunlight
As they watch passionless
She defines new orbits, rotates
On unmeasured circumferences
—arrhythmic
they shudder
She paints the galaxy of gods
with graffiti of her lightning
She spews the breath of her
ballads into their conch shells

JapNeet Kaur
The Goddess Fallacy

JapNeet Kaur illustrated Kashiana Singh's debut poetry collection, Shelling Peanuts and Stringing Words. In 2019, Japneet gave visual life to Kashiana's three part poem about the Sikh Sahebzaade, His Own Magnificent Sons.

Kashiana Singh
Reclaiming Kali

Invitation to my nectar
I offer, as I kneel into
my firmament
    almost
     in prayer
unraveling
a moaning of absence
as I churn into myself
and flow full
into the earth
    the cosmos
    confessional
    as it constricts
    and contracts
    shredding itself
into a cyclical
flourish
adequately
reclaiming itself
at the altar
of my flames
my Kali[1]

[1] *Kali – Kali is one of the Goddess Avatar's in Hindu mythology and represents a complex origin deeply rooted in tribal folklore and history. In simplistic terms, she is the Goddess representing power, Nature, the force of time. In the context of the poem, she is simply being used to refer to the symbolize the primordial feminine force – the duality of nurturing, yet devouring which is a woman's relationship to her own body, acceptance of the menstrual cycle and the cosmos*

JapNeet Kaur
Reclaiming Kali

JapNeet Kaur

Kashiana Singh lives in Chicago and embodies her TEDx talk theme of Work as Worship into her every day. Her poetry collection, Shelling Peanuts and Stringing Words presents her voice as a participant and an observer. Her chapbook Crushed Anthills is a journey through 10 cities – a complex maze of remembrances to unravel. Her poems have been published on various platforms including Poets Reading the News, Visual Verse, Oddball Magazine, Café Dissensus, TurnPike Magazine, Inverse Journal, and many others. Kashiana is the winner of the 2020 Reuel International Poetry Award. She carries her various geographical homes within her poetry.

JapNeet Kaur's foray through this project in illustrating for poetry is an extension of her passion to design the life she loves. Recognized for her art in various forums, she creates bespoke art-pieces and has had the privilege of creating for renowned celebrities like JohnLeguizamo and Tiffany Pham amongst others. She also had an opportunity to showcase her artwork for UN Women: She Innovates Global Launch on Women's International day 2019 in NYC, to spotlight the global problems being solved by women and girls. Recently her artwork dedicated to women's issues made it to the front of the book cover 'Ripping Off The Hoodie': Encouraging the Next Generation of STEM girls authored by #1 International Best Selling author Shannon Wilkinson; a STEM Advocate and a women who are changing the face of Technology as recognized by Las Vegas Women in Technology. JapNeet lives in NewYork and besides art, her life revolves around the two men that are her anchors – her husband, Sumit, and son, Armaan

Kavita Ezekiel Mendonca
Arranged Marriage

I was born in the land of arranged marriages
My birth and the land were not a choice.
Three types of unions traveled with me across this land
Arranged, semi-arranged, and love marriages made this journey.

If the horoscopes match, the planets align and the families are happy
With your color, height, education, cooking skills, and dowry
Named 'bride' price in other cultures,
You had an arranged marriage, a story to tell your children,
Extolling the joys of such a union as subtle encouragement.

If, by the strong power of suggestion, you are introduced by family
    friends
Subtle but overt matchmaking, he's a nice guy and she's so pretty,
Getting a chance to connect on Facebook and meeting over coffee
Your union was 'semi-arranged,' like the one my parents had.
There was no Facebook in their days, but my father was a poet
So my mother went to a Poetry reading and was charmed!

If you fell in love, arranged your own affairs, with some approval
(If they disapprove you can tell them you'll elope)
A compromise can be negotiated, as in my case,
Appease the parents with statements like 'Love is blind', so I can't help
    it
If I love him, and apologise profusely, grovel a little for their
acceptance.

My father asked if I could stay home a little while longer
It was too early to leave home, according to him
At twenty-six, and in love, age was a factor for an Indian girl
Wasn't he kind of making an arrangement or semi-arrangement for
    me?

Perhaps, I was not born with the arranged marriage gene
I had escaped to freedom.

Death by Dowry

My mother's nightmares saw my burning body
While her daughter cooked his meal in the kitchen.
The kerosene was for the stove, not for human flesh and bone.

My mother read stories of dowry deaths
In the morning papers before we awoke.
After she fried the onions in the kitchen,
Her dreams turned the onions into charred remains
Of her precious daughter, her tears 'bittered' the curry.

My mother had me pack my trousseau with cheap sarees
She had no flat, or phone or fridge to give us
My old clothes to be worn in the husband's home,
Tell him and his mother we don't believe in Dowry
Or find another man to love your beauty in worn sarees.

I did not serve him his dinner
Nor eat after he had eaten
Though that was the family tradition
We ate together.
I was his dowry, no diamonds in my ears.
And my mother slept peacefully
And stopped reading stories in the newspaper.

I was one of the lucky ones
The kerosene was for the stove
I was free to write my own destiny.

*(**Bride burning** is a form of domestic violence practiced in countries
located on or around the Indian subcontinent. A category of dowry
death, bride-burning occurs when a young woman is murdered by her
husband or his family for her family's refusal to pay additional dowry.)*

The Poet's Breath

Walk gently here, careful how and where you step
For here, where girls discarded like candy wrappers,
Where female fetuses destroyed in the still of night
Wrapped in ragged shawls or torn scarves
Are left to be devoured by wild animals
In the jungle of survival,
Or drowned in rivers
Not fortunate enough to be rescued
Like Moses in the bulrushes.

I am she who
Born free in the land of the free
Speaks for them.

In that same country, in a hospital
'New Hospital for Women,'
I opened my eyes to my first cry
As a 'new woman.'
Later I would rename the hospital
'Hospital for New Women.'
In my mind alone, of course,
Some things are prophetic, time makes those revelations.

A poet with a different philosophy
Entered the room
Listened to my first breaths
Cradled me in his arms
Breathed a name on me
Speaking it quietly, almost a whisper
Yet, loud enough for all to hear.
Mother was deaf to my cries,
She had hemorrhaged badly,

Father rejoiced at the birth
Of a girl, his girl
A daughter, born in the land of the free.

He believed his daughter was a gift from his God
She would be named *Kavita*, symbolically.
His joy would shower poems on her
While others with girl-children
Knit their brows, puzzled.
Is he crazy, a little touched in the head?
Maybe his poetry made a fool out of him.
What shall I protest?
A girl wanted in a country
Where girls are unwanted?
He wanted me and took me home
A girl, his daughter, his first-born.

Indian sweets were distributed
Neighbors raised their eyebrows
Surprised, but with silent voices.
'Light-skinned, and hair of golden curls
At least she will not have much trouble
Finding a marriage partner,' they said
'We'll have to check her height and cooking skills,'

My darker-skinned friends taunted and teased
While Michael Jackson later sang
"It don't matter if you're black or white."

My aunts and grandmothers
Simply prayed I would be like Ruth and like Esther.
May all fathers be poets.
And all aunts and grandmothers pray prayers
For their girls to be women of faith and character
Loved for their hearts and minds
Not their colour.

I want to go home to this
Way of life, this kind of land.

(*Kavita is Sanskrit for poem)

Kavita Ezekiel Mendonca was born and raised in a Jewish family in Mumbai. She was educated in Mumbai, with Masters' Degrees in English and Education, from India and the U.K. Her career spanned over four decades, teaching English, French, and Spanish. Her first book, Family Sunday and Other Poems was published in 1989. Her poems have appeared in various publications. Kavita is the daughter of the late poet, Nissim Ezekiel.

Kavita A. Jindal
Katra
May 2014

My sisters
you have been strangled and hung
from the mango tree.
For international papers
you've been
a horrific story

until the next disaster and outrage elsewhere.

My sisters
don't forgive us
our broken world
our exclamations and excuses
our failure to educate
menfolk in decency

our not being able to provide you safe toilets.

You didn't need lavatory buildings
commodes or toilet seats
you needed safety,
be it in fields
or walking the lanes
around your home.

You needed no one to believe they were better than you.

You needed no one to assume
you mattered so little
that you could be killed
you could be child pawns
of punishment and disgrace
and the police would think nothing of it.

My sisters, it was not you who were shamed.

It was everyone else.
Perhaps you were raped
perhaps you were spotted talking
to a male friend
perhaps you were abducted.
None of this is your shame.

It is ours
that it can even be said
that two teenage girls
should be strung up
silenced
by their own dupatta.

We failed you in so many ways.

My sisters
don't forgive
bequeath your souls to the breeze
so the perpetrators hear you
carrying with them always
your unforgiveness.

Don't let them forget; don't let us forget.

(First published in MIR Online, Birkbeck, 2015. Also included in the collection Patina, 2019.)

Faucet

A woman
may buy a tool-kit and know how to use it
may change the washer, adjust the stopcock
swap the ball bearings
fix the leaky spigot with a spanner.

A woman may suggest to Nature
that for the next millennia
men become pregnant
a facetious fractious suggestion;
the woman knows her pleas
are just venting, as ineffectual
as hammering water.

A woman may not drive in Saudi Arabia
may not bike unless in a ladies' only park
may not be seen in public without a male protector.
A woman must also be fertile
dribbling out male heirs;
she may spout songs in private
and dance in full Dior, smeared with make-up
for her mirror and other ladies to see.

A village panchayat in Punjab declares
that mobile phones given to girls
leads them to pre-marital sex;
boys can have cell phones and call for help
when they're in trouble, but females,
young things, must take it on the chin,
remaining on the drip-drip of advancement.

A woman there thinks: what if instead of aborting
the female foetuses, the nozzle was turned off
as if by a spell, a sorcery; no babies were born
to the women of this village, then the new elders
all men, would die out without replacement
and further afield too, the taps would be fixed just so
by the women who knew how.

(Inspired by 'Woman' by Arun Kolatkar. First published in The Feminist Times, 2013.)

Kavita A. Jindal is an award-winning writer whose work has appeared in anthologies and literary journals worldwide and been broadcast on BBC Radio and European radio stations. She is the author of the novel Manual For A Decent Life which won the Brighthorse Prize. She has published two poetry collections to critical acclaim: Patina and Raincheck Renewed. She's worked as an editor for literary journals and she's the co-founder of 'The Whole Kahani' writers' collective.

Kavita Ratna
Ringed in

My ring
slipped unnoticed
except for the clink
and a momentary glint.

Mind leapt
to the image of radiant Shakuntala
gracefully reaching out
to silver ripples.

Was she then lost
pining for home,
or entranced in the vision of
a secure future
reflected in the
shifting mirror beneath?

The band of promise,
coming undone,
sinking deeper
than a desperate prayer.

A costly mistake
for a child-woman
drawn to a powerful one
with a highly selective memory

If the poor fish,
pregnant with gold
had not surfaced
and been split wide open,
by hungry hands,
What finale awaited her?

Would she have been
better off,
without the cursed King,
even if left to return home
berated for her
indiscretion?

Would we have
then not been
citizens of 'Bharatha'
the land of her
thunderbolt of a son,
who conquered and claimed
as far as eye could see?

Would we have
refused to cower
beneath the sword of quest
and power;
and rebuffed histories
crafted by the mighty
who dare to define
realities at whim...

Kavita Ratna is a social development activist working in the areas of children's rights, political decentralisation, and developmental communication for over 30 years. Her anthology of poems, 'Sea Glass' has been published in 2020. She is based in Karnataka with her family. https://in.linkedin.com/in/kavita-ratna-3b2bb9b

Kirun Kapur
Waiting for Sleep, I Imagine Sita in Her Youth

She hid all day in a tree,
ate guavas rubbed with salt and pepper,

stalked the long-haired cat, begged
for rotis, ghee, and sugar,

watched as her mother dressed,
bangles stacking her arms like gauntlets.

From the window she could see
women from every corner of the city

walk into the river, disappear
then rise clean, saris soaking.

She drank milk from a hammered brass cup,
around her aunts, cousins unrolled their sleeping mats.

Of course, a woman oiled her hair.
Of course, a woman lined her eyes.

The inner world was made of women,
they filled her stomach, mouth, breath.

What do I need to see embroidered
in my mind's own dark? This girl

young enough to fall asleep. This dream
taking her into its current

so we might both rise ready
to wring out the story.

Reincarnation Ghazal

I have looked back to see   my own body,

    unsure if it could really be my own   body.

The soft wood of the willow tree   splits easily—

    Who has the right to oversee   my body?

On TV, men smile,   white,   in fresh blue suits.

    I fill the doctor's forms regarding   my own body.

I count my breaths,   careful   slow,

    Friend,   refuse   to be a refugee from your
body.

Laxmi was reborn as Sita; Mary carried   God as man.

    Did they ever want to flee   their human body?

Good years,   more years   I've watched her thinning
skin—

    the woman who gave me   my own body.

Fixed high on the temple wall,   carved stone couples
twist.

    Tourists wonder: *is that joy*   *a possibility*   *for my own body?*

The tulip   lost its petals   in the spring's warm wind.

    What force   can set me free   in my own body?

(Both of these poems appear in my second book, Women in the Waiting Room, published by Black Lawrence Press, October 2020. Grateful acknowledgement is also made to the editors of the following publications where these poems first appeared, sometimes in different forms: Mantis: "Waiting for Sleep, I Imagine Sita in Her Youth" Raleigh Review: "Reincarnation Ghazal" [as "Incarnation Ghazal"].)

Kirun Kapur is the winner of the Arts & Letters Rumi Prize and the Antivenom Poetry Award for her first book, Visiting Indira Gandhi's Palmist (Elixir Press, 2015). Her second collection, Women in the Waiting Room, was a finalist for the National Poetry Series (Black Lawrence Press 2020). Her work appears in AGNI, Poetry International, Prairie Schooner, Ploughshares and many other journals. She serves as a poetry editor at Beloit Poetry Journal. www.kirunkapur.com @kirunkapur

Kripi Malviya
Mielikki

She holds herself often
Small veins under translucent skin hide on the sides of her
forehead
until the sky hair allow them to be seen

It's difficult to tell whether the purple on her eyelids are her own
or something she takes on from the lakes
but they cause a hailstorm when you look at her just the same

It's hard to look at her.
Like taking in all of her at the same time
will root your muscles to her ashen ground

I have seen the flow of her rivers now
and there are few things so clear and brilliant
as her motion

She is watchful, the forest maiden,
watchful of her hidden terrors
and of yours, if you look hard enough

She holds herself often
and she folds you too,
taking whole northlands with her

(from her first chapbook 'ale(theia)'.)

Kripi Malviya is an existential, intersectional and queer psychologist and poet. She lives in India where she runs an emotional wellbeing organisation called TATVA combining psychotherapy, nature therapy and cultural immersion with creative exploration and emotional awareness She is the co-founder the Poetry Therapy Society of India and her work has been published and performed in literary, cross-disciplinary and psychotherapy journals, conferences and festivals nationally and internationally (notably Psychedelic Press UK, the Four Quarters Magazine and the Sunflower Collective and the Black Warrior Review, 45.1). She is the winner of the 2017 Rhythm Divine International Poetry Chapbook contest for her first poetry collection ale(theia).

Lahari Mahalanabish

The Vegetable Vendor

She walks miles with her basket
heaped with brinjals, okra, gourds, and lemons
to the open market in the lane beside the flyover;
the remaining vigour climbs along her
windpipe as she cries out to passersby,
holding out the freshest of her stock.
Her shop a rag stretched upon dirt.

Rains
work up her wares in the fields
and blood-tinged sneeze and a jouncing cough in her chest.
She feels she would die in the mud.

The day advances, purchasers dwindle.
Did her children go to school
or had they bunked like they so often did?
Was her husband at the gates of the shopping complex
he guarded
or still oblivious of daylight in his drunken sleep?

When stars spark against the lattices of mobile tower,
when the street lamp turns its glowering
 eye on the unsold greens,
and when the shadows slice the lane
into stretches for us and them,
lurks the sidekick of the local leader,
on whose assent she figures in the food market.
No, he never eats vegetables.

Way back home, vehicles grunt at traffic lights,
with women in well starched dresses
in sales and marketing, perhaps,
fanning their tired faces with dignifying files,
but even with a lighter basket on lucky days
the vegetable seller is
a heaving moon in its forced rays of chain.

A Mother like Kali

The soot-coated Devi
separates from the black night
through her halo
like the eclipse.

Rituals flow along the course of the sacred stream,
drums throb up tunes of demon-slayer battles,
the shining, white curve of the scimitar
shells moons for bubbling galaxies.

Skin decays from the severed demon heads
with their repentance frozen as pain
and they turn expressionless skulls
but that too crumbles into calcium
to nourish her off-springs

The skirt of arms also falls apart,
hands that sinned strewn under silt
holding in fingers green germinating seeds,
blood turns hibiscus at her feet.

When the third eyelid parts, the world dissolves
and the pupil blazes out to a celestial quagmire,
in a waltz of elements, in a torrent of white dwarfs
knots disentangle to lives and lives stretch to
the reach of eternity
through unified blasts and frenzied light.

Lahari Mahalanabish (Chatterji) is a writer and poet based in Kolkata, India. Her book of poems entitled One Hundred Poems had been published by Writers Workshop, India in 2007. She had been a finalist in the Erbacce Prize Poetry Competition in 2009 and also in 2010. Her poems have found places in anthologies such as Yellow Chair Review 2015 Anthology and Freedom Raga (2020).
She blogs at http://theserpentacursedrhyme.blogspot.com.

Lakshmi Kannan

An Autopsy

When they cut her open
everything was in order.
Just about everything was identifiable, teachable,
in short, under control.
That is, everything except her brains.

They baffled the white coats, her brains,
for there was a honeycomb
where there should have been grey matter.
Tiny hexagonal boxes could be seen
storing viscous honey

they could almost scoop it up, sticky
with their probing, gloved fingers.

She had stashed away her private moments, this woman,
stored them up,
sheltering them from the dour,
censoring eyes of the world.

And now, they had gold-browned the insides
of her brains in a wild-grown honeycomb
that glistened under their questioning eyes.

(Acknowledgement, Sipping the Jasmine Moon: Poems by Lakshmi Kannan, New Delhi, Authors Press, 2019.)

Don't Wash
(For Rasha Sundari Debi)*

No, don't.
Don't ever clean with water
the dark, sooty walls
of your kitchen, Rasha Sundari.

For the *akshara* you scratched
on the walls so furtively,
the *akshara* you tried to match
with the sounds you heard

They've quickened now, with life.
Even as you wash rice, fish, vegetables
even as you peel, cut, bake, stir and cook
the thieving letters on the wall will take wings.

They fly down to the palm leaf
you once stole from your son.
See how the letters move
in the eyes of the mind,

then leap over, back to the wall
from the page of *Chaitanya Bhagavata*
you tore from the book
when no one was looking.

You need no book, Rasha Sundari
no paper or pen either
you have the black, smudgy kitchen wall
for your magical scribbles

lines, ellipses, curves
all of them your secret codes for
a whole new world.

Rasha Sundari Debi: Also referred to as Rassundari Devi was born in 1810. Rasha Sundari Debi wrote the first full-fledged autobiography in Bangla titled Amar Jiban (My Life). She lived during the times when literacy was denied to women because of a deep-rooted superstition that a married woman who reads, or as much as touches a book would be widowed. Rasha Sundari Debi tore a page from the book Chaitanya Bhagavata when her husband left it in the kitchen for a moment. She also stole a palm leaf used by her son for writing. Then she compared the two, learning the syllables of the language on her own by writing on the walls of her kitchen, and by matching the letters she saw with the sounds she heard. Her autobiography was acclaimed for its lucid and readable prose).

(Acknowledgment Sipping the Jasmine Moon: Poems by Lakshmi Kannan, New Delhi, Authors Press, 2019.)

Lakshmi Kannan has published twenty-seven books till date that include poems, novels, short stories and translations. Sipping the Jasmine Moon (New Delhi, Authors Press, 2019) is her fifth collection of poems. She was a Resident Writer at the International Writing Program, Iowa, USA; a Charles Wallace Trust Fellow at the University of Kent, Canterbury, UK; Fellow, Indian Institute of Advanced Study, Shimla. Besides English, she also writes in Tamil in the name of 'Kaaveri'.

Lakshmi Tara
At the cusp of eternity

Raven-song

Here,
at the edge
of all things known
we may tumble,
like a shared dream, recurring
into reams, (my words, your songs,)
char-black and sown,
once-dormant seeds of
mythical selves,
well-kept secrets,
hidden entrances to the
temple of the old goddesses.
Home!

Here, now,
as our strange paths cross
(womb to womb),
It is the Earth's turn
to reap her harvest and toll
and ours, to dance
through it
all.

Ash, overgrown

Mortal remains at mother's lap

Lakshmi Tara is a self-taught artist and writer based in South India. She believes that art is a perfect tool to explore (and expand) consciousness, and that her inner worlds unfold best through her paintings and poems. Her art process is intuitive, mostly freehand, with minimum references. Her work primarily deals with the transpersonal and mystical; influenced by Jungian psychology, Buddhist and Tantric philosophy, nature, and most importantly, The Feminine.

Dr. Laksmisree Banerjee
Unborn Kill

I felt my throbs
deep within
the frothy warmth of
my mother's insides.

I was she ...
a teardrop on the serrated edge
of being,
a dew on her hidden, clement leaf
soon to be sucked out by
the boiling seas, the hot winds
of prejudice.

I am not sure when
or how my mother
loved or wept ...
not sure whether
it was a blunder, a crime,
an accident
or perhaps moral turpitude ...

But sure enough
I wept with her in pain
while my instant was
blotted out under
the dark arc lights
in an ageless cry.

She

Married off on her eighth birthday
She hardly knew what
That dark red orb
Staining her forehead like blood
Meant.

She heard the bells ringing
Within a few years,
Jingling with her jewels
And knew that it was springtime,
That it was the
Happiest season of blossoming
In her life.

But suddenly the cruel
High tide ebbed,
The efflorescence waned off
Into extinction,
Into the agony of white.

As she was told that
She was a widow
For life.

Prof. (Dr. Ms.) Laksmisree Banerjee is a Senior widely published and anthologized Indian-English Poet. A University Professor of English and Cultural Studies, she is a Sr. Fulbright Scholar (USA), Commonwealth Scholar (UK) and National Scholar in English (India). She has Five Published Books of Poems, Two Academic Books and One Hundred Twenty Research Publications on the Literary Analysis of diverse areas of Poetry including her work on World Women Poetry.

Lathaprem Sakhya
Visibility

Woman
Just body and womb?
A disturbing question!
Her dreams? -
To live gloriously,
Victoriously, with self-dignity
Standing erect and tall,
United, powerful, diligent,
Rising above physical abuse and violence,
Transcending mutilation Philomela like,
Singing songs of fulfillment,
Weaving stories of truth
Overcoming barriers – linguistic,
Economic, political, and cultural
    Destroying invisibility.

The Trapped Bird

The night wrapped its shroud,
Hiding everything under its folds.
She listened to the gentle snores
Of her beloved and her child.
But her heart alone -
A trapped bird fluttered
     From thought to thought.

The reality, the truth of being a woman
Stereotypical images of womanhood -
Abject beings, self-effacing doormats,
Shaped by patriarchal hegemony
An angel of the house,
A perfect woman
 Haunted her.

A sudden vision of unlimited horizon
Opened, releasing the trapped bird
To fly to heights unknown.

(From Nature at my Doorstep, 2011 & Vernal Strokes, 2015.)

Latha Prem Sakhya- pseudonym of the painter-poet rtd Prof. Latha Prem kumari .B. - author of Memory Rain 2008. Nature At My Doorstep 2011 and Vernal Strokes 2015. She is widely anthologized and writes and paints regularly for many online journals and print magazines. She writes stories for children and drabbles. Her poems, paintings, and stories are of nature, humans, and her convictions. Believing in simplicity she keeps her writings and paintings lucid and clear.

Lavanya Nukavarapu
Cursed

Long ago,
when I was in my mother's womb
and didn't know I was a woman,
I heard my mother telling me that I was
CURSED.

Many years later,
when my mother was taken by the earth,
I told my daughter what my mother said to me: you are CURSED.

I said,
you will not be Sita or Ahilya,
you will bring down the Gods from the sky,
you will be KALI.

You will wear the heads of the rapists as your necklace,
you will slay patriarchy and you will kill misogyny with your sword,
and you will bear the burden of all women.

You will remain cursed for eternity,
but, for now,
you are a warrior in training

Lavanya is a professional accountant who used to deliberate only on finance until one day poems and stories beckoned her. She published her first poetry book "Bare Thoughts" in 2018. In 2019, Lavanya published her first novel, "The Captive," a psychological thriller that has received rave reviews. If metaphors and imagery are the mojos in her poetry, it is narration in her prose, manifested in the several short stories and poems.
https://www.facebook.com/lavanya.nukavarapu
https://www.amazon.com/-/e/B07KX45WJH

Lina Krishnan
Sumangali

Thinking about widowhood in India
Makes me wonder about Kashi & Brindavan
Those great embraces of unwanted womankind
Where sati naaris were cruelly exiled
once the pyre was outlawed

My thoughts turn homewards

My mother experienced, firsthand
The taste of being held at arm's length
By people she had known all her life

"We would love to invite you but...."
"The bangles are kept there....for others"
"We cannot accept kumkumam from you"

The friend that wished her on every anniversary
The nieces that asked after my father, no longer call
"Now that their uncle is gone", she says wryly
"I too, have stopped existing".

I don't find sindoor easily at her puja room anymore
And now carry my own when I visit. After all,
"You're the only sumangali here now", I'm told

A strange title to be the possessor of
It exudes little frissons of superstitious fear
Through every irrational bone in my body
I touch wood, and breathe again

So much is made of this exalted state here
Women are told from birth, may you die a
Sumangali. A married woman. Be the happy holder
Of vetala paak, the auspicious betel leaf
And remain a companion to the end, till you
Precede your partner into the afterlife

No wonder widowhood, the absence
Of this male aura, casts such a shadow
Impossible to shake off, or live with.

(Sumangali: A married woman/Kashi: another name for Varanasi/Sati Naaris: loyal wives/Bangles, kumkumam, sindoor, vetala paak: symbols of being married and therefore being acceptable at social/religious ceremonies/Puja room: the altar at hindu homes).

Lina Krishnan's past work as a communicator in India has navigated program work in the UN, science journalism, copywriting, and research and scripting for documentary films. The project she has enjoyed most is teaching art to children in a mountain village. She occupies her thoughts nowadays with abstract art, poetry and photography. Small Places, Open Spaces, her chapbook of nature verse, with Australian poet Valli Poole, was published in 2018.

Lina Krishnan

Lopamudra Banerjee
Oh Men, Comrades

Oh men, comrades, we sing a different song,
Born into the revolution of female birth.
We have labored in war, as your thorn of love
pierced our core, made us bleed.

Oh, men, comrades or rhythmic reminders—
Did the thorn pierce your hearts too?
Our radical feminism holds us in transitions,
From the haunted sadness of thwarted births
To the restlessness of love letters and coquetry,
From the Radha led astray by Krishna's flute
To the Kunti bearing Karna, her first love-child,
Tears, epic-like silences, the wet world of wombs,
Blooming anew with pleasures fought for,
Traded with momentous strife.

Oh men, comrades, we hear you've carved our destinies,
Rowed our boats since our mothers have borne us.
We hear your love is our elixir, your scornful abuses
Our poison. Comrades, we don't know who chose you
As our unsolicited Gods, in this colonized, unaccustomed earth.
Our radical feminism is our desire to be whole,
Between nameless atoms and the magic of our sculpted presence.

Oh, men, comrades in our twilight sky of unending love,
We have been scalded by your liberated, sunlit bodies,
The smug embrace of your masculine arms, the pride
Of us love-sick women, cocooning our nihilism.
Comrades, our souls have been nourished by your fire, your ice,
Our radical feminism—the naiveté and necessity
Our grandmothers and their grandmothers never knew,
The skin of sex and the crescendo of our revolution
Our daughters and their daughters and their daughters will adorn.

I crave to fight and make love, comrade, as sports played by equals!
My love, I hope to merge your roof with my sky,
Your temple with my shrine, your water with my earth.
We, the remnants of blood and earth are changing,
Our rivers gushing, forcing down before you.

Our radical feminism is not a style statement of postmodern
       longings.
Wasn't the blood of disrobed Draupadi feminism enough?
Weren't the coarse wars and solitude of the oldest women scribes
The earliest jargon of feminism?
Wasn't the enraged, trembling body of Sita
Returning to Mother Earth's core a feminist chanting?
Didn't the bold strokes of women, and men entering their moist
core
In Khajuraho, in Konark sow the earliest seeds of feminism
       blossoms?

Oh men, comrades, let your mothers teach you to strip your pride
With your first baby steps, to come to us with a new love born
within
       you,
A wet, nourishing love of the Ardha-narishwar, the half-man, the
       half-woman,
Embracing our spirits warm, our cogent fire, the palimpsest of our
       scars.

(First published online in Women's Web, an e-zine from India.)

Grandmother Mine

*(For my grandmother who was the first one to call me a feminist when I
was only thirteen.)*

Grandmother mine,
I am the legacy of your progeny,
The flesh and bones of your seed, your flesh,
The slow death of your sounds,
drenched in threatened subservience.
I wake, roam around your ancient seas
Birth life, rattle loud, screaming against
Supremacist songs.

This is how I survive—
Cooing your Bengali rain songs,
Building my cocoon around overdose of memories
Your horror stories of leaving behind
The torn, shaken Bangladesh.
The river *Padma*,
Mothering my girlhood revolution.

I am the forbidden dance,
The onset of new seasons
The distant language
The thirst and the rhythm
Of a revolution
which you had learnt well to deny.

Grandmother mine,
I am the déjà vu of your centuries of stories
The unborn cadence of your language
You had wrapped with crushing silence.
I am the importunate one, inhaling hot oil
In your airless room where you sometimes spoke
Of matriarchs and feminists-to-be,
Of nomads whom your cracked earth
Could no longer sustain, or shelter.

I wake, between continents
The skin of my ancestors, planted in my embryo.
I am the renewed song of your thirst,
The hunger of my mother,
Dressed up in a liberation song.

This is how I survive—
Chopping and screwing old definitions
Of the womb, making claims on my body,
Writing down its verses in blood and dark ink.

(First published online in Setu International Bilingual journal from Pittsburgh, USA.)

For Simone De Beauvoir

(A reaction after reading parts of 'The Second Sex' by Simone De Beauvoir, French writer, intellectual philosopher, political activist, feminist, and reflecting on them as a woman from the Indian subcontinent.)

The last time I woke up,
I remember, I demanded a third space.
A space that meandered
from the hopscotch square
Of estrogen games, from the erectile brain
of testosterone urges.
A space of my own desperation of belongings
'The Second Sex', a requirement of my syllabus,
An elusive continent, a vociferous sea,
A torrid landscape of my own making.

Simone, I hadn't known your name
The feel of that fiercely unwomanly woman
When in my girlhood, cascading beauty
Of princesses and heroines spilled
all over our barren courtyard,
from the basket of my grandmother's tales.

Love was the promise of a sanctioned cacophony
Of children to be birthed, the language of coercion
As kings banished queens for sons not born,
Princes' lip-locked with princesses,
'Hail thee, patriarchy!'

The last time you twisted and turned us
In our dreams and sold us a ticket to witness
The vestiges of war between our own troubled selves,
I remember we had pushed some boundaries,
But there were some barbed wires
which were better left on their own.

The last time your words entered my realm,
"One is not born, but becomes a woman,"
I remember the dark hunger, the denial,
The act of letting go, the truth of our beings.
Simone, we, the 'other sex', reborn, recycled
A zillion times have been churned, fermented
Reclaiming our spaces in the fickle humanity.

Lopamudra Banerjee (Lopa) is an author/poet living in Dallas, Texas, but originally from Kolkata, India. She has received critical acclaim and recognition for her award-winning memoir 'Thwarted Escape: An Immigrant's Wayward Journey' and for her five other books (poetry, translation, fiction) and also four anthologies she has co-edited. She has been a recipient of the Reuel International Prize for poetry (2017), a featured author at Rice University, Houston, and co-produced and acted in a poetry film, 'Kolkata Cocktail'.
https://www.facebook.com/lbanerjee.author
https://www.linkedin.com/in/lopabanerjee/
https://www.instagram.com/lopabanerjeeauthor/?hl=en

Madhu Jaiswal
The Murky Night

She looked beautiful with the red bindi shimmering
The jewellery and Red Banarasi saree beautifully adorning her frame
Shiny her face glimmered even in the dim light
Footsteps approaching she withdrew herself
In the farthest corner of the bed
As her husband entered the room
She welcomed him with her smile
And offered him paan, various emotions bubbling inside
He held her closely looking at her dark colour with disgust

Her curvaceous shiny body though
Bringing lust in his eyes
No introduction, no sweet talks
He just pushed her on bed jumping beside

The demure docile now
Lay silently in bed
Clasping her hands tight
Her clothes were shed thread by thread
Pounced upon like a piece of meat
Savoured and licked
Her virgin dreams died
Clutching her heart she cried in muffled tone
As he ransacked her body invading inside
The pain and humiliation
Tears trickling
Bruised and battered
The newly wed
How can she resist her husband's right
That's what she is intended to do all her life.
Fulfilling his demands was her duty to be obliged
Reeking of alcohol and disgust
Love, that she wished to be showered upon
was nowhere in sight!

Madhu Jaiswal is a bilingual poet and social worker hailing from Kolkata, India. She is associated with The Impish Lass Publishing House, Mumbai in the capacity of an executive editor. She has 7 anthologies as an editor to her credit. Her creative contributions have been published in various national and international anthologies and she often gets featured in prestigious e-zines. Her poetry was recently featured in the prestigious anthology Aatish 2 alongside various stalwarts. Also she bagged third prize in Beyond Black Sakhi Annual Poetry Awards 2019. https://www.facebook.com/madhu.jaiswal.56614

Madhu Sriwastav
Unwanted Womb

Unwanted womb
Plastic fate
Grows up in faith
someone somewhere does care
she is not a slave for all
Forced to grow up
Childhood in dumps
carrying more sisters in lap
mother's lap keeps filling up
in wait of brother to land
Each girl decreed a burden to feed
needs to be married off
till then to serve all
not expecting anything in return
A good husband and in-laws will change her life
she is made to believe and pray
fast every Monday to get a lord like Shiva1
who is careless yet divine and unflinching in love
fasting all night with faith in stride
Millions in India fast
to keep the food for the males
and keep serving them in strife
Fast for husband who feeds himself first
fast for son who will feed you in your days, last
But feed not yourself
feed not your desires that burn your state
Dream not of else but service to others
those who transgress are selfish marked
those who transgress are torn apart
Cross not the *Lakshman rekha* in life
for love or ambition of selfish strives
Speak not your attractions
lest you be *Surpnakha* made
Protest not your hubby s wiles lest you have to live
And die like *Sita* died!

(1. Shiva- One of the principal deities of Hinduism. 2. Lakshman Rekha – Circle of protection drawn by Lakshmana, for Sita in Ramayana. 3.Surpnakha – Sister of King Ravana who was attracted to Lakshmana and had her nose cut off as punishment. 4. Sita- Wife of Lord Rama in the epic Ramayana by Valmiki.)

Madhu Sriwastav is an Assistant Professor of English at Bamanpukur Humayun Kabir Mahavidyalaya. She is also a creative writer. She writes poetry, short stories and translates poetry as well as prose. She has many publications in reputed journals and anthologies such as Setu, Teesta Review, Borderless Journal, The Vase etc. She is an Executive Committee member of Intercultural Poetry and Performance Library, Kolkata. Her debut book of poems is Trips Climbs Circles.

Mandakini Bhattacherya
Missing Person

Ushered in the world with glory,
My imagined fairy story;
I vanish through the womb's crevasse,
I am the girl that never was.

No cradle with lullaby sounds,
A pariah on playing grounds,
No report-card cheered with hurrahs,
I am the girl that never was.

No feast awaits my hunger's throes,
A rag doll dressed in cast-off clothes,
No match for a lad is a lass;
I am the girl that never was.

My rainbows often turn blurry,
I'm forced to bloom in a hurry;
Pitchforked from parents to in-laws,
I am the girl that never was.

(This poem was previously published in the anthology My Tears published by AuthorsPress@2019.)

Mandakini Bhattacherya, from Kolkata, is an Associate Professor of English. She is a multi-lingual poet, literary critic, and translator. Her scholarly articles have been published in international and national journals, and also in books. Her poems have been published by international and national journals like Better Than Starbucks, The Dotism Journal, The HyperTexts, Mad Swirl, Setu, Poetry Nation, Hayati, Sahityanama, Different Truths, and LangLit. She was invited by Sahitya Akademi, New Delhi, and participated in the All India Young Writers' Meet organised by it in February 2020.

Mandrita Bose

Do not call me Durga

Do not call me Durga
And hail me as a warrior
When you have failed to respect women.
Do not call me Durga and tell me how well I manage my work and
family life all alone, without any 'help' when my body is giving way,
my eyes are drooping, my bones are tired and no, I do not cover it
up with a smile.
I scream, I complain, I cry, I shout.
That's how women in pain look like.
Do not garland me with jewelry and make-up in front of society.
A woman doesn't look picture-perfect after battling wars, every
day.
When you should have a fair share of cooking, cleaning, and
        childcare
and not just regard it as mere 'help'.
If it's not selfish on your part to not compromise on your dreams,
how can you say I'm being selfish?
My life, my dreams are of as much value as yours. My want for
equality has nothing to do with the love I have for my family.
Equality is what I believe in.
Call me Durga when you believe in equality too.

Do not call me Lakhi meye (good girl)
And tell me I'm an angel
When you only try to teach me wrongly that love lies camouflaged
within your dominant behavior, when you dictate my life, my
opinions and even my thoughts and leave me suffocated with
depression and refuse to take me to a mental health specialist,
because 'loke ki bolbe.' (what will people think?)
Do not be surprised if this Lakhi meye stops being silent, and
screams and shouts one day to live the way she likes.
Call me Lakhi only when you can stand by my side and fight for my
        respect, my rights.
Do not call me Saraswati and be proud of my achievements

When you lecture me about my weight or my looks or what I should
wear.
When your 'expert' opinions have left me with fourth-degree tears
during childbirth and PTSD issues,
When you have refused to empower women about their own bodies,
My body is not a graveyard where I'll bury every trauma and move
on.
Decisions about my body are mine to make, and never yours.
Call me Saraswati when you can support and worship my educated
decisions too.

Do not call me Kali and tell me how bravely and strongly I have
defeated the demon of an abuser
When you were too afraid to protest against abuse and attacks on
women.
When your ignorance, negligence have failed to create a safe space
for women,
Call me Kali when your blood boils just like mine when you hear,
see, and learn about crimes and continue to fight against injustice.

Do not name me after Goddesses without understanding that
I would rather have a world that cares for its women than be called
such utopian names,
than thousands of women taking their own lives.
And if you cannot respect me, stop manipulating me.
Stop insulting me,
Stop disrespecting me,
Stop saying that I am not enough, not worthy, not great,
Because I know I have conquered mountains and moons, flown
across the skies, over the waves
I have danced and taught and painted and calculated and done
everything you told me I could not.
Because I am perfectly happy with myself, and if you can't add to
my happiness,
Leave me alone.

Mandrita Bose is a spoken word poet and works as a senior copywriter in advertising. She celebrates people through an initiative called Pen Portrait (poetry on your picture). She is a Kommune Kolkata Ambassador and her debut book of poems December Waves was published in 2019. Her poems are also a part of different anthologies.

Manini Priyan

My reality

He is passionate
When he loses his temper
I am too emotional
When I raise my voice

He cannot be interrupted
Because he is trying to focus
I am not a people's person
If I ask for a few minutes

He is very busy
And cannot organize team meets
I am not a team player
If I refuse

He must be really sick
If he takes a day off
I belong to a "weak" gender
If I take a sick day

He needs financial growth
Because he has a family
I have a child
And I am no longer "committed"

You see in my country
We are not equal
Casual misogyny is just another reality

The men feel like
We should be grateful
Because we get to work
Unlike our mothers
Whose dreams were
Confined to the kitchen

But I demand for more
I need more;
Because I am a woman
I have the Goddess in me
Who tells me
To raise my voice
So that my unborn daughter

No longer needs
To wake up in this reality

I am fourteen and I am a bride

I watch as the lady
makes pretty designs
on my sweaty palms

She holds me prisoner
But I want to run
and play with my brothers

My mother explains
That this is something
That I have to do
Since there were red stains on my skirt

I didn't really understand
I was just happy that I got sweets that day
But now they are planning to send me away
They say I have a new home
That I will have to obey him
But what I really want to know
If I obey him
Will he let me play
Will he let me dance
Like Madhuri on TV

Today I wear red
When red isn't even my favorite color.

Manini Priyan is a science fiction author and a published poet whose first series of novels are under publication. Her poetry has also been published in several literary magazines and her first collection of poems was published as part of an anthology called Isolocation in August 2020. https://www.amazon.in/Isolocation-Ishmeet-Nagpal-Nirav-Mehta/ Instagram profile- https://www.instagram.com/manini_p

Manisha Amol

Black

Black colour of complexion is misunderstood by all,
Brutal hateful thoughts create a blind wall.
Polluted minds make them feel worthless,
All their efforts are reduced to nothingness.

As was her fate the little girl was born black,
Was an object of mockery, with emotions lack.
Sleepless nights interspersed with dreary dreams all along,
Wiping off the salty tears she was sad and forlorn.

The following next morning at the break of the dawn,
Despite all the misgivings she decided to fight alone.
The peeping sunlight on her shining face,
Woke up with new energy and life at full pace.

Her coming days were bright and resplendent,
With her might directed, her acts independent.
A focused mind fresh outlook thoughts positive,
Coloured the black canvas of life with a new perspective.

Starlit nights were calm and peaceful,
Cool mind riding the waves on clouds playful.
She was competing hard with the sparkling firefly,
Spreading her passionate wings she flew high.

Put her best foot forward through all ups and downs,
Took head-on the challenges without a streak of frown.
Ambitions and firm resolve free flowing like a river,
No one then dared to look down upon her.

Her mind and soul became strong inward,
Changed the game of her life outward.
She was born black there was no reason to feel shy,
Black is Beautiful! her head was held high.

Manisha Amol completed high school from DPS RK Puram and graduated in Science from Hindu College, DU. Post her MBA from IMT, Ghaziabad worked with many corporations at various levels and won many accolades for her achievements. She is currently working as a Director with a Startup. She started her literary journey 15 months back with a focus on English poetry, Hindi poetry, Short Story, and Ghazals She has been associated with numerous online portals that promote English/Hindi literature. She has participated in online talk shows, live shows, etc and have been appreciated for her work.

Manisha Manhas
You Think I Am Not A Goddess?

You think I am not a goddess?
Indeed! I am not
And I cannot be
For I dwell in the din of a house and not in the stillness of a cave.

Neither a "pativrata" nor "a samskari naari", as you say

Though, the 4 am alarm,
my insomnia, the kitchen chores,
the grocery stores, the dusting of home, our kids, their work

My school, the court case
And with you the several hospitals stays despite my back aches and
varicose veins.

And more, the weddings,
its rituals, the siblings,
our parents, the rents,
the electricity, the bills,
the medicines

And more, the insulins
which I inject in your navel
each evening is forgotten at once on my rage?

I bleed, and bleed more.

I wish you forgot that I was not a goddess.

(Pativrata: virtuous wife. Samskari: cultured)

Manisha Manhas is a Poet based in Pathankot. Manisha, when not busy teaching, is collecting memories and fragrances. She loves to travel and experience the heartbeat of nature. Looking at a flower or gazing at the night sky or staring at the mountains fills her heart with peace and beauty. She dwells in her own space where imagination and fantasy are her best friends, the friends which help her in coping up with the brutal side of the world. She also believes in writing her heart out and flowing with the current.

Manjula Asthana Mahanti
To My Father...

What kind of wedlock is it!
Took away me from you
Reared up me with love & care
Used to call me darling princess
Your princess was estranged
How could you...
I had to leave my own abode
My shelter...

You had bid me in gorgeous bridal attire
They returned me in the same bridal dress,
How they could have accepted
A daughter-in-law, without heavy dowry!
Torture, beating, humiliation
Even after all that,
They couldn't accommodate
My in-laws returned your daughter
So what! No respiration, No life
Separated for... For ever.

Dried tears, on my cheeks, ask
Couldn't you keep your daughter with you!
But how can you refrain from the customs,
How can you encounter society!
You are helpless too.
So, final separation

No idea, how many daughters have been
Offerings, in the valley of fire, of dowry,
High flames of Greed, swallowed them,
What dear daughters will receive after the wedding!
Joy, respect, care, smiles
Or, separation
Bidding final bye...

Couldn't somebody contradict
Cruel customs, eternal greed,
Attitude...!

Mahanti is a bilingual poet, author, translator, editor. She worked in a prestigious college as HOD, She last worked as a public school principal and has published six books, both the languages included. published short stories, poems, articles in many national and international anthologies emagazines, OPA, etc. Recipient of Bharat Ratna Atal Behari Bajpai award, Laureate Rabindra Nath Tagore award, Best Novelist Award, Star Ambassador of World Poetry and Art award and has been chosen amongst 25 women of Excellence, Nari Samman by Literoma, along with many other prestigious samman.

Meenakshi Mohan

I am Kali

She sat dried eye on her mother's pyre, alone
far away from the crowd shedding muddy tears.
From the time growing up in an abusive family,
She ceased calling him her father.
He was her mother's husband.
His mother and sisters were
his mother's *steps.*
Her mother's life even worse than Cinderella's,
she cooked, cleaned, washed and mended their clothes –
a slave of their whims.

Why did you stop me, mother?
She sobbed inside, no tears.

She watched as the fire gulped her mother's body to ashes
each spark, a reminder –
the burnt cigarette marks,
bruises inflicted on her mother's body by his belt.
The fire deluged her already scalded body to ashes.
Why, mother, why did you stop me?

His mother and sisters taunted you for not bringing enough dowry
When all your dowry jewelry was kept for his sisters.
Why did you cover all your scars with your sari mother?
Chup raho, dheere bolo,
he is your father, she is your Dadi, and your Buas,
Why, mother, why?

Many times, I peeked through the keyhole,
he sonorously snored while you with soft shuffling steps,
picked the bottle of tincture iodine to apply on your wounds,
Why, mother, why?
"Why did you stop me, and let their impunities flourish?
I was a witness -
when he pushed you in the tub, pouring hot, scalding water on
your
   body.

Today as your body burns, each flame burns as raging anger in
my
   body –
I looked at them with disdain, howling, and crying like a werewolf.

Today, you will not stop me, mother!
I am a witness!
They would pay with blood written on their stones.
I am Kali, and I will dance on their mortality.

She (In all Manifestations of Shakti)

She is there,
Standing at the court of law -
a woman's rights' lawyer
Adorned with all the manifestations of *Durga, Kali, Saraswati, Lakshmi.*
She is all power, strength, knowledge, the restorer of peace –
armed with all the invincible weapons,
Sword, dagger, trident, drum, chakra, lotus bud, whip, noose, bell, and shield
No more from now on –
Cultural oppression of women has to stop –
The iron-man cruel mentality has to stop.
No *Nirbhaya* would beseech a helpless cry.
No assaulter proven guilty would be granted remission of penalty.
She, a fighter for *Beti-Bachao,* and *Me-too* campaign –
would destroy the last drop of blood from *Raktabij.*
Then she with all manifestations of *Devi*
would rest and breathe in peace,
and sing glories of
Rani Lakshmi Bai and many others
and walk shoulder-to-shoulder with men on the road of equality.

(Shakti – empowerment. Daruka – A demon who could only be killed by a woman. Kali killed him. Chup raho, dheere bolo – stay quiet, talk slowly. No more now, Beti-Bachao (save daughters), Me-too – campaign for women rights movements. Nirbhaya – a victim of gang rape. Raktabij – Demon with every drop of his blood, he created more demons. Kali killed him. Rani Lakshmi Bai – Indian queen who became a symbol of courage and strength in her fight with Britishers).

She

Kali is Born

Meenakshi Mohan is an educator, art critic, children's writer, painter, and poet. Her book reviews, art critics, interviews, and poems regularly appear in different journals. She authored children's picture books, The Rainbow in My Room and The Gift, and edited Tamam Shud, poems of Kshitij Mohan. She is on the Editorial Team for Inquiry in Education, a peer-reviewed journal published by National Louis University, Chicago, Illinois.

Megha Sood
Just Another Day, Just Another Rape
(Based on the Hathrus Gangrape)

Body mutilated, eyes scourged throat strangled
Cut and slashed, the body bears the suppurating marks
Welts and blisters, wounds of caste inequality,
the penultimate sin of being born in low caste family
Where the simple touch has been shunned by society

A body so impure; even to the shadow it bears
But like a scavenger, it has been pulled and slashed to shreds
As she fights her battle of being born in a nation
who stands mute and dumb to her atrocities

To millions of daughters before her and countless after her
Dragged and burned on the pyre to prove her marriage loyalty
A shaved head and simple living conforms
the love towards her departed husband
whose death is a fault of hers to repent

Where the upper caste rules this nation with an iron fist
As they lay lien to her soul;
Scavenging the identity, and mutilating her
hasn't been enough for them, I guess anymore

Burned and cremated in the fires,
the nakedness of this nation spills
through the empty eyes of billion souls
as they scroll through the news on their phone
another rape, another news

Stripped of her dignity devoid of the privilege
of being cremated with last rites is too much to ask for,
in this nation which stands dumb and mute
another hamster on the wheel routine
another strip of news to abhor

Streets lined with wails and cries of mothers
losing their daughters in dim-lit streets, in fields
in a thicket of night, in the brightness of the day
Yet their soul's numbing cries fail to reach the privileged ears
Holding the lien to the amicable society
led by the scriptures as they claim.

These streets are now laced with incessant wails and sobs
Only to find them gutted and stripped of their dignity
Brimming with the pain of mothers whose tears are dried up,
An act in vain, an exercise in futility

Gaping mouth like a toothless animal
devoid of any defense bears witness to this atrocity
when another daughter becomes offering
like a sacrificial lamb to this exalted society

A society, which bootstraps itself after falling from grace
every damn time,
And gets ready for the next day;
to read another ravenous killing of their *betis*
as just another scroll on their phone
a nation's favorite pastime.

(Legends: Betis: Daughters)

Mehak Varun

The Kali in Me

Kali
who is death
with chignon on head
tiara of skulls and crescent moon
she scowls, baring her teeth
wild, naked, her tongue sticking out
bursting sheer power.

Kali
who is black
of mind, body, and soul
a divine protector
bestowing moksha
the Adi Shakti
the mother of the universe.

Kali
the shakti
who is fearless
the destroyer of evil
scary, bloodthirsty
of demons, the asuras.

Kali
the true kali
a Devi, not shallow
defying all attempts
whosoever tried to shred her
to tame her to pieces
her force is pure
standing endure

Kali
embodies the
boundless freedom
epitome of Shakti
of strength and power
standing unbound from all
restrictions.

Kali
be the kali of today
she still exists
in each one of us
standing against the asuras
the demons of astray
be the kali of today
the mother of all power
you dance alone
you sing alone
just be, to be
the Kali.

Mehak Varun was born and brought up in Jammu and settled in Chandigarh. She has been bestowed with the 100 Inspiring Authors of India award in Kolkata. She has also been honored with the Women Of Influence 2019 award presented on women's day in New Delhi. Recently she has been awarded the Gitesh-Biwa Memorial Award of excellence for her article on woman power 'I Just Need A Chance' Along with her books, her work has been published in various anthologies and she is a recipient of various other prizes in poetry competitions as well.

Mithi

A recipe

The kitchen is political today.
Which dish will lure the taste buds of democracy?
Perhaps, a bowl of honey crispy chicken.
Perhaps, the spaghetti in white sauce.
Perhaps, tradition dipped in 'Dal'!

I hear women in 'Shaheen Bagh' are shouting slogans. I do not
understand them.
Actually, I have never tried to.
I see posts on 'Feminism in Kashmir' and gulp down a glass of
mango juice uncomfortably like the majority of my colony.

I indulge in cooking dinner.
I dry my hair in sleek flickering daylight.
However, on certain days, when marriage seems overwhelming, I
remember lessons in Civics.
My old history teacher would read out aloud,
"We the people of India..."

Often in noon,
Shabana comes to her terrace.
Does her hand smell of 'beef korma' when she rinses her clothes?
Does she gather in 'Shaheen Bagh'?
Has her husband too asked her not to talk to the 'other women'?
If I ever converse with Shabana, will we fight like men with
conflicting political views? Will we use our spoons and forks beyond
eating?

I feed my husband and wipe his sweat when he returns from a
polling booth.
While he votes, I wait at home, marinating a chicken and making
sure that a strand of my hair does not end up in a curry.

Like a confident citizen who has voted for his preferred party, he
makes love to me at night.
I haven't voted in years.
I have never told anyone that I was in love with a certain 'Anwar'.
Once he stood on a pedestal holding a placard which read, "I am in
love with you, Mira,
Mira Sharma!" and I had slapped him because I was breaking at the
impeccability and impossibility of that love!
Is he shouting slogans at Shaheen Bagh?
Is his wife there?
Or are they at home watching a hubbub on television? Do they go to
vote, hand in hand?

I haven't written in years.
In fact, this poem is an offshoot of a politically aware adult's
impulse to create and create again!
I am a character.
I am a character who wants to sit cross-legged with her neighbour
Shabana over a cup of tea and discuss politics.
I want to ask her, "Does your husband cheat on you? Do you stand
up to sing the national anthem inside theatres? Does he kiss you
before an interval? Will you shout slogans?"
I am a character, a character of a woman who has learned to dive
into 'YouTube' to expertise in foreign cuisine.
I am a character of a woman who has a political opinion and one
fine day, I want to log into my inactive Facebook account and
express it.
Probably, my husband will not make love to me that night or the
following night.
Probably, he will not pay attention because I have become trivial. I
keep becoming trivial then and now.
While I type, my hand will smell of 'Kheer'!
My kitchen will smell of 'Kheer'.
Will Shabana smell it too?
I want her to.

Talk that talk

A young branch peeps from within the pierced navel. A zebra, melanin, and euphoria stripe her skin. Oh! She is aware that you have been gawking at her from the other end of a moving coach of a moving train in a moving city of a moving world. She knows that in all that haphazard movement, your eyes have been stagnant on her immaculate skin. Your guilty conscience, a snake hisses, and you, a snake charmer often say in your own little mind, "She is asking for it!". She knows that you have dropped your handkerchief and the two letters embroidered on it by your docile wife and it is all a trick to gawk a little longer, a little better. She knows that when she will sit down on her reserved seat and the wind will play with her bright saffron collar, you will bend your neck like a crane and prey on the fishes printed on her crop top.

She knows that when she sits down on her reserved seat in a speeding bus, you will repeat the spelling of equality and cleavages.

Repeat after me.

Equality and cleavages.

A thin line separating two breasts that are now tanned. A hair is drying in that vicinity.

Eh! What do you see?

She knows that you gawk at her.

I know that you gawk at her.

I want you to know that we know.

We know.

বেশ্যা। (Harlot/Prostitute)

Do you buy flowers from prostitutes?
No, you shake their beds and cradles.
Had you bought flowers,
they would sell that too!
I see her standing beneath the red light,
an ally to her left,
an illusion to her right,
and she sways like a rusted pendulum.
I don't know her address,
I don't know if she needed the money to pay her rent or her relative
        sold her off,
parcelled her like the popular plate of chicken, boneless.
She started off old and now she is young,
 as young as the sink where she washes the customer's remains.

Fornication is a fancy word,
a word on expensive lips.
Amidst red light, they just fuck and pay.
A child sleeps beneath the bed,
above is his mother's workplace.

I see her standing.
I know she wants to walk out.
Does she know that I know?
I have seen women walking out of the web, only to return,
only to walk back to the spider that preys.
While she pleasures me, I ask,
"Do you want to stop?"
She laughs cruelly, questions,
"Can I want it to stop?"
Baffled, I look at her again,
a fair mirage,
only free enough to earn and eat.

Does she want to quit prostitution?
Who will pay her rent?
Who will pay an extra rupee to buy tampons
and the orange candy that she sucks on till her tongue becomes
   numb?
I say, "I want to know you!"
She says, "No, you only want a heart-breaking origin story and a
   blowjob.
I can do better than your sympathy, sir!"

Can she quit prostitution?
But, you don't buy flowers from prostitutes!
You only shake their beds and cradles.
Had you bought flowers,
they would sell that too.

Red Ruby

Gaze Gazes

Mithi identifies as a queer feminist. If someone is sitting comfortably, Mithi wants them to stir uncomfortably when they see her work. Curiosity saves this cat as she hammers on sexist, homophobic stereotypes. The inside of her head is a zoo of colours and she lets the animals roam. She is pursuing an Honours degree in Literature, B.A. in English.
http://instagram.com/momma_psychedelia
http://www.mirakee.com/accismus

Dr. Molly Joseph
O, Woman!

O, Woman! You have it in you
to stand up against the wind, undaunted
When it blows harsh on you,
merciless, derailing, devastating...

No, not alone you are
or what if you are alone
In you lies the power to sprout
even on arid planes
You, the mother nature ever-renewing
shedding old contours
in tandem with the eclipse of the moon
to emerge anew, afresh on yonder crested hills..

the ever alive fountainhead you are
sprinkling kindness, care, and love
on whoever comes around,
the herd of tired pilgrims..

When the world gropes in darkness
and fret in dismay drooping,
You shower radiance divine
igniting the guiding light..

the barren blooms, birds flutter, nature rouses
in your magnetic touch...

the river that flows covering
caverns of hurts and wounds
you flow, you smile...

your burns turn to learning lessons for you
to walk through
fire with faith and hope..

strong and soulful you
are,
O, woman, you have it in you
to stand up against the wind, undaunted.

*Dr. Molly Joseph had her Doctorate in post-war American poetry. She
retired as the H.O.D., Department of English, St. Xavier's College, Aluva,
Kerala, and now works as Professor of Communicative English at FISAT,
She writes travelogues, poems, and short stories. (for children) and has
published Nine books of poems - Aching Melodies, December Dews,
Autumn Leaves, Myna's Musings, Firefly Flickers, It rains, The bird with
Wings of Fire, It Rains, Where Cicadas Sing in Mirth, and Hidumbi (a
novel, translation from Malayalam).*

Mona Dash

Woman

I am no different from you
homeless, grey saree in tatters
matted hair, uncombed, unoiled
bindi smeared, vapid eyes
running through streets
to the shouts of mad woman
crying for the son killed
ten years ago

I too have buried my flesh

I am no different from you
in glittering cocktail dresses
red sarees, shiny blouse
see through petticoat
crimson gleaming lipstick, flowers
clipped on scented black hair
stoned in public
for the lack of morality

I too have traded my flesh

I am no different from you
attacked when defenseless
touched when asking not to be
nails gouging eyes out
but always failing
to stronger biceps

blood, oozing slowly
a victim's vulnerability
I too have plunderers on my flesh

Always, a different name
a different country
a different life
But the same I.

The making of a Goddess

resplendent goddess
when you become
we will worship you
with flowers, the best
roses we shall decree
lotuses, pink-gold, fifty-five petals no less
incense mesmerising intoxicating

only the pure can visit
they must fast a whole day
and half
pine, plan for a year or two
before they visit you

we will enshrine you in marble
from European shores
inlaid lapis lazuli
outside
peacocks in the garden
fountains bursting colours
we will worship you
your visage, your body anointed
in red, yellow

your face smooth turmeric paste
our lives, our desires, our dreams
shall writhe at your feet

we will worship you

in return you must burn
first from the inside:
dry out the desire
 that keeps you awake
dried-twig-like crush under your feet
those dreams that glisten
forgotten in your eyes
thoughts that anger
want to tear you apart
you must wash it out
wring yourself bone-dry
the hard bones you must crush
then they cannot support
and you will crawl
jelly like amorphous moulding
how we want you to

next your skin
it must burn
flake curl into itself
beautiful eyes unseeing
hands crippled
breast waist fingers lips
conjoined mass
you must burn
the insides the outsides
the brain the mind the soul
the heart the earlobes

the swirls of your stomach
the legs and the in between
nothing
left with nothing

consuming fire
burnt

and now you are a Goddess
we will worship you

Mona Dash is the author of A Roll of the Dice : a story of loss, love and genetics, A Certain Way, Untamed Heart, and Dawn-drops. Her work has been listed in leading competitions such as Eyelands Book Award 20, People's Book Prize, Novel London 20, SI Leeds Literary award, Fish, Bath, Bristol, Leicester Writes and Asian Writer. Her short story collection Let us look elsewhere is forthcoming from Dahlia Publishing, UK in 2021. A graduate in Telecoms Engineering, she holds an MBA, and a Masters in Creative Writing (with distinction). She works in a global tech company and lives in London. www.monadash.net

Mrinalini Harchandrai
Anti-Rape Trousseau

It has to be stitched
in the fabric of our reason

the weft of reading
and writing sentiment, delicately
enmeshed with the warp
of our banyan classrooms
where we are sowed

the bias is cut against petticoats
even the yin in menslip
isn't spared being hemmed in

trousers flirt with musclelust
skirting the veinwork of denouement

Where our pockets seek
      wins of freedom to backstitch
      the source seamstress' name
      onto ours, cavalierly
            thread through a moonless night
            without buttonhole eyes
            staring below the neckline
                  to unknot knots   coarse textures
                  of community honour
                  from our vaginas
                        to embroider #MeToo
                        on our epaulets
                        without dignity unravelling
                        at the seams

                If he comes in
            demanding to suit himself
         pricking fingers in custom reds
        whetting alterations on her skin
            disrobe him
                        his spindle.

10 Hands of the Goddess

In the first hand of the goddess
her true love gave to her
a plastic fruit
to make up and shape her.

In the second hand of the goddess
her true love gave to her
a silver anklet
to betroth her to her lowly post.

In the third hand of the goddess
her true love gave to her
a teeka-red mark
to cover her gash.

In the fourth hand of the goddess
her true love gave to her
a hush broom
to carpet the evidence.

In the fifth hand of the goddess
her true love gave to her
a silken muffler
to cover her spine.

In the sixth hand of the goddess
her true love gave to her
the crushed lotus petals
of her fragrant spirit.

In the seventh hand of the goddess
her true love gave to her
a veena full of plaintive strains
but no pluck.

In the eighth hand of the goddess
her true love gave to her
a rosary of crystal tears
beaded with every time she didn't consent.

In the ninth hand of the goddess
her true love gave to her
an ashen skull
as empty as her financial flex.

In the tenth hand of the goddess
her true love gave to her
the celestial time serpent
to repeat lethal patterns.

Mrinalini Harchandrai is the author of 'A Bombay in My Beat', a collection of poetry. Her poem won first prize in The Barre (2017), she was a finalist for the Stephen A. DiBiase Poetry Prize 2019 and was shortlisted for the Wordweavers Poetry Contest 2019. Her unpublished novel manuscript was selected as Notable Entry for the Disquiet International Literary Prize 2019. Her short fiction has been shortlisted for Columbia Journal Spring 2020 Contest, longlisted for the Commonwealth Short Story Prize 2018, and selected as a Top Pick (2018) with Juggernaut Books, India. Her work has been anthologized in The Brave New World of Goan Writing Writing (2018, 2020) and RLFPA Editions' Best Indian Poetry 2018, and her writing features on several literary platforms.

Mubida Rohman
Kali and the Black Panther

The grandmother lamented and pounded her chest
A mother incessantly wept and cursed her stars
The father furious walked out of the house in a rage
A tiny baby girl wriggled in the midwife's arms

Her mother named her *'Chanda'* after the beautiful moon
The baby gazed at her mother with loving warm eyes
The grandmother laughed, 'What an awful name for a dark-skinned
     Kali'
The father said 'She is born of bad karma, our past crimes'

Infuriated, the grandmother objected, 'Why should we educate her?
     A girl, a Kali girl'
The father detested too, but, thought it might be better than paying a
     huge dowry
Her mother whispered in her ears, 'This my girl will be your chance'
Holding her elder brother's hand, little *Chanda* ran to school in a hurry

During recess when the children in the field ran and played,
She watched from a distance and yearned to join the game
A little boy once grabbed her hand, 'Come, Kali, don't you want to
     play?'
Chanda smiled and uttered, 'Only if you call me by my proper name'

One day at school, the teacher pointing a cane at her said, 'Read the
     next passage',

She read aloud, 'A black shadow stood in the centre of the circle; inky
     black all over'

The class giggled and whispered in a chorus, 'Black just like her, *Kali*
     reads about herself'

She went on, 'Bold as the wild buffalo, reckless as the wounded
     elephant, his skin soft, his voice softer, he was Bagheera, the
     Black Panther'

That night she showed her mother 'The Jungle Book' and asked about
    Bagheera

'Panthers - they are noble and sacred animals' with a loving smile
    answered her mother

She tucked the book inside her small pillow and thought of the Jungle
    and the panther

She walked in her dreams behind a majestic black being who said 'Kali
    one day the truth will be yours to discover'

It was Diwali the day after, on a full moon night, her family around the
    village Pandal had gathered

Her Grandmother said it was a day to adore 'the Shakti of Shiva, the
    slayer of demons and preserver of Earth'

Chanda stared at the alluring black idol with unrestrained hair, her
    four arms, a garland of human heads, and her lolling red-
    tongue

Hands clasped and heads bowed, the family chanted 'Great goddess
    Maa Kali, the protector of the universe, help us find our
    worth'

The stars were twinkling brightly; quietly on her mother's warm lap,
    she placed her head that night

'Why is such affection and admiration missing; when they call me
    Kali?' she asked

The mother caressing her hair replied, 'For they don't know any better'

Sleep swooped her in its arms; she found the goddess and the Panther
    waiting inside the jungle vast

Riding the Black Panther, holding a sword and a blue lotus, the
    goddess asked, 'Who are you, my child?'

'I'm *Chanda*, the dark-skinned girl; they call me Kali and mock my
colour', she answered

The goddess proclaimed, 'You bear my name and the colour of my
Panther, you're fierce, you're Shakti - the immense power'

The words kept ringing in her ears; she woke up and found the doubts,
griefs around her all shattered

'I found my answer', *Chanda* ran and clutched her mother's warm
hands

She exclaimed in delight, 'Within me resides great strength and a sea of
power, mother'

'In your dreams, you spoke last night? Was it the goddess?' pleasantly
her mother smiled

Her face beaming, she replied, 'I'm the embodiment of Shakti, I am
Kali, I'm the Black Panther'

Years later, *Chanda* now rides the bus to work and leisurely stares out
the window

Radiant and fearless Kalis to her left and her right, behind and
everywhere in front of her

Some to school, some to work, and some just about anywhere, all in
different shades, shapes, and size

Delighted she to herself whispers, 'We the Black Panthers, the *Kalis*,
the embodiment of Shakti forever'

Mubida Rohman likes to describe herself as a storyteller, an interculturalist, and a language enthusiast. Suffering from what the Germans term as 'das Fernweh', she is a vagabond at heart who longs to meet people in distant lands, listen and narrate their stories through writings and photos. Write to her at - cultureyogi@gmail.com You can find her journey and jottings here: Blog : www.cultureyogi.blog & www.anecdotesofamadwoman.blog Instagram – @the_wise_robin

N. Meera Raghavendra Rao
My Mother-In-Law Surprises Me

Ever since I got married
In my late teens
Just out of college
Not prepared for marriage
Having fears of my mil
Breathing down my neck
And peck, peck, and peck!
But lo and behold
She took me into her family fold
From day one
She turned my friend and guide
Which made me look at her with pride.
Empowerment begins at home
When two women understand each other
And feel at home with one another

N. Meera Raghavendra Rao, a freelance journalist, columnist, and author is a postgraduate in English literature with a diploma in journalism. She is a prolific writer having published more than 2000 articles including book reviews in leading newspapers and magazines. Meera interviewed several leading personalities for print, AIR and TV and was interviewed over the media subsequent to the launch of her 10 books.

Dr. Naina Dey

Homing Pigeons

Soon they will come in
The homing pigeons
Circling overhead before alighting
Clapping wings
Into dark-hole coops
A wobbly walk

After a minute they will disappear
As the sky gets heavier and the lights come on
Soon there will be a sizzling pan
Scraped off non-stick coat
Double-egg omelettes and sugared toast

The heat will thicken
The blouse moist, stuck fast to skin
Jagged shells in open bin
Nauseating

I wonder what they do
These pigeons inside their coop
Make omelettes perhaps?
While I wish I had wings that clapped
Even for a day.

(Published in The Sunday Statesman, 8th Day, 7 June 2015 and Intercultural Poetry and Performance Library, ICCR newsletter Poetry: At the Heart of the Nation in 2018)

Feminism

And just when your eyes
Are no longer able
To withstand so much love
So much mercy
They kill you
With their praise of a colleague's chastity
Or another's culinary skills...

You sulk outside heaven's door
With dismembered Woolf and Wollstonecraft.

(Published in Setu, Vol.4, Issue 9, February 2020)

Dr. Naina Dey teaches English literature at Maharaja Manindra Chandra College. She is a critic, translator, and creative writer. Her books include Macbeth: Critical Essays, Edward the Second: Critical Studies, Real and Imagined Women: The Feminist Fiction of Virginia Woolf and Fay Weldon, Representations of Women in George Eliot's Fiction, Macbeth: Exploring Genealogies, a book of poems Snapshots from Space and Other Poems and translation of Upendrakishore Ray Chowdhury's Gupi Gain O Bagha Bain. Her latest publication is One Dozen Stories, a volume of translations.

Dr. Naina Dey

Nameera Anjum Khan
The Cursed Birds

Nameera Anjum Khan believes that poetry is a voice that can never be subjugated. Writing used to be her hobby but eventually it morphed into a way of life. Her work has been published in anthologies such as 'World on Trial: The Earth's Grand Vengeance' by Witchesnpink and 'Inked Fables' by The Inked Square. She writes on topics such as women's rights, social issues, politics and mental health.

Namita Aavriti
how to become a dyke or self-improvement

First, forget that you have eyelashes
Remember eyebrows
your mouth can make a small o
no need to O
anymore.
Flick light switches with your tongue
and practice suffering, always
Your hands should lose grace
stuck in pockets,
only your fingers should belong to pianos
the tips to a blind girl.

Namita Aavriti is a writer. She has written on cinema, archives, sexuality, technology, law, feminism, family. She first wanted to be an academic, then a filmmaker, and now she's back to writing without any grand purpose. She's currently the editor of a website that focuses on gender and technology and occasionally also makes media, curates exhibitions, and festivals, especially the annual Bangalore Queer Film Festival.

Namita Elizabeth Chakrabarty
The Indian woman viewing the dancer in the studio mirror

The mirror returned me to the past.
                And I remember now
The sound of gentle bells
Singing with the rhythm of her movements
As her eyes tell me
The story of the pattern
Watching my eyes
Travelling into hers
As she beckons me into the caves.

                And that day
I did not wonder
Is it the sun that shines
Forming a fiery illusion before me
The reflection of my dream
Emerging from the cool tranquil wombs
Of the other time,
The caves of Ajanta and Ellora.

And this mirror arrives
Sometimes
Inviting me to step into your world.

One evening the cloud of North London night descending
We stood among the crowds
And as they dispersed
The karma ascending
I watched your eyes.
For you, the clear black lines
Of the industrial structures
Were translated into a cool silent reasoning.
Then I understood your insight

Into my chaos
　　　　Of East and West.

You disappeared into the shadows.

The question was left unspoken.
My isolation remained the answer.
Until I turned back to the mirror
And there you were still waiting.

Borders in an English Landscape

She sits facing a black and white hill — in life, landscape is rarely
　　　　green like nature.
In dreams too, the green often ends at a cliff edge, like last night,
she
　　　　called out
In her sleep, for help — she's still scared of meeting strangers.

Sometimes she can walk for miles across the greenery, really
relaxed,
　　　　not see a soul.
Then on a hill, when she least expects it, there will be someone, who
　　　　says something.
So when she walks back down, she looks down too; she remembers:

"Your English is good for a foreigner." "Where are you from?"
"Do you live with your parents?" All the questions –
And the arranged marriage one.

When they shouted out "Paki" as they passed her door,
And when stones were thrown at her, down a hillside —
She dreamt of drowning.

Often she just sees surface. Acid surface.
In Bombay, she told Daddy about the stones. He laughed, but
        nervously —
When she turned, she saw his eyes: he didn't know what to say.

Then he told her how he found England's green and pleasant land
So beautiful, after the dry landscape of Maharashtra — but, how
        could he put it?
Its people aren't always like its nature. Why he left. Why he cries.

Back in England, she understood what he meant, why he left,
Why it was just her white mother and herself now, and
Why they got called names in the street — who's seen as not natural
        in this landscape.

Now, years later, she's an adult, and her father's long dead.
She still faces a black and white hill, but rather than names now, it's
        whispers
Behind her back. She tries to sleep, she tries to forget each day.

But now she has started to dream of meeting her reflection,
someone
Who would see the black and white hills, but make of them soft-
colored Alpine Idylls, rainbow-hued tropical forests, or the infinity
of a desert of gold.

Namita Elizabeth Chakrabarty's poetry has been published @visual_verse, short fiction @DahliaBooks, critical race writing by @routledgebooks, and as Elizabeth Chakrabarty, her debut novel Lessons in Love and Other Crimes will be published by The Indigo Press in 2021. She lives in London. Twitter @DrNChakrabarty

Namita Rani Panda
The Pleading of a Corpse
(A Victim of Gang Rape)

I was not a Sita
For whom Mother Earth tore her bosom,
I was not also a Draupadi
To whom Lord Krishna blessed with endless costume,
I was an ordinary girl
Whose prayers no one could listen,
Whose body was ruthlessly torn,
And soul was cruelly crushed
And dumped into the drain!
Now I plead from the gutter,
I am no more anyone's sister or daughter,
O' inhumane men! Please preserve me for your pleasure,
For your satisfaction you can put me in any posture,
There is no need to choke me for fear of uproar,
You can suck me like a mango though I'm yet to ripe fully,
I promise, I will never scream when you squeeze and bite my flesh
repeatedly,
You can exert your manliness into me as many times, as forcefully
as you can,
Believe me, you will not face any opposition.
Please preserve me to pacify your salacious desire,
So that, at least, a few of my sisters can breathe a puff of safe air!

(Published in 2019 A Slice of Sky and Other Poems By Authorspress. Also published in 2019 in the anthology Resonance [English Poetry from Poets of Odisha] and published in 2019 in the anthology, Speak Your Mind by Impish Lash Publishing House, Mumbai).

Namita Rani Panda is a multilingual poet, story writer, and translator from Sambalpur, Odisha, India. With the experience of teaching English for three decades, she now works as Vice-Principal in JNV Cuttack under the Ministry of HRD, Department of School Education and Literacy, Government of India. She has five solo anthologies of poems Blue Butterflies, Rippling Feelings, A Slice of Sky, A Song for Myself and Colours of Love to her credit. Her signature words are love and optimism. She is an active member of Cosmic Crew, a literary group of female poets in Odisha working with the motto "My pen for the world" and co-authored with the members Radical Rhythm Volume 1, Volume 2 and Volume 3 with the editorship of Radical Rhythm Volume 2.

Namrata K.
Don't kill us

in the womb	for a genetic quirk of fate
in the crib	for needing our mothers
in school	for being smarter than our brothers/father/uncles/friends
on the bus	for not wanting to be groped
in the college parking lot	for talking to a boy/man not of our caste
in an auto	for earning more than our fathers/brothers/uncles/peers
in our marriage bed	for saying no
in the kitchen	for not wanting to choke on empty plates
in the bathroom	for singing too loudly; for bleeding; for having a body
in our mother's house	for loving another family
in our children's house	for living beyond our life
in your minds	for taking up too much space
in our minds	

in our minds

Namrata K. is a nitpicky editor and poet who lives in Bhopal with her madcap family. She also manages music collaborations between international and Rajasthani folk musicians for a prestigious music festival while singing and learning nirgun geet, baiths and other folk forms. She believes poetry and music are two sides of the same coin—expressions of our deepest, most unnamed ways of being.

Namratha Varadharajan

To future queens

The future queen-slaves of homes
can roam (more or less) freely in their cages
Only
else their bodies shall be considered public property
to be explored by anybody.
Archaic mindsets posted outside every door

Granddaughters of witches light that pyre!

clapping with one hand is impossible
that must have been consensual
jeans are provocative
blame
her
honour lies in her vagina
Hence, the future queen-slaves of homes
can roam (more or less) freely in their cages
only

Granddaughters of witches burn that down!

Come, my sisters, breathe out words of fire through your pain
crush that blame-game, cinder those mindsets, melt these chains
Repeat -
me too, me too, me too, they are the rapists
Shout it out, repeat, me too, repeat, march, repeat.
Then, one day, one day, the future queens shall breathe

Granddaughters of witches drown them ashes!

(Poetry form: THE BOP; Submitted to Poetixu.)

If 'Men' Were 'Men'

Men are kind, men cry, men have empathy,
men are nice, men love their women softly.

Men understand no means no.

If all men were men then--
there wouldn't be a rape reported in our country every fifteen
        minutes
Our country wouldn't the most unsafe place for women on this
        planet
We wouldn't have to rely on social distancing to reduce the number
        of rapes by 83 percent in the nation's capital

Men are kind, men cry, men have empathy, men are nice, men love
        their women softly.

Men understand no means no.

If all men were men then--

Billions of women will not have to cry themselves hoarse "Me too!
        Me too! Me too!"
It would not sound anymore like an endless endless reverberating
        echo
Women would be able to breathe freely everywhere
and pursue their dreams without fear

Men are kind, men cry, men have empathy, men are nice, men love
        their women softly.

Men understand no means no.

If all men were men then--
Aruna Shanbaug would have lived a full and fruitful life
Jyoti Singh would have made her way back home safely that night
Priyanka Reddy would still be home with her family
And no one would have had to mourn the loss of India's daughters

we like-

Men who are kind, men who cry, men who are empathic, men who
        are nice, men who love their women softly

Men who understand no means no
Men who take consent before they touch you
Men who hear you when you say no

Isn't it time we redefine what it means to "be a man"
And let a man be a man.

(Submitted to Poetixu)

Namratha Varadharajan stumbled into the magical rabbit hole of writing when she paused her career in engineering to indulge in motherhood. She writes poetry that explores human emotions and relationships, our connection with nature and tries to chip at the prejudices that plague us. She has her poems published in various anthologies including "Indian Summer in Verses" and "Rewind". Blog: http://namysaysso.com. Instagram handle: @namrathavaradharajan

Nandini Sahu
Letter to My Unborn Daughter

Tiny limbs smeared with my fresh inflamed blood
oozing out of the womb, gushing in fact.
I knew. I had lost you. Then and there. Shattered.
The sadomasochist burped, then casually farted, and snored

in a short while, when the maid rushed us to
the local hospital. I heard what you never uttered.
Ahh heal 'us', protect 'us', you and me, me and you,
Mom and her little girlie, wish to take the world in their stride.

Today, a letter to you, my unborn daughter, after
long two decades of quiet travail
telling our tales to your younger brother,
with a bleeding heart, I smile with exuding tears.

Smile to see my dream daughter alive in
her brother little; so full of love and compassion, so much a
feminist-humanist male, so strong to hold Mom's head high,
so much you, so as I would have you.

Ah! There was such rage over a female foetus
growing up to be a girl of power and conviction, like Mom dear.
Or like the *Pancha Mahakanya*. And the marital rapes, the threats
to snatch you any given day, if I dissent; and then the termination.

If at all there is a next birth for you, my little fairy,
come back, come back to my womb, life minus you is such dreary.
You need not play the games that the heart must play.
Pronounced before birth, you are not gonna be the woman of clay.

Like Ahilya, never fall prey to Indra's trickery; and if ever you do,
do it by your choice, not anyone else's, neither Goutama's nor Indra's.
Your penance need not be broken by Lord Rama, the one who
judged his wife; you need not regain your human form

303

by brushing his feet. Remain that dry stream, that stone,
till you find a way to my womb again, in another life, another *Yug*;
you need not be condoned of your guilt, you never were 'guilty'.
Let Indra be cursed, castrated, concealed by a thousand vulvae
that eventually turn into a thousand eyes. Or like Draupadi, take your
birth from a fire-sacrifice, be an incarnation of the fierce goddess Kali
or the goddess of wealth, Lakshmi; but never be the sacrificial goat
to accept five husbands just because someone else deliberated.

If any Yudhishtir drops you at the Himalayas because you
loved Arjun more, look in his eyes and declare, loud and clear--
it's your right to live, love, and pray. While never deriding
the Duryodhan and Karn of your destiny, live laudable my dear.

Nor Kunti be your role model, but if ever you propitiate the sage
Durvasa, who grants you a *mantra* to summon
a god and have a child by him, then take his charge.
Don't you recklessly test the boons life grants you by haze?

nor invite the Sun-god, Surya, give birth to Karna, and abandon.
An unborn child is better than the one dejected, forlorn.
Or if ever you are Tara, the *apsara*, the celestial nymph,
who rises from the churning of the milky ocean

be the Tara, Sugriva's queen and chief diplomat,
the politically correct one, the woman in control of herself
and folks around. In the folk Ramayana,
Tara casts a curse on Rama by the supremacy of her chastity,

while in some versions, Rama enlightens Tara. Be her, the absolute.
Or be Mandodari, the beautiful, pious, and righteous.
Ravana's dutiful wife who couldn't be his guiding force,
Bibhishana's compliant wife, the indomitable grace.

Be you, the elemental, candid, real woman who is my ideal.
Don't ever let another female foetus be the victim of
sadomasochism, unlike your fragile, fledgling Mom.
Be all that she could never be, be her role model.

I send you my prayers, *the prayer before birth.*
Moon, rain, oceans, and the blue firmament,
shining stars and a sun aglow are all that I have--
you must call them your own, my unborn daughter.

Forgive me my love, for you died with all the petals
falling from my autumny breast, the breast that you never suckled;
you rain on my being and burn my heart, but calm my soul
like simmering snow slowly concealed yet revealed.

You will stay indomitable, taking new lives every single day
in Mom's prayers, poetry, social responsibilities, ecofeminism,
messages, voices, layers of thoughts, and action. My girl,
I am what I decided to be after losing you, that's the euphemism.

I am not just a woman since that fateful night, but entire
womankind. Now I am a woman of full circle, within me, there is the
power to create, nurture, and transform. I rediscover pieces of myself
through your unborn narrative, in the resonance in my quirky
confluence.

Prof. Nandini Sahu, Professor of English and Director, School of Foreign Languages, IGNOU, New Delhi, India, is an established Indian English poet, creative writer, theorist, and folklorist. She is the author/editor of fourteen books. Dr.Sahu is a triple gold medalist in English literature, the award winner of All India Poetry Contest and Shiksha Rattan Purashkar. She is the Chief Editor and Founder Editor of two bi-annual refereed journals, Interdisciplinary Journal of Literature and Language(IJLL) and Panorama Literaria. Her areas of research interest cover New Literatures, Critical Theory, Folklore and Culture Studies, Children's Literature, American Literature. www.kavinandini.blogspot.in

Nayana Nair
in the light that smiles nonetheless

that's where my anger lives.

on the mud stains of size 7 shoes
swimming on the white floor of my small apartment.

in the plants uprooted, in the marigolds strewn
and trampled on, in the light that smiles nonetheless.

on the streets where lives my fear – that finds me
and almost kills me. every time i hear footsteps behind me.

on the patronizing attitudes that i dutifully respond to with
gratitude.
on the potential dangers, the possibilities of violence that every
        intimacy invites.
on the things i say yes to with a breaking heart.

in the mirror that only prizes my delicate frame and my weak wrist,
that tells me i would at least beautiful in the missing posters,
in the files housed in grim police stations,
in the videos and photos i would never get to know of (if i am
lucky).

in the speeches that tell me that i am safe,
in the compartments and corners made for me.
soundproof corners where either
i would finally end up believing the façade- the lie of a safe world
or where i would learn how to stay silent to be spared the worst.

that is where my anger lives.

The Darkness that She Sings for Me

I am in love
with the woman who sings and
becomes the background
of my every night.

I like to listen to her voice
as she takes my every second
keeps it out of my reach,
teaches me some really suspicious ways
to keep myself safe from her demons.

She glows in the darkness that she sews
only for me,
for me to hold her hand the way
she will never be held,
the way I will never be held.

I hate to cry,
I have cried for a long time
for people who called me their option
when I was out of earshot.
My tears are cheap, now all they do
is make me feel equally cheap.
But the tears I shed for her life are beautiful.
The tears I shed for her (who feels so much like me)
stops me from taking pills I don't need.

Another lover of hers sat opposite me a few days ago.
She looked so much like her.
It made me wonder if I looked like her as well.
I wonder if she knows that her lovers are running amok
in the world that she paints with her pain.
I wonder if she knows that we are catching all her fears,
staying away from guys who speak like her ex,
staying away from the patterns she has pointed out.

I wonder if she knows
that we tell strangers "She sings well. She writes well"
when we want say
"She made me embrace the woman in me
that I have been trying to kill for a long long time.
She stood in my moonlight
counting all the daggers that make her bleed every day,
the same daggers that I fear to acknowledge,
telling me about the exact number of days it takes to collapse again,
about the face, her heart, and her womb that are for anyone's taking,
about her rage, her mind, and her will that she was allowed to keep.
How she wanted to give up last night.
How giving up can become a concept of life every easily
but she didn't want that,
because she didn't want to be
the sad pathetic corpse of the woman
that the world said she would eventually be."

I am in love with the woman
who wants me to be more than a silent background.

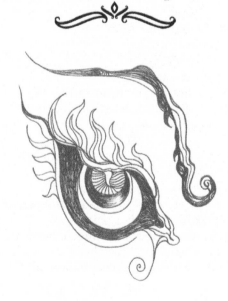

Too Easy to Imagine

I ran past the entry gates
and just as I thought that I made it in time
I heard the noise on the rails above me.
Twenty footsteps away, many tiring step high,
what I ran for and who ran towards went by
without giving me a second thought.
I took my phone and called a friend who would like to hear
how I forgot that there is a distance between the ticket counter
and the scary automatic doors of metro, that there was still a long way
      to go,
who finds it amusing that I am defeated and frustrated so easily
by something so small.

I covered the distance of twenty steps
listening to the phone ring on the other side.
I waited by the stairs thinking about the weight I must burn
but necessarily not now.
She picks up and tells me, as if continuing my favourite story,
about a friend of friend who is locked inside home
for loving someone.
She tells me about the boy her parents are looking for.
She tells me about the marriage that everyone says must happen
before the girl does something stupid.

We both wondered what "stupid" meant.
Probably running away from home or an attempt at death.
Probably we are thinking too much,
probably "stupid" meant
saying yes and giving up
and walking into a bedroom of stranger with a smile
not meant.

It was so easy to imagine this girl
that it didn't hurt us when we spoke of her,
it didn't hurt when we knew it could be us.

We talked of it as we talk of news,
as we talk of the new viral meme,
as we talk of the forecasts gone wrong.

And the girl died as her mention died
and we never looked for what happened to her.
We didn't want to.
Maybe the end, her end would hurt us,
would really hurt us.
Maybe we knew that really well.
So we talked about grander skies and dirt.
Something, anything far away from us.

It was easy to imagine this girl being happy
as long as we didn't get to know otherwise,
as long as we didn't pry.
We made a mental note
to never ask her about happiness
if we ever came across each other.

She knows as we all know
being locked up for love was a reasonable end - the easier end,
the end in which we get to live.
We know of too many examples, too many names
who didn't find this luck?
I don't remember their names, nor does my friend.
If we retained their names and fates in us
we could never complain about the missed trains and falling grades
and love not returned.

Nayana Nair is an engineer and a technical writer who moonlights as an amateur poet on her personal blog (itrainsinmyheart.wordpress.com). Writing for Nayana is a process of self-realization and an effort to understand what is ever elusive. @slingtheink (Twitter)

Nayona Agrawal
Kali – fierce

Nayona Agrawal and her partner Venky, reside in Bangalore and are passionate about two things; their kids and good food. A mom of two - Sid (human) and Groot (no, he's a French bulldog), her daytime job is in consulting, while dabbling in "creation" to unwind from it. She teaches herself new forms of art and finds it to be very meditative and relaxing. She is the proud child of Avinash and Snigdha Agrawal. Snigdha, her mom, is also a "creator" and writes winning prose and poetry.

Neelam Chandra
A Handful of Clay

*(There is a tradition as per which the purohit (priest) has to go and beg
for a handful of clay from a prostitute before the statue of Durga is cast
or installed. This poem is written from the prostitute's point of view when
one such Purohit comes to her to implore for a handful of clay.)*

O, Purohit! I refuse to give you
A handful of clay!
Today you just can't force me-
After all, it's my day!

Ill- treated I am by likes of you,
I can't even walk by your side;
Shunned, looked down upon,
Isolated, I feel; disparaged and despised!

Clones of you, at night, at my house arrive,
Play with my nipples, at my vagina eye;
But when the day spreads its cloak,
Your love disappears like a butterfly!

Heard I have that even Maa Durga
Had to dree Mahishasura's bad gaze!
Her wrath and powers thwarted all such attempts...
But...what about us? Aren't we innocent preys?

Hypocritic that the entire society is,
You come to my verandah today for a handful of clay!
Revered I am for only this moment,
And before me you beg and pray!

O Durga! I invoke you today!
My anger that continually burns is aflame-
I yearn, bless not these pretenders of faith,
And uplift my likes from this life of shame!

Neelam Saxena Chandra, has authored 4 novels, 1 novella and 6 short story collections, 32 poetry collections and 13 children's books. She is a bilingual author, writing in English as well as Hindi. More than 1500 of her poems/stories have been published in various journals/anthologies/ magazines. She holds a record with the Limca Book of Records, 2015 for being the Author having the highest number of publications in a year in English and Hindi. She has won several international and national awards. She was listed in Forbes as one of the popular authors in 2014. Website: http://neelamsaxenachandra.com/
Facebook page: https://www.facebook.com/NeelamSaxenaPoet/
Insta: https://www.instagram.com/neelamsaxenapoet/

Neera Kashyap
Reversals

When the lockdown eased, the maid finally came.
I saw her slippers outside - purple plastic thongs,
one white flower free, a strap hung.
I saw her hands and feet were large, her face
hidden behind a mask so tight she sucked for breath.
She moved speedily through accumulated dirt -
floors, cobwebs, clothes, pans, dust clouds that had settled.
As a tribal she once was equal to her man;
with hoe, they sowed the land, owned it,
shared wealth from surpluses – together.
With plough and arms of war, they were vanquished, their forests
burnt;
women enslaved as maids, men yoked to plough, both labelled lower
caste.
Because she bore children, she was a 'pollutant' to the conquering race,
cast out forever from her knowledge of what it is to be equal;
for 'pure' blood must course through the veins of a conquering race.
Slowly, for varied reasons all women became pollutants – of lower
caste,
chattels needing curbs, seemingly for their own protection
under the powerful yoke of men who knew
how to curb women's sexuality and needs
for men had 'higher' trajectories to follow.

Her duster raised a million motes of grime,
her hands slapped chairs till they groaned.
"How were these months for you?" I asked suddenly.
Surprised, she pulled off her mask, then thought:
"My menses. I had to go back to washing old cloth. Everyone saw."
She pulled on her mask and rapped a sofa hard.

In public - night vigils, protests against rape, changes in gender laws.
In a one-room home - a woman yearns for a pack of sanitary towels.

Tall dreams

This year I dreamt of more women in company boardrooms,
more women in law courts, on planning bodies, in Parliament.
So women could care more for Nature, for humanity, for equality.
At home, between intensive online work, I served –
meals on time, clean cupboards, stocked larders, yards of washing.
What legal space will I claim on company boards,
in law courts, on planning bodies, in Parliament?
When I claim none at home?

Neera Kashyap has had a career in environmental & health journalism and communication. She has authored a book of short stories for young adults Daring to Dream, (Rupa & Co.) and contributed to five prize-winning anthologies of children's literature (Children's Book Trust). As a writer of short fiction, poetry, essays and book reviews, her work has appeared in literary journals and poetry anthologies published in the USA, UK, Singapore, Pakistan and India. She lives in Delhi.

Nishi Pulugurtha
Time For The Goddess

bright blue sky with tufts of white
that float by – the autumn sky
grey, black and white, the colors change
as the light dims, to shine out again
that time when we decide to think of the
goddess – *shakti rupena samstitha** -
throttle her at other times,
strangle her, brand her, curse her
stop her from doing what she likes
curtail her choices -
well, why does she need to voice
what she feels like? assert herself?
let us pray to the goddess
*buddhi rupena samsthitha**
an autumnal reminder
let us pray to the goddess,
it is time for her arrival
*ya devi sarvabhuteshu**
the blue sky and white clouds
portend her arrival
let us pray to the goddess.

*(Lines from Durga Stuti, Prayer to Goddess Durga.
shakti rupena samstitha – one in whom power resides
buddhi rupena samsthitha – one in whom all intelligence resides
ya devi sarvabhuteshu – O omnipresent goddess.)

The Goddesses Around

On that station that day
She lay motionless – dead
Hunger and fatigue had taken their toll
She tried to fight – tried to -
That child by her side -
She had to fight
As hard as she could
Till she could no longer -
The child held on to her saree pallu
Tried to wake her up
Crying and calling
She didn't answer, she couldn't answer –
She was just a woman
A migrant returning home
To uncertainty and poverty
A woman for whom each day was a struggle
She was not alone in this
There were many other
There still are many other
Trying to work things out
Holding onto to life
In the best way they can
The goddesses around us
No, ordinary people like all
Struggling, fighting, living.

The City Decks Up

Every year in autumn the city decks up, like a resplendent bride, shiny and radiant. The glow shows clearly, a happiness emanates – it reflects all around. The lights, the decorations, the clothes, the food, the festoons, the banners, the festivities – all speak loud. It is the time of year when the daughter comes home from her Himalayan abode to her maternal home. With her children in tow, she comes – Durga - to be loved and cared for by her parents, by all at home. After a few days of pampering, it is time for her to go back.

The joy is short lived, the radiance is there for a few days. As things settle back, back to the way they really are. Most of the time camouflaged, disguised, behind masks. That hide the cries, the tears, the pain and suffering of myriads. Muffled, throttled, strangled, killed. In a land that worships the goddess. The dark goddess comes after a few days - Kali -accompanied by more lights. She is needed to awaken the power in each of us. To stand up to, to fight – against wrongs, against injustice. To stand up for what is right.

Nishi Pulugurtha is an academic and creative writer and writes on travel, film, short stories, poetry and on Alzheimer's Disease. Her work has been published in various journals and magazines. Her publications include a monograph on Derozio (2010), a collection of essays on travel, Out in the Open (2019), an edited volume of essays on travel, Across and Beyond (2020) and a volume of poems, The Real and the Unreal and Other Poems (2020).

Nitya Swaruba
she is enough

this world is a universe
for *she* is a world
in herself
at every turn beautiful;
a billion flowers
in any garden of gloom
will bloom to her smile;
her existence is life
her instance pride
with sadness shied away
the swooned heart
travels miles in a beat;
every sweet smell
reminds me of her
the earthy perfume
rain sends forth
the exquisite air
from a bakery, I pass by
or that nostalgic whiff
of swirly memories;
every sweet smell
reminds me of her
    the woman
    is everywhere
    I see her in all your blank faces
    you fail to retain her

crescendo of rage

she was a commodity
now a supremacy
beautifully she evolved
more than he
    he, who hasn't grown
    out of his evil
    desecrating
    the pages of history
    defacing modernity
    and her,
    if weak enough
    and no,
    it is not enough
    that a fraction of hims
    become tolerable
    it is not enough
    that a few are good,
    and enlightened
    while the majority still frighten
    the daylight out of
    parents' minds
because it's men they fear
more than the dark
it's men that make
people keep doors locked
the truth is stark
'cause it's men that
steal the life off *her*
rape that precious pearl
cut her into a million pieces
her mind becomes a sadness shelf
where she sits in filth
never ever to return
to her own beautiful self

senses ravished

her sinuous ways enslave me
with those dewy eyes she plays me
intrigued and intoxicated I go along
I become dissolute
in her ravishing charm;
her existence kindles
an inexplicable fire
I lose my conscience
I become a liar;
with insidious gestures
she beckons
lured into her aura
my heartbeat quickens
I melt in the heat of her
piercing gaze
she's predator
this prey wants to chase;
an ardent urge
surges through
her embrace engulfs me
we are glued
and she becomes *you*

    my eyes grace the tip
    of your fingers
    the cerulean veins that
    run up your arms
    I caress the shoulder
    and fall in your
    clavicle space
    I stay there a while
    before I trek up your neck
    until we're face to face
    a tug at the heart
    noses ready to hug
    my eyes close...
    your touch then
    stirs me awake

Nitya Swaruba is a copyeditor from Pondicherry. She is a writer and poet and is a member of the Pondicherry Poets group. She published her first book of poems 'One Flew Over The Heart' in 2018. Five of her poems have appeared in 'Weather of the Soul', a collection of nature poetry, published by DGG (North Carolina). Her latest collection 'Words from Under the Burning Bridge' came out in November 2019. She recently self-published a colorful e-book of tiny love poems 'Hues in My Thoughts'. Nitya writes prose as well, her musings about the world. She loves nature photography. Her books are available on Amazon, Google Books, and DriveThruFiction. https://eternityspoems.wordpress.com

Nupur Ghosh
Shakti the inner warrior

Art has been Nupur Ghosh' passion ever since she can remember...being totally self-motivated and self-taught she allowed this passion to take her where it will. Today she is able to create through all kinds of mediums, be it acrylics, oil, graphite, charcoal, pastels, and so on. Any surface can be her canvas!! At present, one of her strengths is hyper-realism in still life, wildlife, and portraiture through the medium. She loves to push her boundaries and create great expressions of love through her passion.

Nupur Maskara

Noor Jahan, Mughal Tigress

Dad made sure I knew
Languages, art, lit, song and dance
I chose to leave nothing to chance
Preferring shooting to all those.

I was seventeen when we wed
Sher Afghan Khan
Our daughter Ladli came a decade later.
Politics took you, husband
Led me to my second, Jahangir.

Thirty four then and women today lament
That they are past their prime when they reach my age.
From Mehr-un-Nissa I became Noormahal
Expanding to Noorjahan, a year shy of forty.

I remember hunting four tigers
Just regret I wasted two bullets
Taking them all down.

Was Jahangir looking for a mother figure?
A wife is a mother under wraps
I decided matters of state for him
Undercover, with a pat on the back.

A woman's world is supposed to be her family
I made mine all the world's
My father and brother were our ministers
I strengthened the web I wove
With Ladli wedding my stepson.
My niece married Shah Jahan
Stretching my seed across Mughal generations.

Jahangir gave me a bad birthday gift
A year before I completed half a century
Captured by Kashmiris.
I too fell, in front of Mahabat Khan
Only to rise, pulling an army out of my sleeve
Escape, with the king.

My own brother jailed me, winning by stealth
What others in the open never could do.

My last two decades were quiet
Finally, a lady of leisure
Architecture gave me pleasure
My monuments are my legacies
They don't let me down
Unlike miserable men.

(Published on my blog nutatut.com & part of my self-published book on Kindle – Insta Women: Dramatic Monologues by Drama Queens.)

Nupur Maskara is a freelance content writer who lives in Pune, India. She is married and has twin toddlers. Nupur received the Orange Flower Poetry Award in 2020. She has authored two poetry books– Insta Gita: With Arjuna's Perspective in Poetry and Insta Women: Dramatic Monologues by Drama Queens. She is currently working on a historical romance. Nupur blogs at nutatut.com. Tweet to her @nuttynupur.

Padmaja Iyengar-Paddy
The Vrindavan Widow...

Wed at nine, widowed at nineteen
Has this "woman" any life at all seen...?
Her family has dumped her in Vrindavan
To lead an abysmal life of utter damnation!

Abused and neglected by kin,
Treated worse than a dust bin,
She leads a colourless, wretched life.
Her fault - she is a husbandless wife!

Clad in white and with her head shaved,
She's the epitome of every penny saved!
Her life is spent in the "fasts" lane
Thought of a square meal – insane!

No one cares for her menial existence,
She is often on a perennial penance
For a husband long gone and dead –
Not perhaps, even shared her bed!

Yes, these Indian women do exist -
At Vrindavan, they actually subsist
On some charity and some dole
Leading a life without any goal...

When she comes or goes,
No one ever really knows.
She is perhaps just a statistic
Of my great India's body politic...!

*(The land of Lord Krishna, Vrindavan is considered as a holy place for
Hindus. Thrown out of their homes, these widows get to stay at a home in
Vrindavan where they spend most of their time praying and begging.
Many of them have been lured by their family into leaving their house to
go to Vrindavan in the 'name of God'. With no money, these hapless,
uneducated women – most of whom are from the hinterland – end up at
the mercy of landlords who force them to beg and earn money. The*

conditions that they are forced to live in, amply demonstrate how poorly they have been treated by their families. No one knows why so many widows come to Vrindavan, but it has been so for centuries. Nothing substantial has been done to stop this atrocity.)

I Am Who I Am ...

I run, I rush
I walk, I stride
I fly, I soar
I pilot, I glide

I drive, I lead
I steer, I ride
I talk, I discuss
I argue, I chide

I multi-task, I serve
I score, I achieve
I suffer, I bear
I reinvent, I live

I am the storm
I am the calm

I am the hunter
I am the hunted

I am the seeker
I am the sought

I am *Shakti,* I am *Bhukti*
I am *Siddhi,* I am *Riddhi*
I am a woo-man
I am a wow-man

(Shakti = Power, Empower, Strength, To be able, etc.,
Bhukti = Enjoyment, Consumption, Limit, Possession, etc.,
Siddhi = Accomplishment, Attainment, Success, Perfection, etc.,
Riddhi = Prosperity, Good Fortune, Growth, Magic, etc.
The above four words are from Sanskrit).

Nocturnal Timepass

She thought her life was on a pause,
Oh, to think so, what a fool she was...!

This dashing young man one day came along,
To sweep her off her feet with his arms strong.

He painted a picture in a style warm and witty,
Of his life and dwelling in this big, bright city.

He said, come, my love, come with me,
I promise I'll always keep you happy.

His love and sweet talk made her blind,
And with him, she fled to happiness find.

Indeed, his place was big and bright,
And he loved her all day and all night.

This city made her forget her dull village.
Each day opened like a fresh, new page.

Ah, with stars in her eyes and spring in her steps,
This rustic girl soon transformed into a lady hep.

One day, he took her to a strange place,
The events thereafter, to her, are still a haze.

He left her in this black hole that had no exit,
Where she was showcased as a vulgar exhibit.

Daily, she is devoured by ravenous vultures,
Who come from all over, across all cultures.

She stopped feeling anything long, long back,
To be senseless, she had developed the knack.

Over a period of time, nothing of HER was left,
Feasting by vultures had left her of all bereft.

The simple and innocent village girl that she was,
Is today, every seeking man's nocturnal time pass.

She hears the anguished cry of her soul,
That wants to break free from this hellhole ...

She now eagerly awaits her Judgement Day,
Hoping He is convinced by all she had to say...

Padmaja Iyengar-Paddy, poet, writer, reviewer and editor, and Advisory Panel Member, ISISAR, Kolkata, and Editorial Counselor-India, International Writers' Journal, USA, is a recipient of several awards. She is the editor of 'Amaravati Poetic Prism' 2015-2019, international multilingual poetry anthology series, recognized by the Limca Book of Records as "Poetry Anthology in Most Languages". Paddy's poetry collection 'P-En-Chants' has been recognized as a Unique Record of Excellence by the India Book of Records.

Pankajam Kottarath
Constant Fear

Being the mother of a daughter is no easy task
The newspaper reports scream in your head
The TV channels make you almost mad
You feel for the miseries of parents of girls abused
and you are in constant fear.

For perverted minds, an infant or a girl is a woman
You try to rewrite old stories, cook up new ones,
with morals diverse to instill fear in her,
those taught at school for eons may be in conflict
because you are in constant fear.

You insist her to keep away from all
 be it a lonely place or a crowded one,
estrange herself from relations,
not to accept gifts from the old or juveniles
for you are in constant fear.

When she waves hand to the guard at the gate,
Your anxiety rises at an alarming rate
You advise her not to smile or befriend people
be it her neighbour, teacher, classmate or even cousins
as you are in constant fear

When she goes out during the day, you grow nervous
make calls after calls to tell her to rush back home before dark,
dreadful dreams wake you up during the thick of nights
and you keep watching whether the doors are all bolted.
Being the mother of a daughter is no easy task.

Oppression

An animal, two-legged
known to you or maybe not,
his claws and paws are hidden,
carries a storm inside, yet has a smile.
Lust makes him ugly from within
Lecherous gazes on the goblet of sin.
His body attains abysmal might
like an ogre from an eel, aiming insult.
The organ of shame dictates
and his brain submits.
The filthy message upwards
busts all conventions,
breaks all prohibitions.
Deaf or dumb, distracts him not
for he knows too well
little does it wane his joys
and the devil in him wins.

Tongues may be mute,
Tears are not.

Being a Woman

In quiescence I preach;

I take pride being a woman,
would like to look feminine
with sweet shyness and blushing cheeks,
yet blanket my feminine trails
like the 'touch-me-not' leaves
annoying compliments don't enslave me.

Melanin in skin decides ones attributes
soft rhythm in trots accentuates traits
my body is a temple of nurturing powers
none assigned with rights to relegate it.

I wish to admit my mistakes,
to show my strength through it and grow,
not a weakness it is, I counter,
Don't take for granted, or brand me timid.

I want to be everything,
nothing at all at the same time
be smart, but not appear smarter than you
in your guess precisely, not to hurt your ego,
maintain peace between us is my motto
as we travel together between life and death.

I want to be independent,
be on my own to boost my confidence,
not that I do not need you,
you can be the shade I embrace to be in light
like the maple leaves to the butterflies in rain.

We are different, but no discrimination
mutually reliant we are, none superior.
You and I are fed with the same milk
both at birth, and after death too.

Pankajam is a bilingual poet and novelist settled in Chennai, India. Her poems, book reviews, and articles are published in national/ international journals. She has authored 25 books including fourteen books of poems, out of which one book has been translated into French. Three books on literary criticism feature her works. A book titled "Poetic Oeuvre of K Pankajam" containing critical essays and research papers on her poems is forthcoming. She has won many awards including Rock Pebbles National Literary Award 2019.
Social media Link: https://www.facebook.com/pankajam.kottarath

Pooja Sharma
A Thousand and One Ways

It's quite easy actually,
The poetic among you
can use words
The intellectual
can use logic
The scientific
can use nature
The pious
can use commandments
The political
can use fear
The academic
can use history
And the brutish can
of course, use force.
There are a thousand ways
You can kill a woman
or more, now that I think of it
Why even the foolish can use
their fool-proof prejudice
But for her to live
there is just one
impossible way
That you simply
let her be.

Pooja Sharma is a Delhi based writer and poet. She took a break from her job of writing headlines to write poetry. She is also doing her Ph.D. in Folk Narratives from the University of Delhi. She can be reached on Twitter at @poojabirdword.

Pooja Ugrani
To the boomer who called my baby a burden

A throwaway remark
dished out at lunch,
oozing slyly,
at the colleague/husband
by someone who has never provided for me,
and never will.

You have no idea,
how and why we choose
to live with each other
nursing our soreness
standing up to face the world,
while a little being observes us
closely, intently.

As I step out to earn
he steps in to rear
I let her fall, dust her wounds,
wanting her to be tough
he dresses her up, makes her look
into the mirror to feel beautiful
I teach her to live with what we have
he allows her to indulge
every once in a while.

There is no space in our lives
for unmeasured judgments
or unimaginative minds
weighed down by the beliefs
of yesteryears

You cannot begin to fathom
this magnanimous, beautiful chaos
we have painstakingly worked on.

We sit
on each other's shoulders
we are our own giants,
learning, dancing, fighting, fluid,
filling each other's voids
with everything
that is anything but a burden.

Palimpsest

I witness a child,
wronged inside a temple
and vow I would never enter one,
its sanctity, polluted for me
to a point of no return.

The horror that child
must have gone through,
contained there
conflicted hard and battered
my image of a temple

of stone walls dimly lit,
of facing light, of bowing down
eyes shut, to keep in and not keep out,
silences where your voice is heard,
assuring you that you are safe.

I shut down,
impotent, helpless
hugged my young child
and cried each night.
I cursed myself for having brought her
into this messy cocoon,
filled with pervading, engulfing,
nightmarish possibility.

I quietened a million what-ifs
I wanted to forget that face
I wanted to unsee and unremember

A few days ago, I took my child
with her grandparents to a temple.
It didn't feel traumatic.
Enough time had passed,
enough for this mute observer
of Facebook forwards
not having to clean up
and deal with the mess,
not getting daily reminders
of horrors from the past.

A new patch
stitched over old clothes
like fresh memories that cover older ones
into gentle oblivion
accepting, not negating, nor normalising
only, very, very selfishly,
finding my peace.

(Both poems were first Published in Cafe Dissensus Everyday, 7th April 2020.)

Pooja Ugrani is an architect by education, a teacher by profession, a poet by whim, and an artist by choice. She was invited to read at the Bangalore Poetry Festival 2019 and by the Champaca bookstore at the Bangalore International Center on the occasion of International Women's Day in March 2020. She considers the cities of Mumbai and Bangalore, her twin homes, draws from personal experience and memory to write about the small everyday things in life that intrigue and engage her.

Dr. Pragya Suman

Amrapali

I was bride of a city that was a story
 of splendour
Assailants and hoofing riders laid down their sword
only my wistful wavering glance was enough
I was a victory,
victory was mine.
Father and son both came to my door
for a mere glimpse of my anklets.
I will tell you about my magic that waved up to the ethereal world.
Zenith of my vainglorious boost!
When spellbound Buddha came to my door
My supreme victory was!
You know that day I conquered God!
Do you want to know the secrets of my spell?
I lost my soul of sprouting love in bloody slain
Sun melted down drop by drop on rose petals
wriggling soul erupted in metallic one
That day I became an iron petal.

Dr Pragya Suman is a doctor by profession, from India. Writing is her passion. Her poems and articles have been published in multiple magazines and anthologies. She is a Gideon poetry award winner of summer 2020. She is posted in Shri Krishna medical college, Bihar.

Pramila Venkateswaran

The Verdict

In his chambers, the Madras High Court judge sits across a large mahogany table. He asks my mom softly, Did you drive your daughter-in-law out? No, mother shakes her head. She is welcome to live with me. I never asked her to leave. She could not stand my nurses and therapists in the house. She said they disturbed her peace. The judge prods, Is your son violent? She does not answer. Did he threaten you? Once, she says. Did you press charges? My daughter went to the police station, she confesses.

I cannot keep mum. The high ceilings and the ghosts from the British era wearing their fancy dress are too much. He hit her, he threatened to kill her, I yell. The judge lifts his hand to stop my stricken tones from reaching his brain. My brother stands silently by the door, his face impassive. His wife speaks up, Amma, we will take care of you. On hearing her honeyed words, the judge says, Amma, try to get along with your daughter-in-law and son.

I am seething, the judge's hand, a tape over my unruly mouth. Can't he smell the stink of violence? My voice tears the humid air, How will my mom be protected? He says benignly, Don't worry, be positive. Your brother and sister-in-law are gifts. Help your mother see that.

Portrait of Hyper-masculinity

He was mischievous, got into scrapes.
"Just like a boy," they said, in voices
sugary. As a teen, he fought, cursed,
cruised the town. "Sight-seeing,"
they called his girl-craze. His dad said,
"Man up," so he sailed and knew the oceans
better than any cartographer, but failed
to hear the storm brewing within him.

He drank to drown his unnamed grief.
Since his people saw only his actions,
no one heard his true voice. One day
he threw the crew's pet tubby into the
Suez. He threatened his wife, showed off
who was boss in the bedroom.

His kids cowered, their voices settled
like stones in the bottom of their growing
bodies. His wife learned how to sharpen
her knives, how to cut him into little bits,
inside out. Soon he became a shell, blustery,
hollow. When you pushed his raised arm,
it fell limply by his side.

It did not take long for him to draw
a knife at his mom. The police reprimanded him.
She must have provoked him, they reasoned.
He repeated the cycle. People said
age will mellow him. Instead,
the storm burst out of him.

Pramila Venkateswaran, poet laureate of Suffolk County, Long Island (2013-15) and co-director of Matwaala: South Asian Diaspora Poetry Festival, is the author of many poetry volumes, the most recent being The Singer of Alleppey (Shanti Arts, 2018). She has performed her poetry internationally, including at the Geraldine R. Dodge Poetry Festival and the Festival Internacional De Poesia De Granada. An award-winning poet, she teaches English and Women's Studies at Nassau Community College, New York. She is a founding member of Women Included, a transnational feminist association.

Preeta Chandran

Ash

Vodka, disco lights, kohl; her eyes are kohl-rimmed.
Galena, or ash?
I don't much like disco lights; starlight is better.
It's somehow more honest.
Will you dance with me? Yes. Her smile.
In that moment, every banal tread
falls into rhythm; from the rustling up of the supper
to the cleaning and washing and the dabbing on
the lipstick for him, everything.
She tells me her truth. I feel dizzy; is it the vodka?
I release my own truth from its trenches.
She makes a promise. She's like starlight, I think.
Home. He steals the red from my lips.
I feign headache; too much vodka, I say.
I can see he's upset. Boys don't cry, I think.
Hilary Swank as Brandon Teena would make anyone cry.
I've really had too much vodka.
It's a dark night, just like that one, many seasons ago.
Ten years ago, to be precise. No stars.
Only darkness and whiplash and echoes.
Queer. Queer. Queer.
Wandering freak. Whiplash. Sobs.
My vision swims. It's not just the vodka; it's the tears too.
Wandering. An ironic epithet for an existential blank,
teetering on the fringes of anatomy.
I think about trenches; I think they are no good.
I consign my truth to the flames, and I toss in her promise too.

Fire. Ash.

Cold clouds envelope the ether and smother the fiery dust.

Preeta Chandran is a writer/poet and a CEO with a digital media company, eWandzDigital. She is also a former Assistant Vice President with a global conglomerate, Genpact. She is the author of two poetry books (The Painted Verse, The Portrait of a Verse), and a children's fiction book (The Chemical Drones), co-authored under the pen name "HashWrite". Preeta has been featured in several anthologies, both Indian and International. Her session at the International Kolkata Book Fair 2017 was telecast on Doordarshan News, the national television channel of India, and her children's fiction book has been on Amazon bestseller lists.
https://in.linkedin.com/in/preetachandran
https://preetawriter.com/books-and-works.html

Priya Pramod
She

Somewhere,
She was in the womb.
Will she be born?
Her shrill cries echoed -
through existence.
Soul as the torch,
She navigated through darkness.

Somewhere,
She made breads
for the breadwinners!
Knowledge denied.
Being not the family-name bearer.
She learned the harder way.

Somewhere,
She silently existed.
Vulture eyes caressed her body.
She was at fault,
for no fault of hers.
She was substantive,
beyond what they saw.

Somewhere,
She was a bride.
Circumambulating the fire.
It was a celebration for others.
To erase the memories of,
who she was till then.
Behind the veil,
She held her identity.

Somewhere,
She was walking her way up.
Tongues spewed venom;
How could she even dare?
Dreams were reserved,
Not for her.
Unapologetically she walked.

Somewhere,
She looked up above,
head held high.
Eyes on her wrinkled face,
still gave a sparkle.
She the fighter.
She the woman.

Priya Pramod is an Engineer by qualification, an Observer who loves to think, read & write, She is a Blog Writer (https://priyasvisual.com/), a Mother, and Homemaker. Her poems are featured in the Life in Quarantine project sponsored by CESTA, Stanford University, and on the blog Brave&Reckless.

Priya Sarukkai Chabria
The Gathering of Time: Dialogues with Kalidasa*

Grishma
"...the wayfarers' hearts are scorched by the fire of separation;
nor can they bear the wind-blown parched earth sizzling under the
sun..."
— Ritusamharam by Kalidasa

Summer
Burnt sky, burnt earth, burnt water
surround me. Burnt hopes too.
You're right:
Time has charred me.
See what I've become:
Stretched sand of a riverbed
too hot to walk upon,
and this breeze –
from a phoenix's wings

*The celebrated Sanskrit court poet Kalidasa's dates are uncertain: he is thought to have lived anywhere between 1BCE to 5 CE. An early work in six cantos, Ritusamharam (The Gathering of Seasons) speaks of the joy of conjugal love with scarcely a note of brooding. Kalidasa also invokes 'samharam" or the "Great Gathering" at the end of Time when all of creation is drawn back into the body of Siva, its ground and source. Ritu is a polyvalent word meaning cycle, season, order, menstruation and fertility among others. I see my cycle of poems, The Gathering of Time as a sawal-jawab, a verbal joust with Kalidasa's view of compliant women. My translations of Ritusamharam (The Gathering of Seasons) are adapted with the help of my mother, Smt. Saroja Kamakshi from C R Devadhar's Works of Kalidasa, Volume 2.

(First published in Not Springtime Yet, HarperCollins Publisher, India, 2009.)

Priya Sarukkai Chabria is an award-winning poet, translator, and writer who is acclaimed for her radical aesthetics across her eight books of poetry, spec-fic, literary non-fiction, novel, and, as an editor, two anthologies. Her writing has been published in numerous anthologies, including Another English: Anglophone Poems from Around the World, A Book of Bhakti Poetry: Eating God, Adelphiana, Asymptote, Drunken Boat, PEN International, Post Road, Reliquiae, The Literary Review (USA), The Gollancz Book of South Asian Science Fiction, Language for a New Century, The HarperCollins Book of English Poetry, The British Journal of Literary Translation, Voyages of Body and Soul, etc. She edits Poetry at Sangam. (http://poetry.sangamhouse.org/) www.priyawriting.com

Priyanka Sacheti
For All the Girls Who Cannot Make Round Chapattis

I

Listen,
we are cartographers:
mapping new countries,
birthing new languages,
words for love,
things to sing about,
lakes to swim in,
and mountains to climb.

II

We are countries,
not chapattis:
no can pull
flatten
shape
bake
us.

III

Melted sunlight rivers
across speckled lands,
tributaries running together.
We eat an atlas for lunch
but never ask once
the cartographer's name.

What My Grandmother and I Didn't Know

The summer I turned twenty,
my grandmother told me a story
about her twentieth year.
How she was able to leave
her home and enter the streets
only when inside
a pink cloth tunnel:
a rectangle of sky above,
the only thing visible to her,
the only thing visible of her,
her ankleted feet.

The day she shared her story,
I walked those same streets
she had once upon a time,
young and unknowing.
The sky looked different but it
was still the same sky.
I wore no anklets on my feet
but I felt them all the same.
I thought I knew more than her
and yet, at the end of the day,
I learned I knew nothing,
nothing at all.

A Nameless Woman Goes By Two Names: Pinky/Gauri

Pinky was Pinky only till the day she left the house where she had
come into life twenty-three years ago to start anew in her husband's
     house.
A fugitive now, from an old name. Pinky has been Gauri since the
     moment
her bridal feet crossed the marital threshold, trailing red boats in
     her newly named wake.
Gauri sometimes forgets she was once Pinky: Gauri sometimes even
     forgets she is now Gauri.
What is in a woman's name, after all?

Pinky runs bare feet, hair streaming behind her: a flag fluttering
     in unfettered glee.
In two months and three days, she will become in the following
     order:
a bride, daughter-in-law, wife but for now, she is just Pinky (the
     surname, silent).
Pinky sleeps till noon, skips lunch, bathes at three pm,
and eats paani-puris, as if they were oysters,
a food she will never taste but simply likes the sound of.
At night, her favorite time of the day, she will breathe in the stars,
thinking of all her life's undreamed dreams, waiting to be let out
one by one, like minutes in a clock.

Gauri wakes before dawn, silencing her hair in a bun even before
     brushing her teeth.
In the space of the time, it takes her husband to drink tea,
     phone-scroll, and bathe,
Gauri will boil milk, make tea, and conjure up breakfast and a
     three-tiered lunch.
Her husband sometimes forgets to comb his hair so she will place
     the comb inside his palm,
like a found pair of lost glasses, and watch him slowly run it
     through his hair, as if seeing it clearly only for the first time.

He will vanish for the day and Gauri, in turn, to placate angry pots
       and pans in the kitchen,
the pressure-cooker hissing at her if she is even a minute late.
In that minute, she forgets she has a name, ever had one at all.

Pinky dreams every night in technicolor, writing her dreams down
in the morning, each one tasting of milky unsweetened tea.
Pinky no longer takes sugar to ensure her bones fit into
a wedding dress she does not know yet she will never ever wear
       again.
It will occur to her only later that sugar and bone are the same
color but by then, both will cease to matter in her life, much like
her once upon a time name.

Gauri unbuns her hair to wash it before slowly coiling it into silence
       again
in the ten minutes she allows herself to drink sunlight
and cupboard her dangerous chaos of thoughts.
Gauri does not dream and even if she does,
she is too frightened to remember her dreams let alone their color
      (black and white).
She remembers only this, the nightmare accidentally dreamed
      months ago:
she is dancing on a stage in a rose-pink saree, head uncovered,
her hair flying around, an ominous, darkening storm.
She woke up gasping, clutching the dying life-jacket of her hair,
      deathly afraid.
What are the almost-drowned thinking when their feet finally touch
      land?
The earth shaking beneath her glacier feet, Gauri had just two
      thoughts to spare:
1. I despise pink
2. I have no more a favorite color
than I have a name.

Pinky laughs in her dream before turning over:
a tarot card in making.
A tree is starting to bloom outside her balcony
and if she cares to notice it, she will see that
its petals are bright pink but the hearts, a startling yellow.
This tree goes by many names too: pink trumpet flower, pink
        lapacho, pink ipe.
Yet, for all those who unsee it, it has only one name: tree,
nothing more, and nothing less.

Priyanka Sacheti is a writer and poet based in Bangalore, India. She grew up in the Sultanate of Oman and was educated at the Universities of Warwick and Oxford, United Kingdom. She has been published in many publications with a special focus on art, gender, diaspora, and identity. Her literary work has appeared in Barren, The Cabinet of Heed, Popshot, Terse, The Lunchticket, and Jaggery Lit as well as various anthologies. She's currently working on a poetry and short story collection. She can be found as @anatlasofallthatisee on Instagram and @priyankasacheti on Twitter.

Puja Rai
I, an Illustration

I often grab a paper and a pen,
some handful of seeds in my vein,
and stair my way to meet the remote past.
The virgin memory,
unlike the body I share,
Stagnant like my favorite mother's recipe.
Yet again so sweet is the taste,
that varied flavours explode in every cell...
Submerged in the ocean of secrets,
I pluck words, phrases,
voices, incidents
and recollect my ten year old self curiously asking Baba,
why being his own daughter,
our skin looked so different?
Mine fair, his tanned;
Mine soft, his rough;
followed his witty reply,
"Just an inevitable fruit...
It's easy to relish tea and befriend a book,
than romance amid the bushes,
bearing unwanted heat, the terrible rain, some prickly insects.
So better savour its delicacy and aroma...
Take time to create- your space, your name
more for yourself and less for us... "
This utterance matured with every sunset,
Obediently sheltered within the gray matter...

Enjoying weather and fewer friends,
10-12-15-17-19...
Life continued with the same
conventional formulae and mathematical expression,
Somewhere in between these numbers,
I realised, I exist loosely
like a micro-organism in a petri dish,
Minute in the graphical axis,
No numbers define me,
No lines parallel me,
I carry a peculiar structure,
An ignorant picture,
A mere quark in the universe,
I was reduced to an unborn child
Without a parental history,
Illegitimate was 'I'
surviving in the Forest, like an undiscovered living fossil;
Gasping.., I limped down the stairs, with multifarious seeds in my
arms,
Trying to plant,
the colour, the race, the sex
and the language of sunakharis, chaamp and guras,
Outside their positioned margins...
Yet again, in between these numbers,
I realise, I exist- impure and hybrid
An art ephemeral and biotic,
A simple period to confirm and connect,
A naked spot within an infinite frame...

Puja Rai is from the himalayan region of Darjeeling. She is working as a lecturer at St. Joseph's College, North Point. She completed her M.A. in English Literature from the University of North Bengal. She is interested in reading, writing and nature photography.

Punam Chadha-Joseph
The Women of Today

We are the women of today
The global women of today.

Bound together by a common bond
Intelligent, independent, educated, informed
Well-travelled, aspiring, inspiring and empowered.

We are the women who march on regardless
Not just breaking, but in fact, shattering the glass ceiling.
We are the ones who have the power to produce a new life
No man can ever compete with that.
Sometimes we are also blessed
With supporting partners, family and friends
Who encourage us to take the road less taken.

We are the women of today
The global women of today.

We don many hats and juggle many balls
As we continue to fulfil our roles
Of being a daughter, a lover, a wife, a mother, a friend.
Yet we continue to be dedicated, determined
Extremely hard-working, excelling at being
Professional women.

We are fortunate
That we are not the downtrodden
Underprivileged, stifled women
Who still constitute a large part of our country.
We are the privileged ones
Therefore we have the onerous responsibility
Of not just enlightening
But in fact leading those less entitled.

We are the women of today
The global women of today.

We are here to celebrate ourselves
Our talents and our achievements
And also to demand and ensure that we get our due.
We are not here to compete with men
But to gently remind them and ourselves
That we are a large part of the workforce
And that we deserve our half.

Our physicality though
Does put us at a slight disadvantage
And that's where we require
Some support from the men we work with.
But neither are we the weaker sex,
Nor inferior in any way
We just need a little compassion
And protection sometimes
To help us to do our best.

We are the women of today
The global women of today.

We are flawed and fabulous
Emotional and empathetic
Energetic and active, nurturing and symbiotic
Vocal and vulnerable, irreverent and impulsive
Unapologetic and intimidating.
But we are also often the ones
Who make the most meaningful connections
In our modern world.

We are the women of today
The global women of today.

Our lives are real and random
Chaotic and even unexpected.
We are not just characters in a story
But living, thinking, feeling beings.
The ability to engage with our memories
Brings structure and reasoning to all that we do
Making us a mighty, powerful force.

So dream on dear friends
Dream big and find your place in the sun.
Continue to live, continue to love
And continue to shine on
As only each of you empowered women can!

We are the women of today
The global women of today.

The New Woman

I believe that crossing fifty is a very liberating age
The beginning of a new chapter on a completely fresh page
A finding of ourselves and a certain acceptance too
Observing our world from a different point of view

Physically for a woman, freedom from a lot
A definite moving away from a predefined slot
Responsibilities continue towards the young and old
But with a lot more determination and a stronger hold

Though women are undoubtedly the unifying force
It's something that men find difficult to endorse
But with actions and deeds, we prove our worth
Of women bold and outspoken there is no dearth

We need to break free from shackles and norms
There is no gospel telling us that we must conform
But we are fearful of messing with beliefs that are set
So we bow to them reverentially and then rationalize what we get

Years go by and we diligently play our part
Internally battling demons or even a broken heart
And then one day we realize that we too have a life
Beyond working woman, daughter, mother and wife

We decide that the time has come to spread our wings
Throw caution to the wind and experience new things
With a determined smile on our lips and a spring in our step
We approach even the routine with new vigour and pep

Leaving those around wondering what is this fuss
Confused, they don't know how to accept the new us
And as we inwardly rejoice and enjoy this new space
It's this version of ourselves that we must embrace!

Punam Chadha-Joseph: Hotelier, advertising professional, writer, poet, and artist. Punam's much-acclaimed book of poems - 'The Soulful Seeker', features sketches and the cover done by her. Her achievements include poetry readings at various literary festivals across the country and watercolor paintings adorning homes within India and overseas. She is the recipient of several awards for writing and poetry, with poems in the 'Portraits of Love' coffee table book and 'She the Shakti', an anthology of poems about women.

Punam Chadha-Joseph
Kali — Contemporary

Punam Chadha-Joseph
Kali — Adrogynous

Punam Chadha-Joseph
Kali — Ornamental

Radhika Puttige
The Dark s(k)in

*The Dark S(k)in focuses on the fairness mania ingrained deeply in us.
This poem is a story of one such dark-skinned girl, who is unable to cope
with the barrage of taunts society throws at her. Her emotions rile her
and she questions goddess Kali, about the judgemental mindset of people
and their absolute disparity in attitudes.*

My birth marked a black day
gloom knocked on our door
for I was
dark and a girl,
the two major handicaps
defined by society's
narrow minded norms.
"Baa baa black sheep
Oh! Who will marry you?"
was a constant echo, all through
my growing up years.
Maa scrubbed my face with homemade lotions,
bought a dozen fairness creams,
hoping for a magical transformation.
"Our neighbor's daughter is lucky!"
they often said.
"So what if she failed her exams?
Her fair complexion
is sure to get her a prized groom."
My excellence in academics
seemed irrelevant, for
I failed the major exam of beauty.

I shut my ears to their whines,
but my heart broke into infinite shards,
each time, she blamed her fate for birthing me.
I seek solace in the night sky
for it has a face like mine.

Exasperated,
I look at the picture of goddess Kali,
hanging on the wall,
If her dark colour is worshipped,
why is mine a sin?

Becoming ME

Becoming ME celebrates the freedom of a woman emerging out of the trauma of physical abuse. Though educated, many women still continue in abusive ties. It takes immense courage on their part to break free from such a relationship and move on with dignity.

It started with a single slap
followed by a profuse apology.
Brushing it off as a one-time mistake,
was a mistake I made,
for it kept repeating,
 and a naive me,
falling prey to his empty promises.

His sadist attitude turned him demonic,
mottled me blue and black.
Each time he towered over me,
in silence I bore it all.
The walls of our home were
a mute witness to his savagery.
Grappling in the dark, lonely
I drowned in my endless tears.
Shrouded by emotional debris
absolutely numb,
I began to asphyxiate.
Until I decided,
No more...

Refusing to write my epitaph,
I extricated myself from
the fetters of his abuse,
leaving the grisly darkness behind.
Gathering the remnants of me,
I walked a lonely path
taking my bruised heart along,
cared and nourished it.
Time healed my wounds,
though the scars remain.

Today,
After a long time, I feel emancipated.
I smile again
for now, my soul is liberated
I live to be ME.

I am a curse

I am a curse could be the story of any girl in one of the Indian villages. Being born as a girl is a curse she feels. Her young shoulders are burdened with the responsibility of household chores and physical labor. School and toys are something she has never been exposed to. She is married off at a vulnerable age, thus having no experience of a normal happy childhood. This is a bitter account of child labor and marriage, where the society feigns ignorance to her ordeal, all in the name of outdated customs and traditions.

My
 soul scavenges for memories
into the past, scouring for moments
of smiles and happiness.

Alas,
only to meet a murky wall
 of gloom and darkness
bias and prejudice
 abuse and scorn

burden and guilt
hunger and loneliness
pain and sorrow.
My
delicate hands forced into labor,
books and toys only a fantasy.
The hollow love, tyrant family
leave me bereft of emotions.
The wedding celebrations
shatter my tender dreams.
For,
tonight I shall be crushed
abused and crumpled.
Silently,
wiping the bloody tears
silencing the screams
hiding the bruised body
a lifeless muted me,
will mourn and lament
my birth as a girl.

(This poem of mine was first published in my book, Eclectic Verses).

Radhika's writings reflect her thoughts and ruminations on life. While she mostly writes poetry, her blog radhikasreflection on WordPress is a potpourri of photographs, prose, and musings inspired by everyday life. A couple of her poems have been published on online literary platforms. She recently published her first book of haiku and poetry titled Eclectic Verses, which is available on Amazon and other online platforms. Facebook: radhika.puttige Instagram handle: radhikasreflection.

Raina Lopes
Shades Of Womanhood

Her hairline was filled with vermilion,
tiny hands tinted with henna,
served *gujiyas* holding a heavy platter,
her childhood was tainted by filthy customs.

Wearing all the colors she could find,
dazzling beauty stood in the night,
wooing men wasn't her choice,
shunned by the society, who painted her face black.

Timidly she masked her bruises,
it wasn't her dream to be beaten black and blue,
bright red lipstick and buff hue,
were the only colors she ever knew.

Their lives are colorful, aren't they?
But none could express their daily pain.
The universe sheltered many such daughters,
distanced from colors of joy and laughter.

Voice of a Mortified Body

Often, she looked in the mirror,
cursing at her own reflection,
food she once loved caused resentment,
as everyone addressed her a 'Plus size baggage'.

Hairy skin and frizzy mane,
wished her soul to get rid of,
as they bullied her calling 'bushy nest',
her own visage she considered a bane.

Empathy gushed in her veins,
nobody cared, since she wasn't fair,
color was significant not a golden heart,
white defined beauty because brown didn't elate.

Blemished face, short stature,
'who would marry you?', was all they could muster,
Bogged down by society's denigrating credo,
tarnished minds still existed in a burnished universe.

Thin and tall, she believed she was saved,
Well... that was just an illusion to soon fade,
suppressed and suffocated as she stuffed her chest,
grueling it became to even grab a breath.
Fairy tales were crafted for books and novels,
Miraculous love was movie magnetic,
Facts long ago they had made peace with,
when true colors of folks surfaced their pupils.

Raina Lopes is a software engineer by profession at a renowned MNC and a poet and writer by heart. She loves spending time observing nature and finds solace in reading and writing.
https://m.facebook.com/raina.lopes.14?ref=bookmarks

Dr. Ranjana Sharan Sinha
Ellipsis (...)

Spreading out into different
spectrum of colours:
Iridescent, kaleidoscopic,
I am a woman-- the creator--
chiseling, carving, scratching!

At times a SITA
walking through the flames,
agonies buried deep down,
tagged as being 'weak' or 'vulnerable'.
At times a fiery captivating DRAUPADI,
disrobed and humiliated!

A HOMEMAKER with a clammy face,
making bread for my hungry children,
my eyes fixed on the watch
to catch up morning session;
the distance between the
rolling pin in the kitchen, and
the driver's seat in the car--
I cover in one stride!

On dark days
I become an AVATAR of KALI:
The true badass
rocking the earth and the sky!
With long mane of hair,
the bloodied sword and a necklace
of the heads of my victims,
I crush the god of destruction
under my feet!

Slicing through my subtly
changing and surprising selves,
I find too much worth analysis:
How do I weave a thousand years
into a single moment?
Inscrutable are the ways
of a woman's heart!

A FUNAMBULIST
walking on a tight rope,
the rope a thin long line
ending with an ellipsis...
Many unexpressed
monochromatic truths:
The truths with different shades
of the same colour,
linger in the cobwebs of heart
waiting to be filled in the blanks!

The poem Ellipsis (...) was published in the anthology of 11th Guntur International Poetry Festival", 2018 titled "The Tranquil Muse".

Missing Pearls

The night,
with its unrelenting darkness,
buries the mother
beneath a starless sky:
The moon,
distorted by mist,
conspires with darkness!

Mind in anguish,
soul in agony— The woman
feels the pinpoint needles
of the traumatic memory
that has left indelible
wounds and scars on her being!

Why oh why
the female fetus inside her womb—
The unborn SHE
with her legs and arms curled up
was denied justice and destroyed?

She was not allowed
to go through the glorious
odyssey of nine months!
She couldn't wake up to see
the beauties and wonders
of this amazing world!

"It's a girl, eliminate her," insisted
the so-called guardians of society,
And soon the unborn and
the womb were split apart!
The mother felt the ravages
of deprivation and brutality—
Oh, umpteen possibilities
were nipped in the bud!

Think and stop!
Where're we going?
Such a heinous act in a society
that venerates female deities—
Paradoxical! Paradoxical!

Say no to patriarchal culture
that breeds injustice
against women— the mother.
Arise and awake:
Let the girl child blossom
To save the endangered species!

('Missing Pearl' was published in the special issue of the magazine "Pinkishe", New Delhi, 2018, Crime Against Women Special)

A poet-author-critic and professor of English, Dr. Ranjana Sharan Sinha is a prominent voice in Indian Poetry in English with many awards to her credit from prestigious institutions. Received commendation from the former President of India, A.P.J. Abdul Kalam for her poem "Mother Nature". Two of her poems have been included in the university syllabus prescribed for 4 semester M.A. (English). Authored and published 08 books in different genres.

Ranu Uniyal
The Audacity of Living

As and when you came into this world, did they tell you
there will be no flowers, only twigs to welcome you.
Your eyes will search for a miracle, but your skin will
refuse to glow. Your mother will crush her nails and
dip her fingers in kegs full of acid. You will encounter
siblings dressed as vampires. There will be nuns in
school asking you to join the convent. You will sink with
grade eight girls into sockets of fresh blood. Your menstrual
cycles will go unchecked as you rub the unhealthy sheets
of cotton on your wet thighs. There will be seasons of
cigarettes and cheap vodka. Sex will be more out of curiosity
than lust. The roads will smell of cologne in your twenties and you
will be eager to savour the pill of romance. Chrysanthemums
will add some meaning to your life and you will hope some
gentleman would pick up the thorns and make the road
worthwhile.
Suddenly the ghosts, the vampires and the witches, the nails,
the blood, the dark alleys, the crush, and the pain, the womb,
and the twigs, will all get together, and bring your stretch
to a standstill, but you will once again refuse to die.

Holding on
(For a son with special needs)

I have you gaping with mouth wide shut,
your glasses indifferent to the glare, I follow you.

I have words searing my ears, to tongue
I wish there was little to spout.

I have a drop of rain that lies frozen
in a sea of fire. Despite the storm, I prefer quiet.

I have you still, in my arms, anaphylaxis, they say.
Unfettered. I know your heart beats inside me.

I have you my little sparrow, chirping in the twilight,
this beauty is enough to keep me sane.

I have you as my last morsel, hungry,
but content, I pick you at leisure.

I have you as my only shroud, in full view.
And I am left without a cover.

I have you as my heir, bent with the burden
of my damaged psyche. Full of kindness.

I have you in me – imperfect rhythms.
Whispers swell inside the belly. We dance together.

A Dust Storm in the Middle of the Night

It was one dark yellow evening and the stars had gone inside the
shell and the sky shameless but proud of its early naked flesh
opened its arms for the moon to recline nothing stirred in the winds
as if there were enough sins to wrap around the earth distant and
quiet had enough of blood sweat and tears to cope with there on
that daring night not out of nowhere but from the hungry bellies of
pregnant mothers from the uneven mouths of half-clad children the
disembodied spirits of the young who had been raped on the nights
when her husband was not around the silent fire of Godhra the
unshed tears of Bamian Buddha the blasts at the trains ripped
nameless bodies lost in the acts of vengeance unaccounted tales but
few to narrate sullied wombs gripped with fatigue and tireless
determination to hang on to life to nature to mother earth to
mothers of all the fathers sons soldiers statesman to all who had
once been inside her womb a burning question a haunting disquiet
how often will history repeat itself leaving her to write another
script without rain without sunshine.

(From Across the Divide, Yeti Books Calicut, 2006.)

Ranu Uniyal is a Professor of English at the University of Lucknow. An author of six books, her articles, and book reviews have been published widely across the globe. She has published three poetry collections: Across the Divide (2006), December Poems (2012), and The Day We Went Strawberry Picking in Scarborough (2018). She was on a Writer's residency in 2019 in Uzbekistan. Her poems have been translated in Hindi, Oriya, Malayalam, Spanish, Urdu, and Uzbek languages. She also writes poetry in Hindi. She is a founding member of PYSSUM, a center for people with special needs in Lucknow.
She can be reached at Website: ranuuniyal.com

Reena R
Other Tongue

From being hissed at too much, we have become venom
gliding glibly over your bristles, our skin speaking a new language
you cannot decipher without a forked tongue

Feeding you your poison, remaining untouched at the core
Strengthened by the knowledge you lack
Mimicking your insecurities
but also mocking them while being subdued by the weight of your
bones

The chains have shifted from soft bodies to minds mired in myths
pampered by obedience and shrunken from disuse
The knots are no longer where they were once put
The fabric has changed and the woman in it has ridden off

Liberty now moves like a breast drummed upon by the rain
and no longer wears heels, fishnet, or your name
What you still clutch at is clay of your making
How little you read of what we write on our skins!

*(First published in a mini-anthology on 19th August 2016. An Anthology
of Poems Dedicated to World Humanitarian Day.)*

Changing The Hole Narrative

The street light is blinking
yellow, grey, red. Repeat
Blood messed up with semen flows unchecked
The street is an agori's paradise
The moon hangs from a shredded hymen

Go out girl, you have nothing to lose but your fucked up existence
Let them prove your resolute convictions right
Fear, your only birthright, dread, your acquired one

Herds wait to sniff out
The skin over your degree
The down over your baby skin
A hole is all they lust after
To pour into it the wretchedness of their infirmities
See them swirl their insecurities in a bottle
And gulp it down
Before they take turns
To stick their ugliness into you

The street light goes red and then black
The moon hangs from a smudged eyeliner stroke
Nothing matters to you any longer
But your hole has engulfed them
Pulling them under
into a blackness
worse than the night under which
the rest of their miserable tribe cowers

Nothing sticks to the moon though
She is a savage. Be like her.

Reena R's poems have been published in The Copperfield Review, First Literary Review-East, Angle Journal, Poetry Quarterly, York Literary Review, Duane's Poe Tree, GloMag, Mad Swirl, etc. She is the Destiny Poets UK's Poet of the year (2014) and one of the editors of The Significant Anthology (July 2015). She won awards at 'World Union Of Poet's' poetry competition, 2016 and at "As You Like It International Poetry Contest', commemorating the 400th anniversary of Shakespeare. She won the Reuel International Prize for poetry, 2018.

Richa

Landscape

I feel like
A historical landscape
Explored by Archaeologists
They found my womb
In an excavation
And called it a centre for
Creation and recreation
They found my dreamy eyes
And called them
Lake
Pond
Lotus
They found my dead hands
And assigned them cookery
They found my breasts
And declared them
Mountains and hills
To be bombed for the
Sake of development
They found my hair
And made it the rope
To hang their clothes to dry
They found my organs
Here and there
And connected them
Into shame
Those promising archaeologists
Failed to find
My hopes
Desires
Dreams...

Richa is an Assistant Professor in the Department of English, Patna Women's College, Patna University, Patna. She pursued her Ph.D. on "Gender and Ecology in the Novels of Amitav Ghosh, Arundhati Roy and Kiran Desai" from Banaras Hindu University. She is keenly interested in theatre and poetry. She has written street plays, poems, and short stories and wishes to utilise the academic and creative spaces for affirmative social change.

Rita Malhotra
Leela is sixteen

a year limps by in nano steps
as Leela the widow
remains incarcerated
in the messy, confined core
of everyday struggle
carrying the burden
of invaded virginity
and ostracization
Leela the widow
turns sixteen today
in a threadbare white attire

the customary tears dried up
long ago, in her dark journey
from shunya to nothingness
when destiny deceived, when
dazed emotions lost colour
through sinking sensations
on the painfully pious bridal night
when her glass-shattering shrieks
broke the consciousness
of the unity of her being,
when oozing red, spread its
menacing tentacles to engulf
the fragments of kaleidoscopic
glass bangles-- her dream-bangles
Leela the widow turned sixteen today

as the candle of life
burns at both ends
Leela continues to mirror
the distorted face of tragedy
her silence has no secrets

monsoons do not sing
broken stories pile up
into heaps of abuse and abandon
as Leela the widow turns sixteen today

Molki* *(for a male heir)*

sold from village to village
man to man
it is business as usual--
carnal pleasure betrays
the play of emotions
as, the primate in every "him"
grazes along pastures of blind lust

time has crossed over to
the other side of reason
emptiness circles her huddled self
by the dying wood-fire
in a thatched, dilapidated dwelling,
amidst acrid smoke and garbage stench

her body is her only sin
every inch under the scanner,
the soul torn out of her being,
she is labelled a molki, a paro
a trafficked bride for a male heir
religion of humanity shamed,
another history subsumed in its rubric,
steps into a retrograde phase.

the visceral anxiety for her little girls
born four in a row, traps her in
the claustrophobic cobweb
of misplaced notions
the virus plays no role here
only primeval convictions thrive
in the antithesis of rationalism
in heavy debt of compassion
in the overflowing urn of gloom

was that really the Shiva-Linga
she worshipped from girlhood
to womanhood
or merely a piece of rock? else
why would those intense prayers
for a Shiva-like husband
lead her to the wolves' den?
in her silent pain, is heard
a soul-wrenching call
"Draupadi, i beg you
to circumscribe me".

Call her paro or a molki
her only mask is the metaphorical
burqa of primal fear
as days sink in deep despair,
haunting visions of phantom nights
leave brutal scars
on the skin of a mortified sun
skies stay shrouded in grey monochrome

a stranger
even to the ground, she treads upon,
her mute screams of protest
drown in voiceless echoes
drown in the deep abyss
of a menacing, dark silence
dissipate, in seismic tremors
of an alien time
tomorrows trace a question mark.

(*Bride buying in India remains a prevalent social evil despite the current extraordinary times. The brides, forced into marriage, are referred to as "paro" —from the far side— or "molki" —one who has a price. Molkis are often sexually exploited by all the males of the family.)

A National Science Talent scholar, Rita Malhotra is a mathematician, poet, essayist Poetry editor and translator. Former principal, Kamala Nehru College, University of Delhi and Post-Doctoral Fellow in Math, University of Paris, she is President, Poetry Across Cultures India and Executive-Committee Member, Poetry Society (India). She has fourteen published books including nine poetry collections and has been conferred recognitions by The World Congress of Poets, W.I.N Canada and The Romanian Government besides other International Bodies.

Rochelle Potkar
Key holes

We hide our wet lace behind a trellis of plants, our voices honeyed
      from jaded soap operas.
Our requiems are parties inside our heads, earphone to earphone.
Tolerance in the diorama of this rented place.
No door of solace or shame left open.

They will keep boyfriends. And.
They will come with trouble. And.
They will eat meat. And.

But sometimes we translate into vixens: late night-girls with eye
      masks,
returning on the stairs – *shush!* the landlord is insomniac
to stilettoes and side-slits of little black dresses,
books, menstrual cups, and spandex.

Who will take responsibility for them? And.

Emerald nights pass into agate mornings,
the sapphire of our head scarves and prayer mats
from insular to secular near our 2 by 2 boxes.
We curl each night against thoughts of saffron eyes, bloodshot.

If the nights fall over our skin, our bodies become bottles
of wine, with a crack against it. Dripping... dripping...

They will get raped. And.

Wooden cages with wooden birds flapping to horizons,
we scrape air like parchment,
peeling secrets from walls of adopted jailhouses.

They will grow wings. And.

Serpentine winds belching histories of women
who left when they heard the bricks squeaking,
Shush! And not again! And please behave yourselves.

But we play safe in dog-chewed *chappals*, our cycle tyres gripping
the road's ruggedness
as alleyways sugar-lip the broken sky
of old whispering neighbors.

All this for only one proper peg to place the key
of our russet city-freedoms.
They will wear short skirts. And.

(First published at The Daily Star, Bangladesh 2017.)

In that land under the sun, where dry heat hits bone
and in your pocket you keep a red onion
to peel flakes at 46-degrees centigrade,
male poets speak of Kamala Das and her feminist poetry,

entering a friend's wife's kitchen
and directing her to abandon her breakfast preparations.
They are getting late. There are no cafes in the neighborhood,
yet they depart with a caravan of 15 ravenous townspeople.

Under an angry sun, hunger hitting inside their guts,
Pied Pipers talk of timeliness, reaching a nowhere-wilderness,

while the woman in her four-walled, steeled cliché
keeps away a mountain of grated coconut over flattened rice,
sugar, coffee, and unused milk, par-boiled.
Her father was a village radical... but she tucks her wet sighs
at the edge of her sari.

As onions shrivel in our pockets with intense upheaval,
men use Urdu and Marathi verses to fight God

and the women can't even fight the men,
who are not their husbands
because they know no poetry.

(First published at Anomaly #28, South Asian Subcontinent.)

The girl from Lal Bazaar

sips divination off cups,
laced in ginger over a saucer of zodiac signs
in dark-dusky mornings after wine sediments in beer mugs
of last evenings,

gorging eyes off popped cardamoms -
brittle bones of promises,
unspooling the wedge of her mother's sari under umbilical,
swallowing the rain in vertical pills,
a land-locked dream gathers vapor,
through the thick glass of a *cutting-chai*
for storms in teacups.

As Chinese lanterns blow, she predicts smaller surfaces
for her future without straining dregs
that stir the night to cinnamon kisses,
like stars smudging daylight.
In maps of doubt, enmity, falsehood,
spade-shapes of fortune, mountains of hindrance,
patterns in camels, dogs/ letters in heart, and a ring.

She starts at the rim like the white women did (after independence),
holding teacup handles to their spiral bottom,
reverse-imaging white-negative spaces in clumps of flavor,
breaking potencies of freedom - on a stain with satin.

The girls were then from Europa, Nippon, for the English soldiers.
Now Madama drinks brew through her yellowing teeth,
stalking the labyrinth of dark snakes in hot water
from a kettle by the pimp,
bittering in tea-garden time – one hour ahead of the zeitgeist
present.

What's left is 14 lanes of women of Nepalese and Indian origin
in the old brewing market of flavors,
and she, the daughter of a *randi* who is into
the beatings of drums – even has a new track for an international
album.

She won't let ripples in the saucer of lip-smacking liquid,
quivering with delight, decide her near and far futures
in scaffoldings of condoms and collarbone-consciences.

*(This poem was shortlisted at the Gregory O' Donoghue International
Poetry Prize 2018, and first published at the Southword Journal,
Ireland.)*

#metoo size card

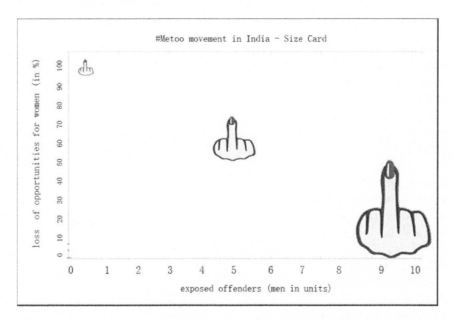

(This visual poem is part of the yet-to-be-published book of poetry.)

Rochelle Potkar is the author of Four Degrees of Separation *and* Paper Asylum *– shortlisted for the Rabindranath Tagore Literary Prize 2020. Her poetry film* Skirt *was showcased on Shonda Rhimes' Shondaland. Her story collection* Bombay Hangovers *is due soon. She is an alumna of Iowa's International Writing Program (2015) and a Charles Wallace Writer's fellow, University of Stirling (2017), and has read her poetry in India, Bali, Iowa, Macao, Stirling, Glasgow, Hongkong, Ukraine, Hungary, Bangladesh, and the Gold Coast. https://rochellepotkar.com. [@rochellepotkar]*

Roopali Sircar Gaur
Rape and the City

Woman,
walk wearily
your honour lies
between your legs
One act of vengeance
will ravage forever
your beauty
of mind and face
Blood trickling,
your accomplishments
ground to the dust
you will be
disrobed, dishonoured, dismembered
ceasing to exist
no longer a woman –
a cipher.
Your izzat your honour
looted by brigands
a leper-stoned out of the city walls

Woman
Fix blades on your breasts
Strew nails in your vagina
Let your crimson manicured fingers
Dig out those sin filled lustful eyes
Restrain with poison teeth
those groping hairy hands
Savour
the blood on your tongue
Scatter
dismembered manhood pieces
across the earth

Let no prostate Shiva stop you
Nor a shamed Earth swallow you
Allow no fire to consume you
Let no Gods shelter you

Woman
Walk naked to the temple
Drag the dripping
garland of demon heads
and lay them at the altar
of the dark Goddess Kali
Light the incense stick and
pour oil into the earthen lamp
Lift the Conch shell high and
Blow into it your fire-spitting breath

The siren just sounded its trumpet
The factory doors have opened
The city sounds are jostling
"Hurry up please,
it's time."

Daughters of India

Draupadi, Sita, Savitri
and Putna the Rakshasi
Ahalya Manthra and Kaikeyi
walk alone in our stories and
our crowded cities
with fired brains and
fire in their belly

Daughters of Gods and Goddesses
Kings and Sages
Farmers and Snake Charmers
They do what their
womanhood bids them do
from none other but

self, seeking applause
Prophets and oracles
hunters and archers
leaders and decision-makers
enchantresses and apsaras
warlords and swordswomen
swift of mind and body
filled with curiosity and desire
spurning virginity and chastity
defying restrain
refusing containment

Each day in farms and fields
carrying spades as their shields
braving the desert sand
Trident in hand
on ramps and in studios
in hospitals and in morgues
in boxing rings
and on wrestling mats
in offices and factories
changing fearless trajectories

From villages and towns
In search of golden crowns
leaving the stench of the ghettos
in buses, trains and metros
pushed and shoved
scrambled and trampled
they defy patriarchal laws
with self-sharpened claws
hidden in powerful tiger paws
fighting deathly cannibal jaws

Abandoned and cursed
damned and demonised
violated and beheaded

branded and brutalised
Medusa's snake hair flowing
turning men into pigs and stones
Kali's tongue lapping blood
and a garland of red hibiscus

Our Battles yet to be done
Our Trophies yet to be won
Our Songs yet to be sung

The Sky Above And The Mud Below

Just the other day
in a village in India
a man with a sickle
slit open
his wife's expectant womb

"This too is a girl"
the vermillion-marked temple priest
had told him
swearing by the gods he peddled
Five frightened little daughters watched

The morning paper grieved
"Panna Lal's dream to father
a baby boy was laid to rest forever
with the death of the male foetus
inside its mother's womb!"

Kiran's slit-open belly
the dark red blood spilt
the amniotic fluid on the floor
The agonising howls of pain

and the dead child
pulled out of her broken womb
found no mention

You see, her womb housed only daughters.
His sperm lodged those girls inside her
nobody told him
She was just a tired hired womb

That is why Rajeev the city slicker
strangled his wife for
some more dowry
Without the money
The woman was a cipher
The colourful wedding feast
had only heralded
the hiring of a womb
She couldn't breathe.
A four-year-old son
watched his mother die

A small column
in the morning paper
let out an excited shriek
"Get ready soon to see a woman
tear into the skies
in the new omni role
Rafale fighter aircraft
It can also deliver nuclear weapons
Look out for those two women
on the multi role helicopters
take off from front line warships!"

The deafening screech
Of swept back sleek metal wings
the whirring rotating
sound of combat helicopters

drowned the cries of wailing women
even as the drums begin to beat
signaling the coming of the warrior Goddess
battle weary from destroying the disguised demon
Mahishasura

Roopali Sircar Gaur, Ph.D. is a columnist and writer. She is the Founder-President of YUVATI, an organization working for girls and boys across India. Roopali was a professor of English at Delhi University and taught Creative Writing at the Indira Gandhi National Open University. Her book The Twice Colonised: Women in African Literature is a seminal text on women's issues. She recently co-edited the anthology, In All the Spaces-Diverse Voices in Global Women's Poetry (2020).

Roshnara M
Scientfic Thinking

Roshnara M is a chronic reader, trying to take her first steps into the world of creating her own works. She was born in India, grew up in Oman, and now lives in the UK. When she's not studying, reading or writing, she can be found in her kitchen or haunting local libraries. You can reach her at roshnaramohamed@ymail.com

S. Rupsha Mitra

Girls of India

This is not the silent dark of mud-brick villages and forests of
        night –
Or the melancholy of soft wails clogging the tributaries of the mind,
This is not *Cover your heads with ghoongat* or
Hide the fire of your soul and power of your voice in burqa, bodice,
        corset, mold
Now we listen to the howling of the wind, the trees, the breeze and
Scatter as free as the luminosity and freed will –
We build homes with tattered hopes and remake faith in this
Body of brown bough, muddy quarry, and granite.
We stand with unfree hands held like auspicious weapons of Shakti.
We. Gather, we parade through the new light of Equanimity –
We rise
Alighting, terrific,
From the macabre, to transcribe our tales, our secretive
Congealed veils and divulge them in fire – alive.
Our voices vibrate together – tempestuous timbre of an ocean, of
Roaring girls
As we come forth, barriers fall, break
Curtains unleash, raise.

I am Woman

They christened me as the river.
So that I flow, and fill the voids,
So that I quench thirsts
As I begin my journey from the foot of the mounts.
They narrated me stories, of caged birds,
Clay pots, jasmine skins
So that I let myself, be moulded, rolled, beaten
And shaped like some malleability
They glorified my softness and naivety,
They asked me to sit down whenever I wanted to stand.

They taught me essentialities of lajja, that admonishes me
To wear a veil,
However they told I need not feel lajja for
Remaining quelled like feet stuck in mud, and
Mouths silenced for eternity.
But – let me proclaim
I have known the myths of ten handed Goddesses,
And Kali
Trampling Shiva with her feet.
I know how the ocean turns vehemently into a loud roaring wave –
A catastrophic tornado.
I have discovered the beauty of my deodar skin,
I rise, from the clods of mud beneath,
I emerge out of the sable of ashes
I emerge as the fire, from the worn wombs of foraged forests,
I come out of my veil, like Razia did, ages ago
I come out as the Chamunda – the raging goddess,
I come out like your nightmarish dreams,
I burn down the wilderness, I break the iron bars, as I
March forward.

S. Rupsha Mitra is a student from India with a love for writing poetry. Her works have been published in literary magazines including Hebe Poetry and Indian Periodical.

Sabreen Ahmed
Song of a Madwoman

An heirloom of psychosis
Is infused in her genes,
Hemlock of neurosis
Ooze in the blood of her kinfolk—
Mania, hysteria, insomnia,
Schizophrenia and paranoia
Etched in her creed's paraphernalia
Sister, mother, cousin
Join hands in the insane ring.
One drank the hellebore
One knocked the asylum's door,
Their sleepless eyes blazing ember
Look for succor in the doctor's chamber
She is no Bertha Mason or Sylvia Plath
Neither Virginia Woolf or any female Lear
Mad out of a discordant fear—
Fear of ignominy,
Blame of blasphemy,
Of dishonor

In every social corner.
She is no Medusa
Or a feminist seer
Nor a Minerva out of wit
Or Saraswati dispossessed
of her Lotus seat
She is the bleeding Kali
She dies to relive
She is me she is you

Mad behind civilized veils
With glaring eyes
Indifferently she trails
The saga of dominance
Forever entails.

Touch of death

The mutilated body,
of raped human justice is
slit open with gendered hatred
in sucking
the savage taste of murder
from Manorama, Nirbhaya
to Manisha are all agape
as you and me

scream at the butchered and burnt
remains of
a dead civilization
fragmented and festered
divided by class
and repeatedly torn apart
by the sexist dictates
and misogynist media
of free online obscenity
with caste orgies
of a fiendish fetish
untamed by the rulers
of the game of law
or the fatal fear
of a castrated hanging.

Dr. Sabreen Ahmed received her Ph.D. from Jawaharlal Nehru University, New Delhi in 2013. Her area of interest is Gender studies, South Asian English Writing, and Contemporary Theory. She has published an anthology of poems entitled Soliloquies (2016) and has also edited a UGC Sponsored National Seminar Proceeding captioned Indian Fiction in English and the Northeast (2016). Currently, she teaches in the Department of English, Nowgong College, Nagaon, Assam, India. She writes poems, short stories, articles, book reviews etc for several webzines in India like Cafedissensus, The Thumbprint, The Citizen, Feminism in India & The Assam Tribune.

Sahiti G.
In this fairytale

In this fairytale, I become the monster and revel in it.

When a man feels entitled to my body, tries to grab my hair, it turns to snakes.

I sharpen my teeth with my words, laugh without covering my mouth, so he knows that this bitch bites. Stare him in the eye and watch him turn to stone, watch him struggle to raise a hand against me.

I'd place my claws against the side of his face; make him stare at the awful, at my grotesque rage.

Make him think about how this time, he better be scared, scared of a monster hunt with the roles reversed. Where the warrior runs, where the wild women make him pay for his crimes.

How does one make a monster?

In one easy step: take all the pity a human has left.

Burn a witch at the stake and ask her for mercy when she shows up unscathed, playing with matches.

Say, "Bad things happen to good people".

Try to guess which category she falls in this time.

Cross your fingers and hope for a hero who doesn't let you down.

I'm afraid this world has run out of them.

Maya

The other day I read about somebody who fixed a butterfly's wings and it made me want to cry.

Maya, I can't think about such tenderness without flinching away. You taught me how to throw knives in self-defense and now I can only anticipate violence.

Maya, I cried in front of a room full of strangers and when they came closer to hold me, I wanted to scream. I don't know how to let others touch me without being afraid of hurting.

All of me feels like an exposed wound I can't let anyone put their fingers on. It's easier to live in fight-or-flight than have the strength to hope.

I've been dreaming of drowning, Maya. I dream I'm in a glass tank and everyone outside is taking photographs, capturing how I look as I try to punch through the glass. Anger makes for good art. Collateral damage is often worth it. I wake up with bruised fists. I am a warning sign, a tense guitar string ready to snap, a red blinking light. I almost understand why they would watch instead of breaking the glass and risking a flood.

I don't know how to uncurl these fists. To let someone touch my hands as gently as a butterfly's wing. To let them look at my jagged edges as something other than a threat. To believe I'm injured, not damaged. I saw someone reach out the other day, and I let them hold on to me. I became more anchor than someone drowning. I think I'm scared to admit kindness lies closer than expected. That I've already made space for it.

Sahiti G. is a counselor and a poet on the side. She has previously worked at online magazines such as Winter Tangerine, Andromedae Review, and Monstering Mag. Her literary projects often address topics close to her heart, such as mental health awareness, feminism, and LGBT+ advocacy.

Samaa Burte Nadkarni
Womanhood is blood

womanhood is blood;
history is decorated
with the carcasses of women
killed in wars crafted by men

womanhood is blood
it is generations of female grief
bottled up inside us
like neat Russian dolls

womanhood is blood
the only blood that is pure
the kind that brings life
the kind we are shunned for

womanhood is blood
it is a quiet rebellion
to buy her battle armour
that prevents further bruises

womanhood is blood
it is a movement;
a culmination of broken dynasty
taking back her birthright

womanhood is blood
and it runs thicker than water.

Samaa Burte Nadkarni is a sixteen year old girl who lives in Mumbai. She is passionate about dancing, reading, music and poetry. Poetry is special to her since the abstraction of the same creates new, very different meanings in each mind. She thinks that this is remarkable since you can tell a lot about a person from the way they understand poems.

Sandhya Sharma
Indian Matchmaking

Only when you are in love, you wouldn't care
If his name is Amar, Akbar, or Anthony
Only when you are in love, you wouldn't care
If he is tall, short, fat, or lean
Only when you are in love, you wouldn't care
About his bank balance or the money he makes
Only when you are in love, you wouldn't care
If he is an MBA, a school dropout, or just a B.E
Only when you are in love, you wouldn't care
If he is a single child or a mama's boy
Only when you are in love, you wouldn't care
Of his vices and peculiar point of view
Only when you are in love, you wouldn't care
Of his ancestral history or inheritance
Only when you are in love, you wouldn't care
About the alphabets in his blood type
Only when you are in love, you wouldn't care
If he is a divorcee with a child
Only when you are in love, you wouldn't care
If he shares the aspiration to travel like you
But who am I to think love is important
Love is blind and I am naive
Only when you are in love, you wouldn't care
If she is fair and lovely or short and dusky
Only when you are in love, you wouldn't care
If she is slim, trim, flabby, or healthy
Only when you are in love, you wouldn't care
If she's an independent entrepreneur making more money than you
Only when you are in love, you wouldn't care
If like your mother she can cook for you
Only when you are in love, you wouldn't care
If she has qualities of an ideal Stepford Wife
Only when you are in love, you wouldn't care

About her past lovers and sexual life
But who am I to think love is important
Love is blind and I am naive
Only when you are in love, you wouldn't care
About the city in which they reside
Or if they are mute or blind
Only when you are in love, you wouldn't care
The past baggage they carry
Or their medical history
Only when you are in love, you wouldn't care
If they want to have kids many or none
Or if your birth chart scores don't confirm
But who am I to think love is important
Love is blind and I am naive
To not partake in this
Transaction based marketplace, where
Compatibility is disguised as a checklist
Created with reasonable care
That needs to match in this affair
But only when you are in love, you wouldn't care
Of these qualities inconsequential and bare

Kanyadaan/ Indian wedding ceremony

I don't want to spend time
Being all prim and proper
Getting every nip and tuck done
Like the Versailles garden before the tourist season
Browsing countless catalogues
Of banarasi, zardozi, and sequin prints
Bookmarking posts on Instagram of
Wedding planners, fashion magazines
And high-end wedding couture designers
Who have decided
What's the colour of the season

And the next wedding destination
I don't want to spend time
Parading around shopping lanes
Surveying if they have what's trending
In the celebrity circle at a price I can afford
I don't want to waste countless hours
Fretting over minute details of the
Catering menu, invitations, and flowers to display
In the bridezilla mode
With the pressure to look good
Watching dad run around ensuring everything is in place
All because this is supposed to be my big day?
Is this the day I celebrate our love and commitment?
Or is it a celebration of our religion and culture?
I don't need the fire to be a witness to my vows
Or those 2000 guests who didn't know I existed until now
I also don't need blessings (read as monetary gifts)
From the entire community of our hometown
I would rather elope than check with a priest
To provide an auspicious time to get hitched
I don't need to be adorned or decorated like paintings on the wall
Or for the colour of the henna to tell me
If I my marriage will be strong and if my husband will love me more
Chanting mantras, I don't understand or know
My biggest objection
The concept of Kanyadaan
Father of the bride giving her away to the husband
Like we are objects of claim
A whole ceremony performed to honour this sacred transaction
Why should my dad give me away?
Why should anyone give anyone away?
I am no one's to give, no one's to take
You might think this is just a 3-day affair
of pre-party, party and after party
if you do you are only naive to think that it is because it's not

We've only managed to abolish sati and dowry
when are we are going to start objecting to Kanyadaan
We can continue blaming the patriarchy
But do we have the courage to not be a part of it?

Sandhya is a digital marketing manager residing in Bangalore, India. She is a fitness enthusiast, globe trotter, Netflix addict, and a poet (by passion). She believes it's a brand new world out there and that we must evolve and have the courage to be a part of it. Follow her blog for more inspirational poetry on love, life and loss –
https://wordpress.com/view/sharmasandhya.wordpress.com

Sanhita Sinha

Her Blue Slippers

Her blue slippers,
That walked with her miles after miles,
Might have strolled with her
here & there.
Ran with her happy feet.
Danced in rain or have bathed in summer dust.
Accompanied her wherever she wished to move,
Are the only souls, who know
What exactly happened.
And how...

She left, abandoning the autumn roads, her courtyard,
Her kitchen and the bajra field.
Alas! the Dhritarashtra society
Could not see her blood-stained assaulted body.
Nor could listen to her deafening cry!

But her blue slippers,
Had seen her struggle,
Her pain, her death.
They are waiting on her veranda, washed with autumnal
moonbeam, covered with soft fragrance of Shiuli.
They are still waiting
To kiss her feet again.

(Bajra: pearl millet. Dhritarashtra: In the Hindu epic Mahabharat, King Dhritarashtra is the King of the Kuru Kingdom with its capital at Hastinapur. He was born to Vichitravirya's first wife Ambika. Dhritarashtra was born blind. He fathered one hundred sons and one daughter by his wife Gandhari. Shiuli: Nyctanthes or Night jasmine.)

I Am Red

Once my life was like a red jamdani.
Bright, vibrant.
The vines of threads carried the happiness of love.
But, the day he left me, you said,
Red, the color of love, is not mine.
He who left proving his infidelity, no one asked his color!
But announced black for me!
I smiled and said he was not a bunch of keys whom
I should've tied in my aanchal.

Once, I had a life like red benarasi,
A life that every lady dreams of.
Soft bridal red with threads of golden dreams, beautifully
decorating every inch of me.
The day he closed his eyes
For his moksha, you threw my benarasi in Harish Chandra ghat and
draped me white!
Didn't even think for me!
Can a drowning benarasi bring moksha?
Now Shackles of your do's and don'ts are the bangles of my wrists!

My life was like an elegant red kanjivaram
Till they tear me into a thousand pieces.
I bled and got drenched in a pool of blood.
You didn't look for them but curved your eyebrows, asked my
purity, and hid me behind a withering gray!

You ruled my life, dictated my fate but alas! You forgot,
Neither black nor white or gray is my color,
I am red and red is me.

Sanhita Sinha, native of Tripura, is a teacher, a bilingual poet. Her poems got published in different prestigious national and international anthologies, journals & magazines like Heavens above poetry below, A Haiku Treasury, In our own words, Scaling heights, Epitaphs, Milenge, IFLAC Peace Anthology, Betrayal, Glomag, Kirnokal, Antohkoron, Rupantar, Purbhabash, Galaxy, ICMDR Poetry Anthology, Mahatma: The Living Legend, Banga Bandhu Smarak Grantha etc. and many more. Apart from writing as an elocutionist, as an actor she is actively engaged in cultural activities. Along with stage, she is a regular artist of television and radio too.

Dr. Sanjukta Dasgupta
The Pillion Rider

No one taught me driving
No one gave me a bike
They said, "he has a bike
So what's your problem, you silly wife?"

So lifelong I am a pillion rider
No one asked me
Do you like to sit behind him
Are you scared, are you terrified
Do you want a helmet too
But a helmet for me he just won't buy.

Though I am the driver in his kitchen
They call me a cook
Is that a common noun or a command
Cook Cook Cook
Endlessly chopping, churning, cooking
I know the kitchen is his,
The chopping knife is his
Everything belongs to him
Every plate, every spoon, every bin
As my body too belongs to him

Why am I so poor dear Goddess Lakshmi
I tried to follow all your rules
Fasted steadfastly for the moon to rise
Though I can't stand pangs of hunger and thirst
Lakshmi Devi in you in trust
My silks and jewelry are not mine
Nothing is mine, not even me.
My body is used by him
My body is abused by him
I have no desire, no will, no wish
I am just a poor pillion Rider

I am just a pillion rider
I am just a pillion rider
I can only be directed and driven
I can't be trusted to direct and drive
I can only drive myself crazy
Riding on this dreadful pillion seat
Holding or not holding the callous shoulders
Ahead of me
Not knowing anymore
Whether I am at all able
Or permanently disabled-
A pillion rider on a lifelong traumatic ride

The Hunted
(After watching the web series Delhi Crime in March 2019)

It was just a bus ride home, Mama
Just a bus ride home at ten that evening
But it was a bus full of hyenas
Six of them, or sixteen or were they sixty
Even my friend pawed me like a hyena
While the others watched, licking their lips
Saliva dripping from their wet, sloppy, lolling tongues

They pounced on me, they stripped me stark
They manhandled my helpless body parts
They bit me, slapped me, twisted my protesting arms
They raped me again and again and again
Into the recess from which one day my baby
Could have slid out into this beautiful world
The iron rod tore through
The terrified tunnel of my trembling body

The rest is history, the police, the hospital
My recorded statements, the protests
I died far away from home
I died far away from my homeland
What a first trip abroad it was for me!

But no, I haven't left
Each winter night in December
You may find me
Standing next to that ditch at midnight
Standing on the lonely bus route
My blood-dripping intestines spilling out!
Tell me what was my mistake
Friends, teachers, parents, politicians, and priests?

(These lines refer to the Delhi bus rape case of Nirbhaya (Jyoti Singh) in 2012. The accused are on death row, except the minor. The four convicts, Akshay, Pawan, Vinay, and Mukesh were convicted for raping and brutally torturing 23-year-old paramedic Jyoti Singh on the night of December 16, 2012. A total of six people were convicted, out of which one juvenile was released after a three-year reform facility. The sixth convict, Ram Singh died during the trial.
https://www.indiatoday.in/fyi/story/nirbhaya-gangrape-case-jyoti-singh-convicts-rapists-975462-2017-05-05)

Kali

Her jet black flying tresses
Like dark monsoon clouds
A bright black halo lit up her dusky face
Her dark eyes were bloodshot with angst and grief
Her lolling tongue perhaps a thrust of self-control

Like a timeless ebony sculpture
Her dazzling stark dark silken form
Stood statuesque
On her supine intimate partner

She was a furious doer
She was a restless dreamer
She was a tempest, a tornado
She was the ruthless Redeemer
She was not Bhadrakali
She was Chamunda Kali the relentless slayer
She was Kali who haunted the burning ghats
Shamshan Kali, the ultimate liberator

A garland of skulls around her neck
Gruesome, grotesque, and gorgeous
A scintillating scimitar in one raised hand
The other left arm gripping the hair of a severed head
Her two right arms aloft in a gesture of assurance
 Four-armed Kali the Mother of all Avengers
Stood tall and stark and very dark
An invincible symbol of power and trust

A towering terrifying terminator
Raging like a mother of all tsunamis
Goddess Kali restlessly rushes on
In pursuit of the demons of deceit and lust
The world feels secure as caregiver Kali
Paces the earth like a prowling panther
Tireless vigilante!

(Bhadrakali-Gentle Kali / Chamunda Kali- Furious Kali / Shamshan Kali- Kali of the cremation grounds).

Dr. Sanjukta Dasgupta, Professor and Former Head, Dept of English and Former Dean, Faculty of Arts, Calcutta University, is a poet, critic, and translator. She is a member of the General Council of Sahitya Akademi New Delhi. She is also the President of the Intercultural Poetry and Performance Library at ICCR, Kolkata. Her published books of Poetry are Snapshots (1997), Dilemma (2002), First Language (2005), More Light (2009), Lakshmi Unbound (2017) Sita's Sisters (2019). She is the recipient of the WE Kamala Das Poetry Award 2020.

Dr. Santosh Bakaya
Salt-less

"There is no salt in the *daal*.
Is this what your mother has taught you?
These modern girls are good for nothing.
Simply nothing". The uni- browed mother- in-law sneered,
peering at her daughter-in-law, pouring the third
helping of *daal* on her huge mound of rice
and gobbled it up in a trice, licking her lips,
then her fingers, one by one.

"You lazy laggard! Get me my food",
it is the turn of the husband to bellow orders now.
The wife scurries to get the job done,
shaking like a leaf in an autumnal gale.
"Is this *daal*, or tap water? It has no salt,"
yells the alcoholic husband,
flinging the plate at his wife, staggers towards his cot,

and slumps down in a drunken stupor.
The wife watches in a daze,
a tingling sensation in her eyes,
she touches her cheeks,
wondering how the salt got there.

The Maid's lament

"I bathed and scrubbed my sleepy kids,
they were in no mood though.
Sorry, I was late today, left them mewling and puking, was so tired,
almost had an urge not to come, slept very late last night.

But then work cannot be, shirked,
and what was the point of staying at home,
would have to listen to my hypochondriac mother-in-law's moans
and her perennial cribbing that I am a lazybones.

How I miss my mother! She is unwell too,
dad when young, would beat her black and blue,
he repents now, but what is the point?
 But my husband is not like that, he cares, yes he cares,
 beats me only once or twice a week. "

Kanchan, the twenty-three-year-old maid with three kids
 was venting steam, her stream of consciousness, unbridled,
 riddled with pain.
"Till when will women suffer, madam?"
she went on and on not expecting an answer,
  while I kept jabbing words on the computer,
 giving last-minute touches to my talk on Women Empowerment,
occasionally peering at the bird flying untethered
in the fresh air, outside.

Dr. Santosh Bakaya, internationally acclaimed for her poetic biography of Mahatma Gandhi, Ballad of Bapu, is an academic, poet, essayist, a novelist with more than ten published books. Her TEDx talk on The Myth of Writers' Block is very popular in creative writing workshops. Her latest book, a biography of Martin Luther King Jr. is getting a lot of critical acclaim. She runs a very popular column Morning Meanderings in learning and Creativity website.

Sara Malwiya
Here Lies

Here lies the girl who'd
always stand up for what
she thought was right,
Here lies the girl who was
not afraid of fighting back
with all her might,
Here lies the girl who
fought tooth and nail
for her to be "allowed"
late nights,
Here lies the girl who
adamantly believed that
women deserved fair fights.
Here lies the girl who'd not
think before screaming at the
rape headlines on the news,
Here lies the girl who still
hoped and prayed that the
society started looking at
women as their 'muse',
Here lies the girl who was,
with a feminazi, confused,
Here lies the girl who was
undressed violently,
when she was out alone,
Here lies the girl whose
body had been violated
against her own will,
Here lies the girl who had
become a piece of meat for
the four rebellious freaks,
Here lies the girl whose
disappointment in society

grew the day, it let the guilty
'roam free' and forced her
to become a mime,
Here lies the girl...who
never wanted her gender
to be declared a crime.

My name is Sara and I like to think of myself as an amateur poet, who likes to write about anything that catches her eye, right from topics like love to gender equality. I've been living in India for all my life and thus, I decided to write on how Indian women are denied proper justice when sexual assault and harassment are concerned, even today. My Instagram and Twitter handle are @saradonically and @tragicsara respectively.

Satvika Ajay Menon
Before She Broke

Her mind is a constellation,
each stage of her life a fickle and fading star;
her childhood, teenage years, and wisps of adulthood
are interlinked via invisible cords
that tether her to earth.

Hazy summer nights entwined with the sickly-sweet scent of mangoes
and days spent colouring in clouds with broken crayons find
themselves
amongst the millions of memories in her constellation.
Afternoons walking through the hazy streets of Mumbai,
days spent darting through crests of frothy waves
and mornings speckled with the hues of the sunset
lace together in bursts of blue and ember,
Beneath her eyes, her universe takes shape before her.

Her brain spins out of control as she reaches frantically,
beneath the acidic stench of alleyways and the catcalls from the
drunken men,
beneath the middle-aged aunties clad in sarees who said she wasn't
enough-
was too young, too fragile, too delicate, like porcelain-
beneath all the people already planning for her dowry
and a man waiting to whisk her away,
beneath all the poison that lurks amongst the light,
she reaches for one last sliver of happiness,
tumbling down the rolling hills of Idukki
as the sun slid down her face in flurries of gold,
the dizzying creeper-encrusted walls of her childhood home,
the sashes of velvet that swayed as she swirled
through the night of her fifteenth birthday.
She reaches for one more golden memory
before everything falls apart.

In This Town

In this town, the men stare when they want,
their eyes gleaming eagerly
like the schoolboys in the second grade
when they looked at their tightly-wrapped Onam presents
and didn't care what was inside
because the packaging was so eye-catching,

In this town, it doesn't matter if you're fifteen or twenty-five,
if you're wearing a kurta or a tight shirt.
Everywhere you go, young girl,
catcalls will follow you,
biting at your heels in bold, black letters
that swirl and whisper in the wind,
following you, lingering near your soul,
attempting to get you to whip your head around,
plaster a smile,
to encourage their ignorance, their lust.

In this town, dear girl,
you should keep walking. Don't stumble, stutter, or smile.
For if you do,
the catcalls will curl their way into your mind,
eating your brain.
Do not give them what they desire the most.

Satvika Ajay Menon is a seventeen-year-old from India. She began writing poetry at the age of five and since then has been published in several notable online magazines such as Vita Brevis, The Daphne Review, Shot Glass Journal, Scarlet Leaf Review, Plum Tree Tavern, Pazzage and Uppagus. Her favorite themes are nature, society, and the human mind.

Saumya Shinde
The unfair burden

A female politician is asked to be pure.
To have no faults and flaws
Just a steady upward incline.
No place for a moral decline
What clothes does she wear?
What words does she utter?
How does she do her hair?
Does she put on makeup?
How many relationships has she been in?
Because in an Indian society one thing I've learnt is that honour is
upheld by women.
The responsibility of respect and awe is to be upheld.
But this responsibility is a burden in disguise
Thrust upon us
Chaining us to the very system that perpetuates these harmful
notions
Who asked them to keep their honor in us?
In the leading female personalities?
Why do her clothes, looks, skin colour matter
when she is so much more than that?
Chaining us with the false notion of being the role model
Snatching our opportunities
And then presenting them wrapped up in a bow
Demanding our gratitude in return

Shatter the Silence

Originally created for the YLAC (Young Leaders Active Citizenship) Counter Speech Fellowship

Saumya Shinde is a 16-year-old girl hailing from Mumbai, India. She is an ardent Feminist and is working towards an equitable and safe environment for all. She loves dancing and cooking. She has a strong resolution for working towards social causes. She also believes in the power of dialogue and art in resolving conflicts. Poetry is one of the ways she loves expressing myself. Follow her on Instagram @_saumya_2805

Shalini Chakraborty
Not Girl Enough

Am I not girly enough when I lift those weights at the gym?
When you realise that my biceps are more muscular than yours will
ever be!
Do I see a smirk on your face, glaring at my abs?
Why, do they make me less of a woman?
I see the look in your eyes when you spot me holding a cigarette
Tightly pursed between my lips- talking to my friends about last
night's football match
Comes as a bit of a shock, eh?
I see you wonder open-mouthed
When I shower on my friends every cuss word I know
You didn't expect that coming from a girl, did you?
Am I not girly enough when I seat on my sofa
With my legs spread, gulping down from a bottle of beer
Unaware and frankly, unhindered by the presence of guests?
Am I not girly enough
On days I wear my oversized tee with a dusty trouser to class?
On days I tie my hair into a bun
My face feels like a pathetic excuse for waking up late
Sometimes accompanied by puffed eyes, a result of crying all
night?
Oh, does crying make me enough of a woman?
The fact that stupid videos on Youtube can encourage my tear ducts
to strain my cheeks
That the news of a newborn being killed on account of being a girl
stirs my emotions:
Do these sensitivities make me a woman?
And on days I don't want to be a woman
On days I want to run away from the corset forcing me to conform
to the given pattern of elegance and grace
On days I wish I could flatten my chest, crop my hair short and hide
my curves within my boyfriend's hoodie
Period cramps remind me the escape is a futile effort!
That I can never be spared as long as I have a vagina in which you
can insert anything you freaking wish to
So tell me,

If you spot me on street alone at night in a three-piece suit,
Struggling hard to deny every ounce of my femininity
No touch of makeup, no flick of eyeliner
My lips in their natural hue, my earlobes spared of the gold stud
Would you be man enough to respect my flight from my gender?
Hah! Not girly enough but girl enough to be RAPED!

Colours of my womanhood

Red is the colour of the rose he bought me
As we were passing by the lake
It smells of love and passion, he said, and so did everyone
I wish I could tell him that red only reeks of blood
That Red is the colour of the stain on my bed sheet
A rather rash reminder of my subservience to my body
Red is the colour of the success of a man
As it drips from the thighs of the girl he just conquered
Red scratches her face with disgust and shame
As she is made to recount her tale countless times
Red hangs on my face like the flag of defeat
Red paralyses me for my inability
To translate my anger into action

Pink is the colour of the soft toy my best friend gifted me
It is the colour my room was painted in my childhood
Pink is the colour my cheeks should've turned
As it says in the love poems of Shakespeare
If only I was as fair as the world dictated
But pink is too meek for a revolting soul like me
Pink glorifies the softness that I repel
It upholds the ideals of grace that I seek to shatter
Pink scribbles vulnerability on my body
Sorting beauty into labels and putting tax on them
In a world where Pink drapes its standards on a barbie doll
I choose to put it on Umbridge

Green is the colour my eyes turn into
When the dress I choose fits my sister better
When he praises the curves of a pretty Instagram girl
And I look for slimming belts online
Green adorns me in my fury
Instead of liberating, it confines me
In a corset of strict beauty paradigms
Green traps me in my insecurity
In my irrepressible desire to be desirable
Even with a body and a face that society ridicules
Green makes me feel small
Fussing over these petty, material interests
Trying to fit into their 36-24-36
Yet my eyes don't lose their green
For the green has long seeped into my being

Blue is the colour he imprints on my body
In lumps and patches- souvenir of his love
Reminding me of the tight grasps which smelled like home
But---
Oh But How it recalls the ghosts of my everyday suffering
Of the squeeze at my back in a crowded bus
Or the dash with the elbow in an empty street
In a moment Blue transforms from pleasure to fright
As I fail to distinguish the blue of his touch
Out of the blue, I suffered in the metro?
Blue takes the shape of faceless apparitions
Inching close to me with every unwanted second
Their blue, sinuous fingers plunging my naked skin
As I am helplessly drowning in my silent scream

What colour am I then?
Can you contain my rage, my fear
My disgust, my hatred, my repulse- in one hue?
No- I am a concoction of all the colours
A strange mix of strength and fragility, obstinance and docility
Something that you cannot fathom
So you named me Black

I am the thick black hollow
Which absorbs every raw emotion in its dark envelope
I am the unknown, the inexplorable
I am the vastness you gape at with awe
I scare you, I repel you
Yet you're drawn
Like the black hole I only grow bigger
The more you pour your tawdry debris into me

My mother tongue is SILENCE

If mothers had a tongue it would be called silence
Dipped in mayonnaise and stuffed with cheese
She serves silence in china plates for dinner
While my father digs deep into the fries
For faults he is obliged to find

Her silence lies in her cold look
In her occasional murmurs only when no one's listening
In the pockets of her apron where she carries her knife
Steeped with the ice-cold blood boiling with rage
In her wardrobe full of gorgeous sarees
A bribe she receives for keeping up the performance

Her silence diffuses with the shrill whistle of the pressure cooker
With the whirring of the vegetables.
Slowly simmering in the kadai
With the grumpy sound of the washing machine
Containing no clothes of her and
With the slow moaning of the air conditioner at night

Her silence hovers over the frying pan
As she fries the fish my father loves
Even if she cannot stand the smell
And adorns her body with fresh blisters
That goes unnoticed like most of the work she does
After all, what does a housewife do anyway?

My mother's silence is in the gritting of her teeth
Everytime my father slyly mentions her sister's debt
Or insults her father in the garb of a joke
When my grandpa makes a snide remark
On the size of the bed she brought in her marriage
When my aunt flaunts the 50" inch television she was sold with

My mother's silence is withdrawal
Everytime I scream at her for not keeping my books properly
Assuming that a housewife would, of course
Not know the value of literature
And in one swish I undo my scholarship
Or perform the elitism that I vouched to fight in my papers

My mother's silence is a defence
When my father and I discuss politics and economics
She wears her opinion on her sleeve
Only thrice in every five years
Before the EVM where she knows
She can't be judged, at least for 30 seconds?

My mother's mouth is programmed to say "sorry" and "thank you"
10 times more than a kindergartner
Her language is a couple of set phrases handed over by the society
Beyond which is a sea of words she never got to swim
Her language is the chiselled silence she carries around
Like the sword of a warrior asked to retire early

My mother drapes her nine yards of silence
Like an invisibility cloak
My mother's silence is the steely edge of a guillotine
That cuts across our indifference and dissects the hypocrisies
We are too proud to admit to ourselves

My mother's silence is the armour of resistance
She puts up every morning before we start firing our arrows
My mother's silence is her name
Trying to escape being engulfed
By the men around her.

A teacher at Calcutta Public School, Shalini Chakraborty has completed her Masters in English from Jadavpur University. As a slam poet, she has been associated with Kommune and was featured among the 100 poets last World Poetry Day. One of her poems was published in an anthology on mental health, Mindscape. She has also co-edited an anthology of creative writings called Beautiful Minds, a Bankim Sardar College initiative. She has also judged a poetry slam competition online organised by Shivnath Shastri College, Kolkata.

Shanta Acharya
Alphabet Of Erasure

Begins with a bloody Caesarean,
a daughter, perfect almost, yet relegated
to live in the shade if not in oblivion –

crossed out, the way people looking at you
look straight through as if you were invisible,
hidden from your own timeline.

A life spent pursuing other people's dreams,
never realising yours, is self-mutilation,
leaves you diminished, grief-scarred –

no different to being blotted out, bleached
reefs of coral as the earth's treasures disappear
species by species, glacier by glacier.

Every time we lose a language we lose a view
of the world, a slow sclerosis of vision,
not the same as knowing all is illusion.

When barbarians run the city, legislate on art
and beauty in the name of progress and diversity,
rewriting the past with their version of history,

they deny us the gift of exploring the world,
finding our place in it. Truth is nobody's fool –
not a god defaced by humans pretending to speak

nothing but the truth. Before you know it, life's taken
the fork in the road with no signs down the path
of dispossession, nothing you can claim your own –

country, family, faith, freedom, language, memories.
You learn an alphabet of erasure –
amnesia, anorexia, anosmia, aphasia, ataxia –

experience every measure of loss between A and Z
in silence; not a healing, consoling peace where you
find your voice, but the silence of oblivion.

*(Shanta Acharya, What Survives Is The Singing, Indigo Dreams
Publishing, UK; 2020.)*

*Shanta Acharya is the author of twelve books, her publications range
from poetry, literary criticism and fiction to finance. Her most recent
books are Imagine: New and Selected Poems (HarperCollins, 2017) and
What Survives Is The Singing (Indigo Dreams, 2020).
www.shantaacharya.com*

Shelly Bhoil
Letter to fellow women

Dear woman
are you spreading yourself
out on the floor as a playmat
for that little, long-silenced girl in you
to play and become
the fountainhead of your joy
splashing and purging you off
the thick dust you don't need?

Dear woman
are you planting your feet
in the forest of your dreams
stretching arms for your fingers
to alchemize into fireflies
enough to illumine your garden
and make ash of the axe holders?

Dear woman
are you growing flowers on your tongue
and loudspeakers on your ears
to be velvety soft inside
and bounce back all you are told
in books and nooks of a world
tailored to fit not-your-size?

Dear woman
are you measuring your fragility
by stone
and density by petals?
In short, dear fellow woman,
are you
already becoming
your own man?

The Indelible Ink of December 16
(In memory of Nirbhaya)

On December 16
the day sleepwalks like dreams in languid night streets
and the night sleeps without the pleasure of oblivion,
the world feels like a catacomb rotting to its core
with its zombie residents, those whose hands move with ease
from praying to preying and tearing apart threads of skin
from a breathing bleating woven mass:
performing the living's sky burial
these vultures from a mistaken human culture!

On December 16
the sun refuses to greet the city with its downcast eyes
and roads run into sand rivers, where float fishes without fins
we all with our paper wings fly skywards but dash
against a pretend horizon, soaking the evening's menstrual blood
we come down falling, bone by bone, intestine-roped
ligaments splitting like hair fall:
a body feasted upon by creatures of the wildest wind!

On December 16
not too far above in a familiar sky
a moon was devoured slice by slice
and a lonesome star still mourns
wishing upon stars from another sky
to hide in the womb of a day yet unborn!

Shelly Bhoil is an Indian poet and scholar, living in Brazil. Her publications include two poetry books An Ember from Her Pyre (India, 2016) and Preposição de entendimento (Brazil, 2020), and two academic volumes (co-editor) Tibetan Subjectivities on the Global Stage (US, 2018) and (editor) New Narratives of Exile Tibet (US, 2020).

Shikha Mendiratta

Fight for Pronouns

(Poem solemnly dedicated to Shree Gauri Sawant, an Indian transgender activist.)

She may not be endowed with a womb
A womb where wholesome flower thrives
Or a breast where life giving milk contrives.

A queen she is
The queen of her own domain
Her soul stirs at every mortal cry
She can sense every little one's pain.

Her core caparisoned
With the only requisite of motherhood
Open arms
And heart throbbing
Fertile as much as
The wet soil after rain.

Ordain her magnanimity.
Never rue her pronouns.
Never rue her identity.

Changing the Definitions
(Dedicated to all the working mothers)

Gone are the days
Curly locks merrily dancing over her face
That mirth and florid looks
Head embedded always in books.

Now,
Everyday to office on the way
Carrying her baby in a sling on back
She hears kids shouting
"You mother kangaroo"
No offense
She just smiles back.

An archer she is
Adorned with her quiver
A warrior with all her armours lined up.

She, a sangfroid
Waging wars
Crusading for her space
Changing the definition of womanliness.

Shikha Mendiratta is working as a lecturer in English, at the Department of School Education, Government of Rajasthan, India. She is a fervent teacher and poet. She contributes to the ezine of the District Education Department. Her poems majorly deal with the human psyche and malice prevalent in society.

Shreya Chatterjee
The interview

This story is about a "SHE", one who is like all the other SHEs in
    this world,
Facing similar problems due to her being a creature, referred to as
    girls.
There's no doubt that conditions have improved from what they
    were in the past,
But that's no justification for the situation that still prevails, and
    after-effects that last.

She slowly climbs up the stairs to the stage and notices people
    staring at her, from head to toe.
Just near the stage, a young girl is sitting, her head bowed low,
Her eyes reflecting an unknown terror. She calmly takes her
    position at the mike, and waits
For the questions, while in some corner of her mind, some past
    occurrences play in flashback, which she hates.

She remembers when she was in school and had been appointed as
    the class monitor.
She was a responsible and sharp-witted girl, since childhood, not
    afraid
To put forward her views or to stand by her opinions.
Her classmates weren't happy with this decision which made,
Her, the monitor, for they knew she's strictly against any
    indiscipline or disobedience.
For the same reason, she faced a lot of opposition, even after being
    appointed.

When she tried to stop some boys, who were fighting with each
    other,
She was asked to stay away, lest she might get hurt in 'delicate
    places'.
She was even teased by them.

But when she slapped them, tight on the faces,
The others called her vile. They shamed her for being aggressive,
Something which women are not supposed to be.
What surprised her the most was that the other girls didn't support
her.
They too advised her to 'behave like girls', you see.

When she complained about those boys, she was boycotted by the
others,
For being aggressively dominant and for 'misusing power'.
During the Christmas celebrations, when she assigned tasks to
other classmates, again they revolted
Against her, refusing to do what was the need of the hour.
They called her bossy, accusing her of treating others inferiorly, and
called her callous.
As she grew up, these experiences became more disgusting.
And left a detrimental effect, everlasting.
When at office, she handled some project and made a minor
mistake,
Her ability was questioned. But if it was some male colleague in her
place,
Their fault was thought to be sheer bad luck or lack of efforts.
When she succeeded in some project, the scenario was the exact
opposite, much to her disgrace.
It was thought to be her tiring efforts or rather her good luck, while
it was his innate ability.
His working late was an indication of his determination and
sincerity,
While her working late would raise questions on her morals.
She had faced such situations all throughout her life.
She remembered her elders teaching her to be shy and soft-spoken,
for that's how girls should be.
Boldness is a taint, out-spokenness, a flaw. Denying this results in
unending strife.

Even the television shows, since ages, have portrayed
A bold and aggressive girl as the vamp or the villain, while the shy,
Soft-spoken, submissive one as the protagonist,
Is there some logic? Can you tell me why?
The ones who stand up for their rights, the ones who are bold
       enough to question the irrational laws,
Are tagged as "characterless" by society. The ones who are strong
To make their own decisions and stand by their choices, are
considered as possessive and callous people, who are always
wrong,
And who causes a rift among families.
The ones who aren't happy with the age-old norm of accepting
And being satisfied with whatever comes their way,
And are determined to achieve what they desire are tagged as "gold-
       diggers",
And said to be controlling, as per heresy.
Without even knowing what they actually are,
They are thought to be egoistic and arrogant, full of attitude, self-
       pride, and vanity,
If he is dominating, aggressive, decisive, and authoritative, he's
       praised and
Looked up to as a great personality with these leadership qualities.
He may commit mistakes as well. But 'he' is never judged.

With these thoughts in her mind, she answers the questions hurled
       at her.
Here too, she is praised for her beauty, not for her ability.
Still, she believes in herself, and with the same old confidence, she
       speaks up,
"A she is not just another 'he' with an additional 'S'.
Every she is unique. I am myself. I am an individual with a separate
       identity and existence.
I am bold and I am proud of that. I don't hesitate to admit,
I am not arrogant, but if you ever think so,
Try analysing your own words and behavior which might have led
       to it."

The applauds echo in the room, which she knows, are fake.
People won't be changed so easily.
But she is happy, for she can see a shimmer in the young girl's eyes,
A ray of hope, similar to the shine which her young self had,
And the zeal which helped her rise.

Shreya Chatterjee is an 18 year old student and belongs to Jharkhand, India. The only child of her parents, she aims to become a doctor and make them proud. She has a passion for poetry. She is an amateur blogger and writer and moulds her thoughts into words at her website The Brainy Essays (https://thebrainyessays.wordpress.com/). She stands by the quote "If you want to predict the future, invent it yourself."

Shruti Sareen

Hair

She told me you cut those long black tresses
suli in axomiya, falling to your waist since a time
before I can remember. She showed me a picture
of you with new frizzy hair.
I wish I could have collected your beautiful fallen hair
I wish I could have preserved a piece of you
which you no longer wanted..
I wonder how your juda stick will feel from disuse and neglect now
Will you discard it, throw it away?
Will you keep your hair short now, send out short hair pictures?
Or let it grow long again?
My hair is an emotion for me.
I caress it, twirl it, fiddle with it constantly
when I am upset. You are the only person
who could make me cut it. On an impulse,
I want to cut my hair to be like you.
To keep you in me. To forsake the hair
instead of forsaking you. Hair is precious,
but you are priceless. But that would
be silly. I will preserve the old you for a while longer
My long black waist-length tresses like yours
tied up with a stick the way yours used to be,
Can I keep my hair and keep you too, I wonder?

Someday I will cut my hair like you
(Only you can make me do it).
Some of my hair turned white with Ph.D. anxiety.
Sometimes, when macabre and gloomy, I think of killing
Myself, and presenting all my long cut-hair to you as proof.

I will cut my hair short when it's mostly white
Like yours, or maybe like your sister's
I will prance around with hair, blue, purple, and green.
So my hair is growing ripe and white and I am about to turn 32
You were 32 when I met you first. It's been fourteen whole years.

Shruti Sareen studied in Rajghat Besant School KFI, Varanasi, and went on to do English literature from Indraprastha College for Women, University of Delhi. With a keen interest in Indian Poetry in English, her MPhil looks at the depiction of urban spaces and her Ph.D. on twenty-first-century feminist poetry at the University of Delhi. She also teaches whenever she manages to find a job. She has had over a hundred poems accepted by Indian and South Asian journals, and a handful of short stories. Her debut poetry collection, A Witch Like You, is forthcoming from Girls on Key Poetry (Australia) in April 2021. She is passionate about poetry, music, teaching, Assamese culture, queer love and sexuality, mental health, nature, and the environment! She blogs at www.shrutanne-heartstrings.blogspot.com.

Shweta Rao Garg
Kali in Theatre

The Visitor

Shweta Rao Garg is an artist, poet, and academic based in Ahmedabad, India. Her poetry is about her lived experiences as an Indian woman. Her poems have been published in Coldnoon, Muse India, Postcolonial Text, Alimentum Journal, Everyday Poems, Transnational Literature, etc. A former Fulbright scholar and recipient of Sahitya Akademi Translation prize, Shweta perceives her art as a culmination of her creative and critical faculties. She has had two solo exhibitions of paintings till date. Her second series was based on everyday lives of Indian women, Of Goddesses and Women in 2019. The questions of identity, space, history, and ordinary lives inform her work. Her standpoint as a feminist, and as a gender studies scholar, shapes her subject matter and forms. www.shwetaraogarg.com

Shyamolima Saikia
Of Other Lives

My mother is a woman too,
But there lies
between her and me, her daughter
A wide gulf
I am trying to bridge it;

She belongs to a generation different
When women weren't that equal,
She didn't enjoy the things that I do now,
She was not aware of social media,
Or of girls going alone for travel,
Or of sanitary pads, of what the world can unravel,
But I am trying to bridge the gap;

She was a woman no doubt
But of a different age,
When girls were married and sooner got rid of,
When homemaking was far suitable than a career,
But I am trying to bridge the gap;

She belonged to a milieu
When feminine qualities were looked for,
When outsmarting men was derided,
When being flamboyant was not asked for,
But I am trying to bridge the gap;

She is near seventy
And I ask her to learn
How to use Facebook, WhatsApp, et al.
So that she can connect,
I am thus trying to bridge the gap;

I ask her to voice her opinion loud
And not care what the world says
And chase her fantasies,

I am trying to bridge the gap,
But am I successful?

Much to my chagrin,
She is not willing to unearth the possibilities,
She is attuned to the caged system,
She cannot protest, she cannot be free,
She cannot come out of her shell,
For she belongs to another age...
I am thus left wondering
Will she never live a life real?

Bindi

She wears a 'bindi'
Beneath the vermilion mark,
Which they say holds the universe,
Here in lies hidden
Latent wisdom and strength,
Here in they say the dualities merge,
Become one
And herein is creation itself;

A mark of love and sacrifice it is
That she has to uphold,
A mark of honour, too it is,
That she has to keep to gain her foothold;

But herein also lies a contradiction
Of living one life
And dreaming of another,
For she has forsaken her pleasures
Her dreams and desires,
She cannot be what she wishes to be,
Her people draw a line

And she cannot surpass it,
Their eyes constantly survey her demeanour
Lest she falters and breaches her honour;

She fantasizes of wearing a short dress,
Of letting her hair down,
And pose like the popular actress,
Of hanging out with her friends,
Of having her own space,
Of charting out her own way,
Of being independent;

Yet, she has to hide many things
From her social media accounts,
Her male friends, her finances to her stilettos,
Her mind's ramblings, her heart's emotions
And most of all her secret desires
And her authentic inner self;

She cannot go out in the evenings alone,
She cannot smoke or drink a while,
She cannot talk too much with men,
No, no... these are far outrageous things,
Oh! this list of dont's goes too far
It is only now when I pen down,
That I realize there are too many bindings...

She, therefore, draws a veil of anonymity,
Outwardly, she abides all obligation
And lives her secret life only in her imagination,
For the onus rests solely on her
To not break away from the shackles,
But to carry forward the tradition
Just because she wears a bindi...

Woman: Courage Incarnate

I am a woman
In different circumstances
Sometimes a Dalit brutally raped,
Or a subaltern quashed of all rights,
Or a so-called witch being hunted down,
At times, acid is hurled onto my face,
Call me by the usual attributes,
A weaker vessel,
A vamp, a spinster, a seductress...

I am a woman,
The world is indifferent,
For them, I am as well non-existent
Leave alone bestowing liberty and entitlement,
Thus, I am shunned and forlorn.
So often have I questioned,
What is the purpose then
Of my life?
Shall I play no role?

I am a woman
But a human too,
I long for nothing
But a little affection and care
From the depth of heart,
An admission of my worth
And a space to perform my part;

I am a woman
And for long have I been in misery...
But why?
Why do I act fragile?
Why am I looking for support?

Why do I crave for sympathy?
Why am I being credulous
Of the sinister and false ways?

Have I forgotten
The rugged road I traversed so far?
Hostilities have I not brushed aside?
Hurdles have I not overcome?
Goals have I not fulfilled?

Those arduous journeys navigated by my kind,
Stirs and fortifies me,
Prods me to move ahead
And even lift others of my kind
Who've staggered.

Now it's a grueling path, no doubt,
Yet, these are trivial obstacles
In the face of greater purpose
And I know my destination.
I am bold,
I am ready to strive harder
And prove my worth.

I am a woman
Derision now eggs me on
To fight against this very indifference,
My spirit shall not be vanquished;
Rise I shall rise above all
With nothing but the beauty of my mind and soul.
Caring not for the devious ways,
For the voice within me says
'I am courage personified.'

The Grind

Shyamolima Saikia is working as an Assistant Professor in the Dept. Of English, Gargaon College, Sibsagar, Assam. Besides editing a number of books, she has also published a book of poems titled Palimpsest. Her poems have been published in Borderless Journal, Muse India, Indian Periodical, Virtuoso, an ISSN Journal, newspapers like "The Assam Tribune", "The Sentinel" and in several online platforms and anthologies. Moreover, she has also contributed a few short stories in several regional dailies, magazines, and e-journals.

Simran Wahan
Choked Identity

Wait! So you're telling me that, that's her 'only' identity? Do you also see what's strangling her? Inspired by a real-life incident I was told about this morning. Weirdly enough, just a thought of a woman choking on her inability to leave a man, a family, or a home because of various reasons but one! How her marriage is her only identity all through her life and her suffocation. How the color red beautifies her and chokes her.

Simran Wahan, brand owner, The Amaya Store, Coimbatore, and an Art Therapy Practitioner based in Bangalore. She's been an artist since forever and it's more sort of a calming down therapy to a riot of a mind that she lives with. She conducts therapeutic art sessions for adults & kids. She creates abstract art to survive an actual world. She works with acrylics, watercolor, and digital art.
instagram.com/draw.with.sim & instagram.com/the.amaya.store

Smita Ray
A love like this

It's not your fault, my love
Maybe, that's how we were destined to meet
when shards of my broken heart still cut up deep
Still bleeding...
My soul is peppered with bloodstains...
Though my memory is like a sieve,
I can't forget those moments
When your beastly hands viciously clutched my hair,
You were always so generous with your tone...
And you slapped me right on the kisser
Pummelled me black and blue
Now when we are apart —
I wince at the memory of it
But I know you're such a beautiful person,
A powerful man!
It was all my fault that I couldn't cook to your taste
Maybe my eyes deprived of sleep
and my hands too weary of drying nappies whole night
too lazy to comply with your orders properly
Oh! Where could you find a love like this?
The beautiful soul you are! but I just couldn't measure up...
Sigh! I could never match your intellect, wisdom, manners or
character!
I have plentiful memories like this adorning my plain, prosaic life
I love you, I feel so grateful from the bottom of my heart
I cannot forget when you smothered me with kisses
Panting, altogether...

I know you're a gentle soul, born from truth and love
Now, I have buried my soul somewhere where light cannot reach
I know, there are many like me but I won't meet their gaze
Oh, it's so naked and lonely in the broad daylight
I promise I will keep up the appearances
And feign ignorance
That's how I love you!

Sustainability

Let's talk about oppression and subjugation
Let's talk about suffering and grief
The curtailment of her basic human rights
Think of a woman who not only sustains abuse
But accepts, supports and stands up for it
An embodiment of the most powerful person —
her oppressor, her prosecutor, the maltreater
Tainted with the same dark motives,
Ominous and foreboding, gloom and doom
Thrusting them back to their burrows
How far will she go to bring those down?
Who are struggling,
Who refused to give in,
who refused to be lessened and minimized?
Will she cramp their style?
Her only qualification?

She could be worse
Let us talk about her persecution
Her emancipation
Her degradation

The paedophile and his likes

His eyes sunk into my artwork, a naked woman
He chuckled as he fingered the curved lines
Just as he fondled budding breasts and tiny nipples
He licked puddles of juicy fantasy off his lips
And cackled with amusement then turned his glance to me
His eyes awash with tits and cheeks
One of the girls he molested turned out to be exactly like him,
Clad in convenient spiritual citations and mores and excuses
The number may exceed
The air befouled with the scent of all kinds of manure heaps
That feed and nourish the paedophile and his blooming breed
Never decontaminated

Smita Ray is the mother of two lovely kids and hails from northeastern India. Her perpetual displeasure arising from the hypocrisy in the society underneath the semblance of religion, culture as well as the conditioning for complacency urged her to put down the impressions on her mind. In her spare time, she likes to have some culinary adventures, trying new recipes along with her kids or crafting.
https://thewideblue.wordpress.com/

SmithaV
Enough! No More.

I wrote this in the light of happenings all over the world- violence against children and women. The #Metoo campaign sparked a new wave where those who had been assaulted could come out and talk about it and bring the perpetrators of crime to book. But this campaign was for those who survived the ordeal. What about those who lose their life in the process of violence? The law needs to be changed, not only in India but all over the world to befittingly punish those who violate other people's rights. Rapes, acid attacks, molestation, domestic violence are equal to murder and should be treated similarly.

Daily News
Empty views
Growing aversion
Lawmaker's Inaction
Enough! No More.

Daily crimes
How many more times?
Increasing animosity
Leader's insensitivity
Enough! No More.

This far. No further.
Enough. No More.

Defiant

I see you glaring
It makes me nervous, a trifle anxious
Is anything showing?
My hands move up, I feel anxious
I see you emboldened; you strip me with your eyes

My confidence takes a battering
He's only a heinous coward in a wolf's guise
I tell myself, my courage I find returning

I return the glare
You flinch, and then you glower
How dare I dare-
To shake the status-quo, to challenge the seat of power

I can tell that's what you're thinking, I know your kind
Insecure, incapable, insufficient
Diseased art thou of body and mind
You make me more defiant

Bewitching

Raven hair tucked back
No flyaway strands
Lips painted nude
Kohl-lined eyes
Cheeks sun-kissed
Bloom

And her dress
The fall
accentuated the highs
suppressed the lows
exuded confidence
Discreet

Rain-drops on her lobes
sparkled, as she traipsed
the crescent moon winked

on her décolletage, as she sighed
Quiet contentment
sensuous

How could she be real?
They busied themselves to find the flaws
And when they failed
Disheartened -
they christened her
'Witch'

SmithaV is a banker-turned-writer and a management professional, who embarked on the writing journey in 2016 with her blog Eúnoia (https://smithavishwanathsblog.com/), while still heading the regional cards operations of a bank. After having worked for almost two decades in senior roles in the banking industry in the Middle East, she quit and moved to Mumbai, India in July 2018 with her husband and two daughters. In July 2018, she co-authored Roads: A Journey with Verses, a book of poetry. Other than writing, she enjoys reading, traveling, painting, and going on long nature walks. Her work has been published in SpillWords, Rebelle Society, Borderless Journal, and other magazines.

Sneha Patra
Look at me

You look at me
And you laugh at how absurd I look.
You look at me
And you see nothing beyond the colour of my skin.
Even so, what's so funny about me being brown?
What have I ever done to you
That you try to pull me down
With every chance you get?
How does having different complexions
Make us any different?
At the end of the day,
We'll all be but no more
Than part of the same soil and dust.
So why look at me with disgust?
Why try to create a world of distrust?
I wonder if you even have the answers
To the questions I ask.
Probably not, because society's never forced upon you
The tedious task
Of considering what one might feel
When looked at like they don't matter at all.

And so,
You look at me
And you laugh.
And I don't know whether I should laugh back
In utter distaste or feel dismayed
Because you've never learnt to look beyond
What you've been taught to see.
But I hope we can change that one day.
I hope we can find a way
To learn to look at one another
And not mock each other for our identities,
Nor degrade each other for our dissimilarities.

I hope that one day,
We learn to laugh together
As we look at the sky and marvel
At how beautiful you and I truly are,
And at the wonder
That is life.

Sneha Patra is a senior in high school and has been writing poetry in Hindi and English from a very young age. She strongly believes in gender and socio-political equality. She loves using poetry to express her emotions and ideas, and to talk about oppression, equality, and the need for change. She lives in Doha, Qatar with her family. Find out more about her works on her Instagram handle, @potato._.poetry.

Dr. Sneha Rooh

Will I be courage?

They ask, "Who is your mother? "
I ask, "Who is a mother?
Who nurtures, instigates the impetus
Who feeds and watches things grow?
Who inspires without noise.
I don't know about names
This is what courage looks like to me
Yes, courage was my mother!
Yes, I would shriek before laughing
Would show my incisors when I am angry
I would love knowing I can lick my wounds
I would stretch and rest when I know I should
If courage was my mother
I would be able to fall asleep quickly
Open my heart wider when I hug
They say after a point,
It is best to be your own mother
Knowing the best possible can be done only by you.
Then if I am my mother
Would I like to be courage?

TAKE me

When I look hard enough
Be quiet enough
Breathe deep enough
There is power in the moment
That brings me to me
When life is awe-filled
Love powerful
Courage inspiring
And heart smiling, unguarded

When I feel I am alive and it matters
When I am the sculptor
To the clay of me
When I move beyond habits
When hesitation is met with
Equally present action.
When life is not a slave of happiness.
To that tiny space, malleable space
I say— " Take me!

Dr. Sneha Rooh is a palliative physician and founder of Orikalankini an organisation that is changing narratives around Menstruation and sexuality in India through art theatre and dialogue. She loves to travel and write.

Sneha Roy

Cooking Lessons

When a woman's body blossoms with bruise,
They say, it is then that she learns best how to cook-
Do not beat your eggs like a man of the house beats his woman.
These knuckles shall learn how to steady the fright of a yolk,
When it jumps out of a bowl and never rests to clot.

Learn from the leather belt landing on your back,
What it is to make the finest batter for coconut pancakes.
Whip the mix tireless, rest not for a while to even take a breath,
Until you know by now, the welts waiting to burst on your flesh
Would tire as well.

For the night, grind and knead the flour for the chapatis,
Like how your body shall be treated just after-
There's lesser blood in your body as much as water
Make your dough like how it is to be in your body,
-The deadweight of a moon,
Spread flat each night
For a recurring test of malleability.

Bindi

A coloured full stop worn
Settles in the space,
Like a pebble skipped mid-water
Rippling respect widening its circle
To the point that it soon all vanishes.

Nothing exists outside the text, you say
Hence most have given up
And jumped off the skewed lines
Of my forehead,

Meeting death while
Seeking pleasure.
(How else do I punctuate?)

When I leave
You realise, the glue is so sticky,
Even in my absence, I inhabit your space.

Yes, it shall be easier
To crack this blasted mirror.
Funny how,
God made man in his own image.

So I try a small experiment -
I simply take off the full stop
Like a closed valve
And wait.
The text bleeds, ending inevitably
With a period.

The world is a brilliant red stain.

An ardent lover/ learner of all things art and literature, Sneha Roy is currently pursuing her Master's in English Literature at Jawaharlal Nehru University, New Delhi. One of the Top-30 prize winners at the WingWord Poetry, 2017; her poetry is forthcoming or published in Silverleaf Poetry, Wifi For Breakfast- New Age Indian Poems (Winning Poetry Anthology by Delhi PoetrySlam), Ruptured- A Mental Health anthology, Antargata by Bangalore Poetry Circle, Khushk Zubaan Bebaak Jigaar- a Women's Poetry anthology and other such poetry collections and literary websites. She writes on Instagram under the handle @sylviasroy.

Snigdha Agrawal
Batter Fried Truths

Demons ambushed another life
Dragged her into the fields, body defiled
Set it on fire, as though with it,
their acts would be burnt, reduced to ashes
Leaving no traces to prove the wrongs
that were in plain sight committed
And the parents left distraught
Not only losing a daughter
but at the injustice of it all
fear lurking every moment
When will it stop, if ever,
tormenting the minds of women?

How long will lawmakers make excuses?
"in the absence of sperm, rape didn't happen"
As though that alone is proof of penetration
Like denying there's water beneath
the surface of a lake frozen
Flies daring to buzz, are squashed
with a fly swat and life goes on
as war of words are waged
Clash of swords cutting clean all blame

Life goes on
Till another rape is committed
Again big mouths will blare
through loudspeakers...
"Twas not rape!" "Twas not rape!"
Voices of dissent will be quelled
Through an avalanche of threats
Candlelight marches will be held

Media will follow every detail
dissecting the victim into pieces
arranging, rearranging facts,
to align with thoughts of those
holding powerful positions

Such men will get away each time
For mothers will reason
"boys will be boys, that doesn't
mean you hang them"
Mothers so proud of bearing sons
mollycoddling them from birth
to think they are superior to women.
The irony of a woman insensitive
to the sensitivities of woman
So why blame men alone, when
mothers fail in bringing them up
keeping them on the right trail?

Snigdha Agrawal (nee Banerjee) is from Kolkata, settled in Bangalore (India) for over three decades. She has published two books of poems and contributed to several published anthologies. Brought up in a cosmopolitan society, and educated in Loreto Institutions, she has been exposed to both the eastern and western cultures. Her family and extended family belong to India and countries in the West. https://randomramblings52.wordpress.com.

Sohela Chhotaray
Misspelt

I am misspelled,
or else I am that,
with no boundary,
no source of loyalty,
nor typically your attitude.
Who proves her existence,
beneath you, below you,
sarcastic, enslaved.

Just to prove,
You are anorexic without him,
or petrified, buried somewhere, deserted
and diminished, begging for him.

Lost in lust, loneliness,
In feverishness, longing, fooling yourself,
In the shadow of the greenish softness,
that ruins you slowly,
corroding you everyday
ounce by ounce.

You are destroying,
Your inner core,
with that randomness,
discovering no one but yourself.
You a moulder,
You changed my funda,
My vision and virtues,
just imposed your philosophies,
In the name of lovesick blues,
In my dreamy eyes,
In my shattered life buzz...
no suffusions are mine now.
The blues of togetherness,
Echo somewhere,
I am unwilling to sing.

Sohela Chhotaray is a postgraduate in Botany, B.ed along with a PG Diploma in Journalism and Mass communication. She wrote an anthology in Odia named "RudraTamash" and a translation work of "The Magic Change Metamorphosis". She worked as a lecturer in various colleges and contributed as a poet in "100 poems are not enough","She Express 'Lafz'. She is a regular poetess for Utkal Sahitya Samaj and believes writing is a journey not a destination.

Kapalini

Sohela Chhotaray

Somjeeta Pandey

Flight

The train waited for the clock to strike 11.42 am,
An impatient Raina, seated inside, looked at the other women
     around her,
An old lady, an adolescent girl, a young woman in her twenties, a
housewife tightly holding her little daughter's hands were Raina's
companions.
An air of restlessness lingered, filled with longing eyes and wanting
     hearts.
The old lady seated next to Raina, smiled and said,
It has been thirty years since I last saw him,
I dared to fall for a man outside my religion and when my father
found his letters hidden inside my books he was beaten to a pulp,
He was soon sent to the States by his parents...
I got a letter from him just yesterday...finally we will meet and
     get married...
Raina smiled, not knowing what else to say.
This old lady was firmly holding a piece of crumpled paper in her
     hands,
Her translucent and skinny withered hands were shaking.
Raina felt a peculiar sting of pity for her.
And soon there was an air of muffled approval among the other
     women.
Everybody, it seemed, had secrets tightly wrapped up around their
     souls waiting for an outlet.
I am leaving for good, I will never come back...
A young pretty girl, with oily messy hairs and teary dark brown eyes
     said,
My father set my mother on fire when I was three and married
     another woman,
Both of them would torment me endlessly,
My mother would lock me up in the bathroom for days, without
     food...
But... but ... when yesterday he tried to force himself on me, I
     kicked his groin and fled...

She broke down, sobbing helplessly.

Raina could not believe her ears.

Her clothes were torn and shabby, collar bones protruding, bruises here and there, dark circles around her eyes but an unbeatable spark in them conveyed her strong indomitable spirit.

Another woman, seated comfortably on the upper berth with her daughter, offering some water to the sobbing girl said,

Behind the closed doors of their house, my husband and my in-laws ruthlessly tortured me,

I endured because women are supposed to, that is what we have been taught,

Our mothers and grandmothers are testimonies to this sad truth of life,

But they were conspiring to sell my 8-year-old daughter, how could I let that happen?

When everybody had fallen asleep, I took her in my arms and ran as fast as I could. . .

Raina listened, dumbfounded.

Raina was fuming with rage. She looked at the eight-year-old who was gently wiping her mother's tears.

The horrors of patriarchy sent a shiver down her spine!

Unable to bear the pain, Raina shifted her attention to the newspaper,

Dalit girl raped and killed in Barabanki,

Minor in Bhopal befriended during PUBG game, gang raped and blackmailed,

Haryana woman locked in toilet for husband for over a year rescued,

Cousins killed by the family for wanting to marry each other. . .

Raina, disgusted, tears the newspaper into pieces.

I was just six when my father's maalik had come for a visit,

The woman seated opposite to Raina blurted out,

He had brought chocolates and we were playing hide and seek. . .

All I remember next was lying in a blood puddle and a tremendous pain in my abdomen,

He handed some money to my father and left.

When I complained about the pain to my mother, she said we are
    Mahars, and this is the destiny of a daughter of a Mahar,
For fifteen years I was just a bundle of flesh, but now I want to be
    a human too. . .
Raina, closed her eyes for a moment, trying to recuperate from the
    horrors.
In an impulse, she draws the girl into her breasts and starts crying.
Slowly slowly every other ailing woman comes forward and joins
    Raina extending warm hugs,
The moment witnesses an agency of sisterhood being created
through grieving women, rising in unison against the invisible
hands
of oppression that have battered their souls since ages.
After sometime Raina takes out a letter from her bag, an admission
letter from one of the greatest culinary academies, pride swells up
in her eyes.
She remembers the face of her father, a man who believed that
Raina was a disgrace to her   family, women in her family were
only supposed to cook and procreate,
Fed up of her father's contempt she had packed her bags and
    boarded the train.
Why did our mothers never teach us to fight the filth?
Why were we always taught to be servile and meek, why not break
    some bones instead?
Why does a mother always teach a girl to be the lakshmi of the
    house and not kali?
In a secular country like ours where everybody has equal
constitutional rights, why do we always have to fight for justice
and equal rights?
Is there no end to this distress?
The whistle blew, Raina was jolted back from her daze, she realized
she was just mumbling to herself!
A tinge of victory and relief now replaced the earlier restlessness.
As the wheels slowly started rolling towards the new destination,
Raina saw an eagle taking flight in the pristine blue sky.

Somjeeta Pandey is a poet, scholar, and an Assistant Professor of English. Her research interests are rooted in crime fiction studies, feminist literary studies, and Dalit studies. Her poems have appeared in The CQ: A Literary Magazine and her poems will soon appear in Global Poemic, Faces to the Sun: A Mental Health Awareness Anthology, and Point Positive Publishing's Rebloom Anthology. She can be reached at somjeeta072@gmail.com. https://www.facebook.com/somjeeta.pandey https://instagram.com/somjeeta?igshid=q929r7xsb1vd

Somrita Urni Ganguly
Matla Nodi

There is a river in Canning, called
Matla (n., meaning: intoxicated/ the first couplet in a ghazal).
I would like to be her, someday:

a drunk roaring raging raving poem of a river.

Our rivers never get judged.

(Previously published in A Map Called Home, Kitaab, Singapore, 2018.)

Somrita Urni Ganguly is a professor, an award-winning poet, and literary translator. She was a Fulbright Doctoral Research Fellow at Brown University. She is an alumna of the University of East Anglia's International Creative Writing & Literary Translation Summer School, and currently the Head of the Department of English, Maharaja Manindra Chandra College, University of Calcutta. Somrita's work has been showcased at the London Book Fair. She is the editor of the first anthology of food poems, Quesadilla and Other Adventures (2019), and has translated, among other works, Firesongs (2019), Shakuni: Master of the Game (2019), and The Midnight Sun: Love Lyrics and Farewell Songs (2018).

Sonali Pattnaik
not your nude

the female body
titillates you,
humiliates you
but most of all, it horrifies you
breasts, unasked for,
appearing untimely
and un-underwired,
are cause for fear
when they don't disappear
under the fog of your
objectifying desire

birth and menstruation
scare you. blood. too much blood
blood you want to shed and own
but blood flowing freely, out of line,
blood in no mood to be contained
blood that will not be managed
and erased or soaked
horrifies you, so you try
to tame its femininity
with your masculine name
you give her blood
your name

a single woman with
a child intimidates you
more than a war mongering man
sending millions to their graves
a life saved outside of the normative
dismays you more than one
slain at the altar of patriarchy
a woman must be rightly accompanied

a woman must be rightly occupied
reproduction is her task
her rights over her body must be denied
whether she is giving birth
or not, she must be infantilized
from her own self, kept aside
a mother who knows
what she would do
bothers you

at parties, in classrooms, in queues
anywhere this un-body appears
it un-bones you
how did she dare mix labour with love
and when she could be sexy,
do the hetero thing,
mothering non-threatening
why does she deviate by singling?
why does her haircut expose the nape?
how does a whore file for rape?
the female body
when covered, not covered
slightly covered, forgets covers
intimidates you
so you compensate
your fears in the language of
consumption, you try and fix
that body by wanting
or not wanting her

to have lived so far
from the truth,
have wrapped yourself
tight in the flag of falsity
burrowed so deep into
the cave of masculine make-belief,
living by the lies of self-origination

and women's self-objectification
and other codes of abiding hypocrisy,
having drawn the borders
of families and nations
by contorting, stretching,
manning this body
even a single flash of the real,
a woman living in, through, out of,
her own body, say,
wearing a burka at the beach
or smoking at a bus stand
that woman who
enrages you for not falling
neatly into your
binaryculars of want/not-want
would but naturally
scare the living daylights
out of your fragile mandom
for that body is not
your 'nude'
not the one you remember
from the airport magazine
or the studio table
that body appears instead
as the ghost of all your
murdered truths

—no nation for women

no nation for women this
no place at all
no place for her to grow or be born
when she is burnt, raped and
murdered by spurned men
who's barbaric, inexplicable hatred

is justified and prized or explained
while her death, her scars,
her broken limbs and
her burnt face, her pain, and indignity
still seen as her lot
when like no other object or
sentient being, she is oppressed
manhandled, ripped apart, and left abject
some hiss about it in disgust
others say there are things she
ought to learn, some others shield
themselves from it, saying
it's really about that community
or those other men
shielding entitled and violent
sons, husbands, and friends
and others talk of rape
as male pleasure and appetite
adding girth to a culture of rape as right
a culture of doubt and suspicion
at a woman who howls in pain
most are content to relegate
a woman's abject decimation
to further invisibility
by blaming a person or place
or media manipulation
but you see it's not any of those
no matter where she is in this
living hell, her gender is rarely
seen as her defense, only a slate
for men to write their atavistic desires
and borrowed identities upon
no nation for women this
no nation so from this non-place, she speaks
from this non-place
she will change things
she fights to rewrite everything

that she has learned
to make you unlearn and embrace
the nation's foundation, its constitution
and learn to see her as human first
and begins to take
what she was never given
her right to a life of dignity and freedom
and she demands the nation
a caste, class male prerogative till this day
question itself and thus through her whys
births a revolution
that will create at long last a place
that her sisters can call home
and maybe, finally,
because of her blazing tongue
cut but still speaking truth to power
and her holding up again and again
the mirror to your face
because of a women's revolution
there will be at long last a free nation
for a nation where women are in chains
is no nation at all, no nation of hers
no nation of yours

—no nation for women

water's story

the falling from above
of water reminds us
that the story of water
remains half told
water gives, takes, dances
and destroys
it surrenders without
relinquishing a drop
of its power
it's a paradox,
a talisman of
the truth in resistance
do not let water
and its generous falling
trick you into believing
that she is gentle and appeasing
she flows, feeds, and forms
for herself alone
water is held and holds
without boundaries
banks are contours
to her infinite body
she is not made to be controlled
through the years, ever so silently
she will change
the mighty land's structure
through her meandering course
like love, water only
appears contained
the fount of all birth
water never truly belongs
it is not only fire that undoes
water caught, chased,
choked and harmed

is self-damnation
she will explode every pore
of the parched firmness
you stand upon
water is given to release
and flow not to fall
she will become you as you immerse
in the end over your limbs fold
the falling of water from
above reminds us that
water will not be caught
let her be many,
let her fondle
and enter the earth
to rise again and again
she is here for love
for it is not fire, but water
that ignites many a hunger
and ends many a thirst
water, a testament
to life's divine and delicious
contradictions
was here first
yet her story
remains to be told

Dr. Sonali Pattnaik has a PhD in English and teaches Literature at St. Xavier's College (Autonomous), Ahmedabad. She was formerly Lecturer in English at Delhi University's Kirori Mal College where she co-founded the literary magazine Palimpsest. Her poetry and book reviews have been published in print and online journals including Journeys by Sampad South Asian Arts, The Book Review, The Indian Express, Muse India, Cafedissensus, Wordgathering, Writer's Asylum, Women's Web, Tehelka and Intersections.

Kali #1

Sonali Pattnaik

milk

Sonali Pattnaik

Kali #2

Sonali Pattnaik

Sonali Sharma
She is Might

This morning aglow with zealous air
I pen down a story somehow rare
It begins with 'She'
And ends with 'Might'
Narrating her fortitude
A head splendidly held high.

She thought of paper as will
A pen as wheel
Both of which could carry
Her innate desire to lead.

An identity she craved for
More than jewellery
Resolute her belief was
She will be 'Something'.

There was never a night
When pages won't flip by her side
Neither a day when
She won't walk up to there
A railway station near Hari village
And wait for the whistling train.

A hapless hour would rather say
A compact leeway she passed by
Settling in a thronged compartment
Aberrant eyes fell at her front.

With few, her reluctant look met
Flared up a peculiarity
Lust was displayed through gestures
The desire of her grew nearer.

A rangy chap pulled her unfair
Modesty was defying the nightmare
Cowards abundant watched a game
Didn't speak as if living dead.

Soon came another loathing honour
Infuriated at her fulmination
Pushed her off the advancing train
Spilling blood out from her veins
The penetrating bones tore her skin
Loss of a leg was excruciating pain.

The tears of torment blinded her
Vibrations she could only get
A quiescent ill-lit corner tempted her
An inky silhouette was a fading image
An unconscious mind with a state of affairs
Wearing a blindfold saw aeons fly.

Gore dripped from the cotton pads
Syringes bloated the nervous nexus
The medic was dubious, panic spread
Prodigy if she, marvel be sent.

A passerine chirped on a far off sapling
As if seeking a mature tree
That could feed substantially
The core of sentient perpetuity.

In the dead of night, her fingers stirred
Breath released as an unleashed eerie
The ordeal caught in her forehead
Rang as an entire susurrate.

That morning aglow with a remarkable air
She vowed to be unexcelled
A mentor, a believer she became for rest
Womankind is superlative, the essence went.

Picking up petite anecdotes
She recited her conquer over abominate
Travelled she kilometres away
To restore in damsels an everlasting faith.

She narrated to them with content
You are born on cradles of edge
Civilizations can't spurn my adored
Your pinion is meant for the ether
Divulge your say as a widespread rain
That apart from itself
Replenishes the sea with Might.

Sonali Sharma is a published poet from Dehradun, Uttarakhand, India. Currently, she is pursuing a Master's in Environmental Studies from Panjab University Chandigarh. Sonali holds an extreme passion for poetry writing. Her poems have appeared in "Indian Periodical", "Poetry Magazine", and "Indus Woman Writing". She is the co-author of anthologies "Into The Woods of Rame", "Whispers of Heart", "Shadows of Soul", "Fervour", "Shades of Ink", "Masques", "A Breath of Verses". Social media: https://www.facebook.com/profile.php?id=100012783129912

Sonia Dogra
Women Who Read Break Families

She discovered a firefly between the covers of a book
Its phosphorescent glow unveiling mysterious truths.
"Don't read, Saraswati!" immediately bellowed patriarchy
And they turned around to blow their conch shells
in praise of the 'Devi'!

She stealthily made her way, slipping in through the spine
Gliding her cracked hands over letters so fine.
They buried her books under pantries and laundries
Lullabied her once more with tales of yore
Of knights in shining armours, riding to salvage her
from wrecks of tomes.

For, they said...
Women who read, break families.
They no longer love gol rotis
or sweltering kitchens which they must!
So...
"Don't read, Saraswati!" immediately bellowed patriarchy
And they turned around to blow their conch shells
in praise of the 'Devi'!

Your book's no Sirius, foolish woman
A mere firefly, one day it'll die.
You have no need to write or read
The pages you turn will make you scream
shatter not one but several dreams.

For, they said...
Women who read, break families.
They no longer love gol rotis
or sweltering kitchens which they must!
So...

"Don't read, Saraswati!" immediately bellowed patriarchy
And they turned around to blow their conch shells
in praise of the 'Devi'!

The politics of the state is not to frail's taste
It is too much for you to handle,
The economies way more than new apparel.
You'd do better to manage the affairs of cookhouses
Budget furnishings and save for beautiful blouses.
You need no more, neither fireflies
nor their phosphorescent glows.

For, they said...
Women who read, break families.
They no longer love gol rotis
or sweltering kitchens which they must!
So...
"Don't read, Saraswati!" immediately bellowed patriarchy
And they turned around to blow their conch shells
in praise of the 'Devi'!

The paternal umbrella opened a while
They tuned her well, just about fine.
Ignorance is bliss is the mantra they chanted
You need no books; you need a man.
Burn them tonight; those books, oh! so vile
Burn them if you still care to smile.
They'll tear you apart
the familial fabric is fragile.

For, they said...
Women who read, break families.
They no longer love gol rotis
or sweltering kitchens which they must!
So...

"Don't read, Saraswati!" immediately bellowed patriarchy
And they turned around to blow their conch shells
in praise of the 'Devi'.

The Dance of Rebellion

Somewhere between the wrinkled pages of history,
lie untold tales of many a bravery.
The Revolt of 1857 was one such event,
that also has a tiny list of unsung (s)heroes of dissent.
As the striped flag fluttered in several parts of the country,
an ocean of resentment seethed among the Indian sepoys
of the East India Company.
The second half of the nineteenth century saw what they called a
        'mutiny',
the First War of Independence if you truly ask me!

The military garrisons kindled the torch of rebellion,
with Mangal Pandey, Nana Saheb and Bahadur Shah standing tall
against the English dominion.
But pillars of strength must have foundations strong,
just as leaders always need the ordinary all along.
And whenever we must sing of legends from 1857,
let us remember to mention the sacrifice of
the Cawnpore courtesans.
The 'tawaifs' as they were called were talked of in hushed tones,
their stories had no listeners and they perished unknown.
I promise to bring to you Azeezunbai the brave,
she is hard to find in history books, no eulogies in her praise.

But local legends and archives as also colonial accounts,
speak of a woman in male attire in the battle ground.
Armed with a brace of pistols and mounted on horseback,
she fought courageously along with the Indian sepoys
in the Cawnpore attack.

She opened her doors for secret conferences,
cheering the men in arms, standing upright against the winds.
Along with her comrades she tended to the wounds
of soldiers who returned from bloody battles, hurt and maimed.

Azeezun, let me add was not the lone revolutionary,
Hossaini and Gauhar Jaan were no less ordinary.
They danced with rebellion and raised a charity,
furnishing Gandhi's non-cooperation
with their hard-earned money.
Such resilient women free-spirited and strong,
were hailed by the Mahatma for being the storm.

And yet as it always happens, India chose to forget them
filling pages of text books only with the tales of men.
Hence, I sing to them bringing to you their story,
These Indian women are the muse today
in this rendezvous with Indian history!

('The Dance of Rebellion' first appeared as part of an Ebook, Unlocked: Historical Tales in Verse, written for Blogchatter's Ebook carnival in May, 2020. The book is no longer available on any platform. The poem is based on research work as appears in a paper by Lata Singh, an associate professor at the Centre of Women's Studies, JNU)

Sonia is a blogger, writer, copyeditor, and proofreader. She worked as an educationist for ten years before she was bitten by the writing bug. She is often found grappling with words on her personal blog 'A Hundred Quills' which is a repository of soulful poetry, personal memoirs, and flash fiction. Her poems were part of the anthology 'Poems from 30 Best Poets' published in 2019. She can be followed at https://soniadogra.com/ and https://twitter.com/SoniaDogra16 Read her at https://www.juggernaut.in/books/52454518356a4e9d

Sophia Naz
If I Were a Goddess

Some days I'm seized
by the irrational desire to be a Goddess
it doesn't matter what stripe
Lilith or Kali
any badass Medusa will do
to m/end their ways, make morsels
of beastly, priestly pedophiles

Sadly there's so much to eat
If I were a Goddess I'd excrete
the lot in steaming little piles
that patient village women would feed
to their hungry home fires

If I were a Goddess I would grant
those scum just enough
immortality that even pulped
they'll keep on feeling pain
let them never be liberated
from the suffering of sentience
even when their ash drops to earth, feeding
tiny shoots in the village fields

I'll make each green blade
turn inward in a constant hara-kiri
then and only then
will I take another birth
as a carefree girl and dance
all over the prostrate grass.

Splitting Screens

Broken gram, her
weight and balance, beam, repeat
doesn't miss a single beat

Woman as splitting
headache, bad apple, spittoon for seed,
bossed from on high, sifting

Through shifting feelings, fear
like a clot of flour in the cake
no one would know the measure

Of that furtive cupping, unread blood
would boil over, yet remain
hallways in the marrow, dread

Hollow as a bone to pick
and pick it up she did, knowing
those hated eyes that held

Her pittance hostage like a soft
summer peach biting
her lips to keep an angry dam

From spilling the beans
because par for the course
men were golfers, women holes.

(previously published in Pratik)

Pushcart Prize nominee Sophia Naz is a poet, author, editor, translator. Her work features in Poetry International, Adirondack Review, The Wire, Chicago Quarterly Review, BlazeVox, Scroll, Nether Quarterly, The Daily O, Cafe Dissensus, Guftugu, Pratik, Gallerie International, Coldnoon, VAYAVYA, The Bangalore Review, Madras Courier, etc Poetry collections: Peripheries, Pointillism, and Date Palms. Shehnaz, a biography, published by Penguin Random House in 2019. Twitter @Sophi_Naz   Instagram: sophia_naz_author Facebook @Naznotes Site: SophiaNaz.com

Srabani Bhattacharya
One with Green Fingers

Maa will rescue plants
unwanted on pavements,
come home to wash leftover
pickles from an old jar
or scavenge a cup with
broken handle and force
in a handful of soil, make
a hole and tuck in roots
lovingly crooning baby talk
for good measure asking it to
grow healthy and well only
to repot it over and over again
She will run after the sun
and steal sunny spots from
basking cats to favour her
flourishing flowers, cry if
I throw away banana peels
or drain the rotting pan of
vegetable-washed water
because everything in the kitchen
belongs to her family extended
from children who have escaped
her wing. And I see her call
her new youngling pet names
and think that she has not known
anything better than the time
of day when the sun shines
brightest to feed her brood,
not the tea kettle where she
makes rounds and rounds of
tea to bribe baba to hang pots
on hooks or trim overgrown
hedge of the shiuli. Nor the

rusted gas stove before which
in between her endless chores
and preparation of four dishes
for four people, she studies
poetry when she is not searching
'how to make terrariums' or
'best rooftop garden ideas'
on YouTube. No. She has not
known anything better than
to pile desires and dreams
in compost pits to decompose
with the egg shells and vegetable
peels to feed her children so they
can grow and grow and grow

Lion's Share

That day I felt the familiar anxiety
I feel every day on the road,
in the cab, an instinctive
looking over my shoulder,
the thumping on my chest
travelling on a bus with more
men than women, or walking
alone in late evenings
I felt the familiar anxiety
that day not on the street
but inside four walls
of my aunt's house.
The man who assaulted me
as a child new to puberty
sat there on the bed
I visited after years to
meet the puppy my aunt
adopted to fill the void

of her estranged marriage
and I could not once turn
my back to him even though
it has been years since all that
and he has served his karma
and he lay on the bed,
a vegetable of a man
bereft of the pride and vigour
of his youth but I was still conscious
about leering thoughts he might
have and covered my chest and
lowered my eyes around him like a
newlywed bride before her father-in-law

Aunt said karma has done nothing
for him. She despises her husband
who lost his job because of his
decaying stability and she ran the
family with her scanty income from
a job much below her qualification
that she got after giving up ambitions
she had before marriage. He has no
friends no family but she, who makes
sure to serve him dinner before
retiring to the attic room she
designed from scratch to get away
from her husband-filled home.
She tells me she will be happy
if he dies, that there have been too
many times she thought of murder.
The man, tone deaf, speaks cordially
if we address him not giving mind
to how her wife takes his blame
personally and all the news of
rape she hears on TV slashes
her with guilt for the accused
who goes free to have his meals

served under his nose, a marital
routine she has not been able to
abandon however despicable an
object he is to her. 'Why didn't
you report him,' she asks me. 'I
would have if it were my daughter.'
She struggles in quiet shame rocking
back and forth repeating, 'Are you
not a daughter to me?' I grew up
aware that men, even favourite
uncles, are poisonous but the
family's shame congregated on her
who rejects wedding invitations
and get together for something
in her mind tells her that she
must suffer for a man she
never agreed to marry, and she
condemns herself to life term
atonement serving for fifteen
years and counting because
in our upbringing the biggest
piece will always be reserved
for the man and mothers will
go hungry until the son returns
home at long last reeking of
whiskey and chicken fry late
at night while the women (already
indoors safe from predators, from
a life they could have led) have the
dinner cooked and plates ready
to serve the omnipotent gods

Recipe for Pulmonary Obstruction

I remember childhood days
When I could not spell, my aunt
would come to visit her only brother,
the treasured youngest sibling
whose cares are now to be fulfilled
by his wife, my mother
My grandma, her mother-in-law, would
complain about maa's faults to the eldest
aunt and maa would stand there justifying
herself teary eyed. I would hold my breath
for baba to get home when aunt would
relay thamma's grievances to him
and the three would tower over
maa cowering under the weight of
two children at twenty-three.
Today, maa tells me about the boy
they have found for me, 'he has a good
job and a respected degree' she says.
And I ask how she thrusts it on me
when I have seen her suffer silently in
forced wedlock because her father retired
before she got a job or finished her degree
and had to give her away to survive.
I ask her how she can forgive baba
for not letting her take teacher's training
that would feed us after he retired early
for how for half her life she has looked enviously
at the mothers who go to office and be awed
at how much they spend while she has
to beg every month for pocket money
and wait in line with my brother and I,
as baba would write a receipt in a red diary
and keep tab of spending each week and

frown at the new saree or a piece of jewellery
that she keeps in an opaque jar treasuredly
and smirk at the owl-shaped money bank
where she saved quarters that became
obsolete much before she could use them
on her dream voyage to Andaman.
I wonder at her immeasurable strength
as a new comer in this new house with
new life cradled in her hands
At how she brought us up with the hostility
She vs the in-laws. I wonder at
the unspoken strength of a woman
who never slept in the arms of a lover
who found no time for friends
to confide in because of the preoccupation
with the next meal to cook that would
have ample proteins and vitamins for
her kids ('deficiency will wreck a healthy
life') and checked salt and oil for baba's
cholesterol. I wonder if she ever looked up
recipes that had adequate nutrients her
body needed to survive the constricted
airflow in her lungs at home

Srabani Bhattacharya is a writer, editor, poet, and translator. She recently opened a poetry blog, 'Paperbird: weavesbirdsong with paper', to practice her writing: https://paperbird.me/and-then-the-forest-said-tome/. She is currently working towards starting a creative collaborative project with an artist on Instagram through the account Paperbird: https://www.instagram.com/paperbird.me/.

Sridevi Selvaraj
Bathra Kali Amman

The goddess came with
Lightning speed
She knelt down and danced
Moved with speed and grace
Tender coconuts were poured
Turmeric water was sprayed
Still her fiery soul was
Blazing with sparks
They gave her live fire
Still she blessed every one
She bore the fire with ease
The people watched mesmerized
They knew this year
The harvest will be good.

(Muthar Amman is a mother Goddess from the Southern part of Tamil Nadu in India. She is considered to be a goddess who blesses villagers with good health. She is known as Muthu Malai Amman, Ujjaini Makali Amman, Batra Kali Amman, and so on in different places. South Indian villages worship her as the village governing goddess. Every summer the village celebrates her for ten days during nights. Shamans dance and her words are expressed through them as foretelling. She is also the goddess who cures chickenpox and smallpox. Oral literature is abundant on these goddesses who are mothers to communities and songs are sung in celebration of them. Batra Kali – can also refer to Goddess Saraswathi, the goddess of learning in Indian mythology).

Sridevi Selvaraj is a bilingual poet from Tamil Nadu, India, who writes in Tamil and English. She has written a few collections of poems in English and Tamil: Reservations, Heralds of Change, Naan Sivam, Penn Enum Perunthee and Erkaud.

Sridipa Dandapat
Burn in Earth

A temple is born.
A court adjourned.
A sapphire fire rising.
Two fingers on the throne
Groping to consecrate
The goddess beneath the god.

The white cap/the sapphire fire.
Dadri/Shimoga.
Black veils burnt. Mangalsutras torn.
Silence! Silence! Men at work.
At office/at home.
Glass ceiling and sticky floor. Dowry-burn to adorn.
Delhi/Park Street/Mathura/Hathras.
'A lonely girl/an open vault'.
Wolves howl and grin. Candles mourn.
Rejoice. Rejoice.
A temple is born.
And courts adjourned.

Honour-lost daughters queue up.
A cold, dark, and deep pit awaits.
The Sacred Cow mooing.
Over corpses of honour.
Deafening.
Defeating.
A shut window of the mad attic.
Withered lips of hiding words.
Whirligig of unvoiced agonies.
Of those who deserve neither heaven nor hell.
For being born a woman.
Echoes of silence whisper to their ears,
Burn in earth, girl! Burn in earth!

Still in search of her voice, Sridipa writes to raise the words about the elephant in the room. You can reach her @the imprints in front of your eyes. The black in white. Through the words, she types.

Srividya Sivakumar

Telekinesis in Tamil Nadu
(after 'Bengal's Black Magic Women' by Somrita Urni Ganguly)

1.
Start with English.
Speak it. Love it. Teach it. Preach it.
Nothing qualifies you as a show-off bitch witch quite like a common hatred for this language does. Oh, wait. There's Hindi. But no. English is king. Strike that. Queen.

2.
Dress for yourself.
Wear red lipstick and ditch the *bindi*. Wear a necklace or not. Those jeans work. Those shorts too. That sari is gorgeous. Yes, your hair can have a deep purple streak. Wear bangles or bare arms. Bear arms. Because nothing scares a man more than a woman with wit who has her wits (and more) about her.

3.
Reject the notion of an apology.
Stop saying sorry when someone bumps into you, when you need space, when you want some time away from 'close' family members and friends. Don't preamble a sentence with hesitance. Don't couch a command as a request. Don't end an assertion as a
question. Don't shine less because you are too much for some.

4.
Practise autonomy over self.
Life isn't only about lineage. Choose children or not. Stop explaining
your choices. Live-in or single. Childless or rhythm method. The traditional homestead or a studio apartment for two. You don't need ornaments at the neck, the toes and the fingers, blazing red *sindoor* in the hair, and everything else to 'look' it. You are. And that is enough.

5.
Sex.
Say it, speak about it, write about it, do it. Pleasure yourself. Pleasure your lover(s). Abstain or sex up every day. This three-letter word goes with another—yes. Chip away at patriarchy and the male gaze. Ask questions. Make a noise. Push back.

Spell making in my state, in every state.

(For Vikki. Enchantress nonpareil)

Apartment Complex

I heard something today. The clothes clips tried to get my attention as I was drying a week's laundry. When I had finally pinned the last kitchen cloth to the line, I turned to them and looked, pointedly. They spoke in hushed tones to tell me that they had been hearing things and seeing things. It happens when you've been on a balcony for years, I told them.

After a loud indignant shout, they informed me that the neighbour is a wife beater.

The neighbour? The one in the apartment opposite mine? The scrawny man who left the French doors wide open as he immersed himself in mundaneness on a widescreen? A wife-beater?

Sure, I'd never seen him leave the house. And come to think of it, i had never seen his wife and him talking to each other. But they did sit in companionable silence in the sofa. But I'd never smiled at either on my forays to water the plants. What did I know?

The cloth clips clamoured for quiet.
They'd seen and heard things. Shouts. Bruises. At night, he would push his wife to the balcony and shut the doors. Yes, sad but what can I do?

The clips looked askance. For pieces of wood, they sure were filled with feeling.

The next morning, I searched but could not find. And then I saw. My tablecloth.

Covering a quivering shape on the balcony in front of me.

Poet, teacher, columnist, and TEDx Speaker, Dr. Srividya Sivakumar has two collections of verse- The Heart is an Attic and The Blue Note. Her poem, Bamboo, was nominated for the Best of the Net Anthology in 2018. Srividya wrote a weekly column, Running on Poetry, for The Hindu's Metroplus, for eighteen months. Her column — Srividya Speaks Poetry — currently appears in the journal, Narrow Road.
https://youtu.be/ZxypHGmsVvk #rumwrapt

Sucharita Das Maity
Money Erases All

Leaving aside the path of law
In terms of money
You measure torture
Tie justice
And establish injustice
In the Black eye of the society
Hard pained ,
Forcibly a girl becomes a mother
You offer them the ointment
Called money,
To rub out their pain
In the presence of power
The reaction of the lives
Of the wounded
Generates
The so-called educated society.

A Battle Yet To Win

I heard,
I have a relationship with the
People of the high caste.
But never lucky to go
To the temple or school.
Our face is evil for them.
One day for the first time
They came face to face
Forcibly dragged me into the car.
Then I found myself in the hospital.
Strangled!
Some of the police stood outside.
Then maa tightened

My forcibly opened bun
And held my hand
As the soil holds the tree roots
At that moment I understood
The mystery of my birth
And the battle of an oppressed,
Exploited, tortured Lady
Standing just in front of me!

Sucharita Das Maity is a social worker in the field of disability management and in rural areas as well as a writer, writing in English as well as in her mother tongue Bengali mainly poems, having published a few online and also in print media. She lives in West Bengal, India with her husband and two children.

Her Facebook link is: https://www.facebook.com/sucharitadas.maity.37

Suchita Parikh-Mudul

Daily Routine

Each morning I take a sip
of masculinity
before I am found out,
put on lipstick to cover
any stains, and swim across
a few centuries of inequity
with brazen strokes.
I reach the shore in a shiver
and slip into dry humour
to fend the cold lashes
that sweep across the land.
At work,
I throw sidelong glances
at infidels like myself,
smiling surreptitiously.
There is lipstick on all our mouths
—pink is popular,
as is red.
I move like a well-oiled machine
that pays injustice its own desserts,
marked by steady strides
and some wavering.
I am quiet,
but I feel the uproar;
I serve as needed,
infusing simpering laughter
into each act.
A grim tune slinks across
the airwaves as the clock face
frowns, creaks, slows;
rudimentary roles are taken up
but I keep my eye on the skylight
and the rustle of snakes beyond.
I might stumble over
the male gaze, but I am adept
enough to walk on.

Surviving

When I feel vulnerable
I let the misogyny
grow on my skin
like moss.
I let it flower
over my breasts,
over my mouth,
over my eyes.
I let its spores multiply;
I don't attempt to remove
any of it.
When I feel vulnerable
I allow my body to collect
verbal abuse
like sediments of earth
accreted over time.
Layer above layer,
words that are rooted
in systemic hate.
They begin
to seep through
my epidermal surface
into my veins,
into my arteries,
into my heart.
That is just
how it is.

When I feel stronger
I exhale it all away
into the air
and watch it dissipate
from a dark mist
into nothing.
I exfoliate my body,
cleansing it of the murk
obstructing
neural pathways
and slowing my pace.
I clear my bloodstream
until it sparkles Himalayan pure,
allowing for deep, yogic breaths
unencumbered and free.
I wash the filth from
my sight,
my thoughts,
my breath,
and continue.

Suchita Parikh-Mundul's debut collection of poetry 'Liquid Apnea' was published by Sampark, Kolkata in 2005. Her poems have appeared in Sahitya Akademi's Indian Literature, as well as online journals Muse India, Cerebration, and most recently, Hakara. She won the local Poetry Tournament organised by Dosti House in 2019, and was a runner-up in the national eShe Lockdown Poetry Contest in 2020.

Sudeshna Mukherjee

Feat and Female Foeticide

Our darling daughters have strangely vanished
Wiped off from the face of our earth as if banished

Before the dawn of advancement and technology
The doll was fed with sharp husks of paddy

It pierced her delicate innards as she hemorrhaged
A tiny life packed and bundled in the earthen cage

More and more ways were devised to put an end
To her life by risking the law and tweaking a bend

The tiny tot was fed poisoned milk or simply left to starve
Helpless mothers followed the willful ways that patriarchy carved

Sometimes she would be put in a tub of cold water
She would be wrapped in wet towels to close the chapter

Pneumonia would set in medicines in garbage thrown
A quick grave dug to put her in and a few crocodile tears to mourn

The 'khaps'* would often warn the new mothers
Threatening of dire consequences if she didn't smother

Sometimes a leg of the 'khatiya'* would be put on the baby's throat
Sometimes she would be drowned or left in rivers to float

With the advent of new technology
The process to hoodwink became an apology

Ultrasonography and testing of amniotic fluid
Instantly told of the gender and of quicker methods to get rid

From dark to dark she travels without seeing the light
A world sans her babbles or chortles is the sorry plight

Even those that make it are undernourished
Raised to cater to other demands and
often ravaged

Such is the plight of the abused Durga* and Dusky Kali*
Sacrificed in the burning pyre of desire and actions lowly

Durga invoke your inner Chandi* to surface and slay
Pick up your scythe to destroy the demons as in child's play
Let us not turn a blind eye and worship Goddesses in different
forms
While misogyny continues to deviously kill our daughters as is the
        norm.

*khaps-notorious for their primitive belief regarding girls/ women
*khatiya- a stringed bed with a wooden frame
*Durga - Goddess riding a lion /tiger slayer of Mahisasur (a demon in
the guise of a buffalo)
*Kali - the Goddess of time, doom, and death
*Chandi - Fierce Goddess slayer of demons also called Mahamaya
(magical) and Abhaya (fearless)

Sudeshna Mukherjee's poems deal with varied human nature. A keen
observer she chronicles the happenings around her and writes with a
tinge of humour. "Meanderings of the Mind "and "Mélange" are her
published collections of poems. Her works have been published in many
national and international anthologies and e-zines. She is the recipient of
the "Golden Vase " award for her humorous/satirical writings. She has
won many online contests and awards including 'Kaafiya' and 'On fire
cultural movement'.

Sudipta Maity
Girlfriend Tree

The crane's bill on the Geranium fruit
Began to play the otamatone
In the middle of my secret petals.
At the end of the greed to beat
Monster left the body like camphor,
Smearing ashen glue on the faces
Of all women.
I didn't stop
Wanted to give myself
To the deepwater lap.
Then suddenly saw my girlfriend tree,
Leaving the bark of my stem,
Went towards her
For Warmth.
Like herbs hugging the tree tightly.

Fearless

Stick to the clip Sad Life
Bring resentment
To the damp eyes.
Apply sun ointment
On the back of the whip.
Oh, girl,
Now the mill-stick!
No, turn around with your feet
Look
Whether male grain
Is being crushed!

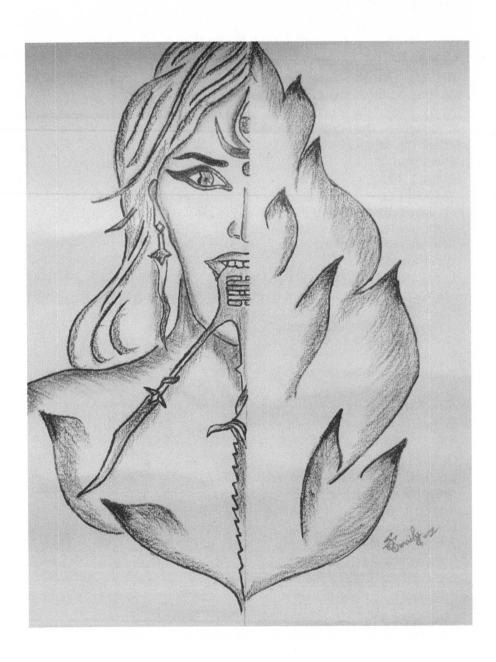

Sudipta Maity is currently pursuing her graduate studies in English Literature. She is an artist as well as a writer, writing in English as well as in her mother tongue, Bengali. Her work has appeared widely in numerous magazines, journals, and anthologies. She occupied the third position in the State Level Essay Competition in 2016 and lives in West Bengal, India with her parents and sister.
https://www.instagram.com/sudiptaamaity
https://www.facebook.com/sudipta.maity.14661

Sukrita

"Women,
and Women"

Sisters and daughters, even mothers
Are hurled into daily abuses and jokes

Trapped in muscular gaze
Frozen as soft targets in epics
dolls in cinema
Excuses for duals
Cause for battle in the past

Possessed as furniture
Or items of jewellery
Kept in vaults
In the royal cellars of history

While Sita greets Savitri
Singing songs of captivity
Shedding tears of loss and regret

The two women on the motorbike
Lal Ded and Akka Mahadevi
Whizz pass through centuries
Multiplying in numbers
As also in Shakti

Each one searching
for her own path
Her own tune...

Draupadi on a Hunt

I am on the lookout

Is this where I might find
What I am looking for

Yes this way
Not that way

Draupadi stomped out
of Mahabharata
became a squirrel and
climbed up the tree
as did Manto's
Toba Tek Singh

Look down
Is this Hindustan or Pakistan?

Barbed wire between
the two lovers
real as their love

On all fours do I crawl
Holding on to the earth's call

Not to fly, nor abandon them
Not to forget the one and only
Nor the rest of them

Rumbling and whispering
with all the tales and myths
gurgling in the earth's belly

I am on the lookout

A noted poet and critic, Sukrita Paul Kumar (born in Kenya) earlier held the Aruna Asaf Ali Chair at the University of Delhi. An invited poet and Fellow at the prestigious International Writing Programme, Iowa, USA, she is a former Fellow of the Indian Institute of Advanced Study, Shimla. She has published several collections of poetry, translations, and critical books. A recipient of many residencies and fellowships, she has also held exhibitions of her paintings.

Sulochana Ram Mohan

A Kitchen Saga

Traversing the distance from
the kitchen to the front verandah
time after time
day after day
she measures the distance
from the inner spaces
of the house
to the front verandah
where the outside world waits in all glory.

Some days, it is done in pure joy,
dancing with careless abandon,
silver anklets tinkling in harmony,
her long black plaits flapping to and fro,
the innate rhythm of the danseuse hidden
inside every female body
choreographing each movement,
she twists and twirls, flowing like a river,
forming a circle and then pausing,
surveying the unseen audience before bowing down
and withdrawing from centre stage
Then, suddenly, as if pushed on by some impulse,
she rushes out to the front verandah
like the waves surging on to the waiting shore
splashing up seawater with fervid energy
and then retreating gracefully,
she pauses by the door to the outside world
to shake out her wild yearnings,
pulsating vitality, fecund imaginings
down to the ground and defenseless,
goes back to waiting household chores.

At other times
it is a silent sedate walk
as if calculating the length and breadth
of the tiles lining the kitchen floor,
as if assessing in square metres
the area she covers daily
to record in the history of the 'akathamma',
the woman trapped inside the homestead
with no knowledge of another world outside,
reserved for the men folk.

Sometimes she sits by the barrier
the undrawn territorial marker,
that stops her desire to walk out
into an unseen world of glamour,
she has an overwhelming urge to
run out and touch the blazing horizon,
so far off, yet so near in imagination,
to return then, satiated, fulfilled,
to don again the role of the docile homemaker.

But best of all
are the mornings that beckon her
with sweet bird songs,
the virgin touch of early sun streaks
She sleepwalks into the yard then
and stands still seeing buds open slowly,
butterflies sinking gently
into their fertile inner petals
birds beginning to spread wings
and soar up into calm azure skies
awaiting their touch,
she feels the caress of the first breeze
damp with the dewdrops of the past night.

Drinking in the sights, sounds, smells
of the fresh day
her senses are aroused,
the soul of creativity suddenly revealed,
It is as if Mother Nature is passing on her
magic of creation
her fertility that pulsates with
passion for posterity.
She then rushes to her own solitary kingdom
the kitchen, revitalized,
and transmits all the energy received
into the clamour of ladles,
the lightning flash of sharpened knives
the powerful rhythm of the grinding stone
the humming of the burning stove.

Feminine creativity,
Cooked and served.

The Aftermath Of Film Festival

Silent night walk, alone,
along dim-lit shadowy paths,
returning after the last show
of the film festival.
I hear no sounds of revelry,
nothing at all of the celebrations
song, dance, merrymaking,
discussions, debates, senseless arguments,
accompany my solitary walk,
it is just me and the silence of the night.

Suddenly before me looms
a *chempaka* tree,
its boughs abloom with golden flowers,

the sharp strong fragrance
spreading into the darkness
as if a woman walked there,
another lonely presence,
unseen, unsung.
I stop and gaze at it
and see that the tree
stands in front of the *Ammathottil*,
the flowers falling softly, soundlessly,
into the cradle set there
for babies abandoned at birth.
As I start walking again,
I cannot but think
Why should this female flowering tree
blossom so very lustily
showering heady golden perfume
over the lone cries
of lost little girls
—babies thrown into the mother's cradle-
born unwanted, carelessly abandoned?

Unsung lullabies caress them
in forlorn dreams,
fallen petals embracing the tiny bodies
like a mother's loving touch.
I remember the female films
showcased at the festival,
full of pathetic wails of women
exploited, deserted,
cheated of dignity and self-worth.
And as I walk alone
deep into the dense night,
the painful fragrance haunts me
as orphaned female agonies—
they tear open my passions
with sharpened nail points,
splinter my cinematic sensibilities

crisscrossing perceptions with cracks and breaks,
all that I saw dissolving
into formless nothingness, endless voids.

What remains is
Life, Reality,
The aftermath of film festival.

A native of Kerala, who writes both in her mother tongue and English, Sulochana Ram Mohan has published four volumes of fiction in Malayalam. Writes poems in English, participated in the poetry reading in the Mathrubhumi Literature festival conducted in Kerala as a member of the Poetry chain. A film buff, she has written several articles on film criticism for popular periodicals as well as souvenirs. She lives in Thiruvananathapuram.

Sumana Bhattacharya
Damsel Dark

I am the pitch dark night that descends on the day and soothes your
      weariness away
The glittering stars adorn me, I wear the glowing moon like a bindi
      on my forehead
I change the shape of the moon to suit my many moods
Like the million twinkling stars, I hold a million secrets,
Some I whisper softly with the night's breeze, some I bury deep
      within me
My soft dark glow envelopes your world, you are in awe of my
mesmerizing beauty. Shakily you hold my hand but let go, for I am
too enigmatic for you to comprehend

I am the dark Yamuna swollen with the rains, I sweep away all that
      you vainly hold on to
Your pride, your vanity, your pretentions, your superstitions
My wild beauty scoffs at you, at the many names that you once
      called me, at the many chuckles of your sympathy
"Ah, a dark girl", "poor you, your sisters so fair yet you are dark"
As I swell with pride and flow like a glide, revel in my newfound
freedom, I sweep away the fairness creams, the *uptons* that your
      pity left behind

I am the cascading black tresses, that softly fall on your face, blind
      you, stifle you, yet captivate you
You know not how to hold on to me, you know not how to deal with
      my many mysteries
Dumbfounded you scorn me, my darkness, my purple glow, my
      intrigue
I shun your scorn, I shun your pity, defiantly with head held high I
engulf you like the inky night, for deep down you are in awe of my
incomprehensible beauty

Sumana Bhattacharya is a PR practitioner by profession and a writer by passion. Her style is simple, she likes to write about things she feels deeply about. In her writings, she sometimes draws from her experiences of having grown up in a small town, Agartala. She runs a blog The Retro Feeling, that stems from nostalgia – a longing or a twinge of guilt for the days gone by or left behind.

Sumita Dutta Shoam
Woman with a Past

Strength bearing shoulders
at times held too taut
She strides
with grace
People notice
She glows
What has she achieved
that she carries herself thus?
Pensive smile
but there's
priceless peace too
She's enveloped in it
Contentment
Knowing
that she chose
to battle long
on arduous grounds
No time horizons
to rest hopes on
And victory is
equivalent to defeat
With society chattering
and plentiful advise
from people
who cannot walk
any distance in her shoes
Thorny desert and
ocean of tears left behind
Daily grind is hers to meet
And bring up her children
Crucible polished

She gleams gold
Let no one belittle her choices
That lulls her to sleep
Soon as head meets pillow

Off-Humour

Misogyny
From unexpected quarters
Hits the solar plexus.
Am I too touchy
To feel that my soul sisters
had insulted my mother?
Take it easy yaar, they say,
When I protest that I don't
Want my tween niece to giggle
Uncomfortably and brush aside
the gaslighting accepting
gender humiliation jokes
As normal, just a little bit off-humor

Sumita Dutta Shoam enjoys the most creative mediums of expression. She loves jousting with words—lining them up with cavalry precision for an incisive attack or gathering them into a bouquet of flaring beauty. Writing has been a passion from her teens, growing out of her obsession with reading all sorts of books. She has a degree in Fine Arts, a diploma in Computer Graphics, and loves photography. The Heart of Donna Rai, her debut novel, has received good reviews. She is the Founder of Adisakrit, a publishing house that takes pride in publishing books in a variety of genres. She lives in Chennai, India, and blogs at: https://zippythoughts.wordpress.com/

Dr. Supriya Bansal
Polychromatic Life

Have you ever seen that numinous hour when its darkness yet not
     quite?
When the sun lies below the horizon, the sky spurts a motley of
light,
A soft red glow swathes the sphere -a tinge of pink, purple, plum 'n
     peach,
A stellar sight, a seraphic sublime, stirs the soul, distant beyond
     reach.

I am that twilight,
Is it ascent into effulgence or a road to ruin? I travail to decide,
But I must survive, till I can ebb and endure to the other side.

I am a Hijra,
A no-man's land, a middle ground for castaways from either side,
Nonpareil, empyrean but enigmatic, a murky, muddled divide.

Have you ever held a tear for so long that it refuses to flow?
And then it melts into the crimson of your veins-throbbing woe,
Scorching n singeing your insides, morphing into a glorious gleam,
Cinders of your passion 'and dreams, drifting in the smoldering
     stream,

I am that river,
A current of rage 'and fury, stock-still yet in motion,
A rush of dolor 'n despair, a yearn to be the ocean.

I am a Hijra,
A rivulet raging to break free, a throttled thunder, a silent scream,
A veneer of calm, veiling tumultuous turmoil, clutters of a dream.

Have you ever savored grey, not yet bleak black nor venerated
 white?
The bittersweet joy of nirvana-a bale of pain, passion 'n precious
 delight.
Have you heard the howls of your soul as it tears through and
 shines?
Relished the redolence of a rebirth, emanating to blur the blaring
 lines.

I am that ash,
A memoir of all that was, a pithy parable of what could be,
Incense of a buried self, the essence of emerging Elysian within me.

I am a Hijra,
I am midway between genders. I am between several births,
Wretched rubble of society stampeded on, as scum of the earth.

Have you ever scavenged on other people's cheer 'n merriment?
Concocted glee 'n laughter at will, sedimenting your sentiments,
Have you romped with resonant claps, twirling 'and twisting
 hemlines?
Sold blessings or your body, beg, borrow but always dress to the
 nines.

I am that vulture,
Vagrant and unwanted, gorging 'n ravaging bits and blobs,
Vulnerable alone, daunting 'n daring when part of a mob.

I am a Hijra,
Labeled loud 'n lewd, cocky 'n crass, formidable yet feeble, loathed
 'n abhorred,
Hoarding praises 'n profanities, a pawn on the sidelines, abandoned
 'n ignored

I am a god- incarnate,
Ardhnarishwara -an androgynous amalgam of shiva and kali,
Isn't that why I die a thousand deaths yet live on for eternity?
And within my scarcity, I find an elixir of ethereal ecstasy.

(Hijra- In the Indian subcontinent, Hijra are eunuchs, intersex people, and transgender people.
Nirvana- Emasculation operation is often termed as nirvana by hijras. The emasculation ritual is considered a rite of passage for hijras. Ardhnarishwar- The Ardhanarishvara (Sanskrit) is a composite form of the Hindu deities Shiva and Parvati. Ardhanarishvara is depicted as half-male and half-female, equally split down the middle).

A Doctor by profession, Supriya longs to live in a world with constant supply of extra dark chocolate and filtered coffee. She and her husband share their home with two extraordinary kids and a lifetime supply of books. Writing is her me-time, her 'happy place'.

Susmita Paul

Ploughing

Susmita Paul is a creative writer and a visual artist. Susmita writes in English and Bengali. She runs a small business 'At a Pen' that serves Zentangle-inspired art. She has been trained in different techniques of drawing and painting since the age of 6. Her recent Zentangle inspired art can be found on Instagram at https://www.instagram.com/atapen.susmitapaul/. Her writing life is cataloged at @susmita.paul.writes. She also runs an e-magazine, The Pine Cone Review (@the_pinecone_review).

Sutanuka Ghosh Roy
Kali

My body odour is green
like adolescent love
my colours are intense,
like the red flame of the hearth.
My wrinkled skin speaks of drudgery
with blood from my lesions
I am a prisoner of unknown desires.
A burnt fragrant rose
with frozen tear-drops
waiting to melt into a mermaid,
singing to the sea-nymphs
dreaming of conch shells.
I am Death and Eternity
like manna and poison,
I am the Goddess of Life
I am the Goddess of Venom.

Dr. Sutanuka Ghosh Roy is Assistant Professor English in Tarakeswar Degree College, India. She has published widely and presented papers at National and International Seminars. She is a regular contributor to research articles and papers to anthologies, national and international journals of repute. She has guest-edited the July 2020 Issue of SETU on "Children's Literature". The title of her book is Critical Inquiry: Text, Context, and Perspectives. She is a reviewer, a poet, and a critic.

Tanvi Jain

I wonder

I am tired of these menacing stares that
always start at my breasts and stay glued there
like someone forgot to tell these men that my breasts weren't made
to stare at;
that they weren't made for man's entertainment;
that they are not their property;
that I can relate to tribal communities taping
their young women so that they never develop an organ
because it will always only be looked at with lust;
that I am scared of leaving my home even during the day,
because there is a constant beacon in my mind that tells me
that someone will meander past, lightly feeling and fondling an
organ I wish I could rip out;
that I am more than the sagginess that droops low and hangs to my
stomach;
that I sometimes question if my body is all that is beautiful in me;
that I often wonder if I would be allowed to live in peace if I get
myself a surgery that would take out the very organ that makes
these men leer at us all the while calling themselves our saviours;
that I wait for a day when I could walk around without fearing for
my safety;
that I wonder if it would take me a whole lot more than carrying a
pepper spray to feel like I will not be attacked;
that if nothing else works out, I might have to resort to growing hair
on my face,
cutting the hair on my head,
walking as if the only species on the planet,
doing as I like without any fear of repercussions,
and have hairy armpits and stinky egos.

I wonder if all of this would be enough
or would you still find the woman in me
lurking somewhere behind my
laughter and in the thousand other ways that you've labeled and
marked us by.
I wonder if you'd take your revenge
for me wanting to live a life as free as yours, if not more.
I wonder if you'd punish my courage
with more atrocities on all of my kind.

I wonder when will all of this stop.
I wonder when will I be seen merely as an individual,
devoid of the burdens of gender and mistreatment and entitlement
and power and control.
I wonder how many more generations of my kind
will keep hiding themselves behind loosely fitted clothes.

I wonder if you see your patriarchy itching while reading this.
I wonder how many times you've already killed me in your head.
I wonder of all the horrid things that your mind has conceived of
me
in the short duration I've tried to unmask the oppression faced by
my gender at your hands.
I wonder if you see in these words more than rage, more than pleas,
more than grievances.

I wonder if you recognize that there's a silent resistance breathing
through us women, and it will come for you, sooner or later.
You may not know it now,
for we only share it with each other through our silent gazes and
smiles and worried looks.
But you shall see the uprising nonetheless;
you will feel it.
Wait for your heart to cry for help,
that will be the day we will unleash our fury, and reclaim our place.

But don't you worry,
our idea of balance is very different from yours.
You will still have your power,
but it will only be over yourself.
Like it should have been.
Since always.

Tanvi Jain is a writer from Delhi, India. She likes to observe the world around her and tries to make sense of it through her words. Through her poems, she tries to wake people up from their slumber and urges them to think. Tanvi regularly shares her writing on her Instagram account Rustpad.

Tejashree Jadhav & Sanmyukta
In My Own Skin

The Colonizers left,
And we claimed we are a free nation,
but the remnants of their shackles remain forever ingrained.

My Reality of being a brown-skinned, Indian Girl.
Colors -White and Brown.
White- Beauty.
Brown- Beauty.
Inside- Flesh and Bones.
Outside- Skin.
Then!
Why the difference?

Gori Gori Paan, Fulasarkhi chaan,
Dada mala ek vahini aan.
At 6,
Hearing my friends make fun of my skin color,
I would storm away into the bedroom watching cartoons.
Cartoons getting interrupted by the biggest product of colonization,
        —"Fair & Lovely" advertisements.
As if the only way I could become lovely was by getting fair.

Ye kali kali aankhein, ye gore gore gaal
and a 100 other songs addressed only to the "goris".
At 10,
Watching the hero rescue the fair skinned heroine from the dark
skinned Villain, I wondered, was I the villain of my own story?
Almost as if I had no representation of my color to look upto.
Who would tell my story?

At 13,
Sitting by the dressing table, near Pond's White Beauty Powder was
        still the same Fair&Lovely,
Staring right into my face, constantly reminding me of who I was. I
would pull out the fairness scale, put it against my skin and frown,
"Still the same, still Brown!"

Capitalism—the new oppressor,
Creating an unending cycle of insecurities,
For?
Money? Fame? Profit?
And, the cost?
45 rupees for the company and a life full of growing self-doubt for
me
   and for a million other girls in this country
who get compared with a fairer girl every other day.
Where do we set the bar of being the fairest?
Or has Fair and Lovely set it already?
And where do I stand in this race of internalized racism?

Passing by the huge billboard signs,
I saw white foreign models posing in Indian attire,
Made me realize how obsessed we are with the color of the
   colonizers! Every time I went shopping,
I would watch the fair girl in the poster dressed up in the clothes I
   wanted, Looking into the mirror,
I would ask myself,
Am I allowed to wear the same?
"Gorya rangala kahihi shobhta"— "Anything suits the fair-
skinned",
   the shopkeeper would say to the girl next to me.
My heart would sink again for he's not the first person to say it.
Well, no one told me what suited me.

A dark-skinned girl can't get married for her color ruins her
"beauty"? Matrimonial sites would say "Tall and Fair girl wanted."
Why is it that the first thing seen in the colourful processions of a
marriage, Is the skin color of the bride?
So much so that the struggle begins,
layers after layers of fairness products,
But, underneath hidden is a real woman
unknowingly subjugated to the societal constructs of ideal beauty.

It's not just about color, but also gender.
Not just about being "fair" but being "her".
Because "she" would look prettier if she was fairer,
"*Gori hoti toh aur sundar dikhti*".

At 17,
I've been looking into the mirror since the day my elders questioned
      my skin color. Trying to ignore it and let it go,
But it creeps back into my life
every time they speak of "beauty",
Why does my color bother them?
Why are we scared of the brown skin?

Can we stop?
Can we stop mentioning the color of the skin in songs?
And reduce the girl's existence to her beauty,
When there's so much more to what she is.
Can we stop filling the pockets of capitalists with our insecurities?
Can we look for more in a bride,
And not whether she falls on the highest bar of the Fair & Lovely
      scale? Can Indians, wear their own clothes, on their own
      skins, with pride? "*Savali ahe tari pan chhan distey*"
Enough of "Even though" and "Tari pan".
She is pretty. Period.
Because her beauty is not defined by her color.

Can we stop teens leaning into mirrors questioning?
Because I've been there and learnt it the hard way.

Growing up, questioning myself with anger and shame,
Why do I have this color?
Why do I feel ugly in my own skin?
I used to wish I was lighter.
How I wished to get rid of what made me!

How I turned to methods of altering myself.
Who have I been trying to change for?
For the so-called friends who bullied me?
For those who grew up with the same insecurities?
I know, I am better than that.
I know, I am me.
And if I cannot accept myself for me, then who will?

Tejashree Jadhav, from Pune, India, is 18 years old and graduated from UWC Mahindra this May. Right now she is a first-year doing Liberal Arts in Whitman College.

Sanmyukta, from Mumbai, India, is 18 and currently studies at UWC Mahindra College. She is passionate about community service, cooking, and petting her cats. She is currently working on Project Sachetna- a feminism centered project working for women's empowerment. She loves using arts and dialogue to facilitate safe spaces for her projects. She discovered her love for poetry after writing her first poem, "In My Own Skin" with Tejashree.

Thryaksha Ashok Garla
Till Death Do Us Apart

Memories flitted across the back of her eyelids,
As she walked past the silhouette of her school,
Trophies and medallions weighed on her back,
Pushing her closer and into the ground.
Why must I do anything at all, she wondered,
If everything would only be an ornament to someone else's name?
It was as if she was invisible to the naked eye,
Rather a looking glass to someone else's world.
The dirt was beneath her fingernails,
But the fruit in another's belly.
The grime and sweat were on her face,
But the bills in another's clutches.
Did anything amount to anything at all?
Always her father's daughter,
Always her brother's sister
Always her husband's wife.
"He's lucky to have you", they said,
"I'm not a possession", she thought,
Oh, but oh! The words that came out,
"Thank you", a graceful nod.
Graceful, because a woman must be with poise,
Her hands delicate and her eyes trained down.
All through her life, she was pushed to excel at academics,
Only for the books to be replaced with the back of a door.
Every stroke she painted and every word she wrote,
Went up the ladder of hierarchy,
Only to kiss the feet of her 'guardians',
The noose tightening just a fraction more.
Of course, 'twas only the beginning of all yet to come,
Training to be a woman lasted a lifetime,
Learning to stay in your place,
Knowing you can win but only so much.
A pretty wife, a respected daughter,
She yearned to be so much more,
A speck on the canvas of the cosmos,
But a pearl in the warmth of her home.

The soil packed further on the route home,
As the soles of her feet pushed deeper into Gaia,
The sense of being protected,
Missing, but putting her on guard.
A fortress built with a moat encircling,
The spires of the tower kissing the sky,
Could be to keep what is inside trapped,
As much as it can keep the outside at bay.
So, which is it, you ask?
As her palm connects with the metal of her gate,
Pushing, pushing, pushing it away, nay, open,
Trapped, she responds, definitely trapped.
His gaze on her like the naked rays of the sun,
His words like the harsh rasp of a vulture feeding,
His touch burning her yet cold, like ice,
His embrace nothing more than the walls of a cell.
All her tears wiped by the rough hands of those around,
For her life was merely another thing to comment on,
All her screams muffled by the baritone of patriarchy,
For what happened to her was in the hands of her 'husband'.
"We can't change what happens behind closed doors",
Not even when it looks you in the eyes?
"We can't meddle in someone else's life",
Not even when she might not have a life if we keep waiting?
Waiting for whom, you ask,
No one, I tell you, not even the powers that be,
For there's no law to turn the wooden doors to glass,
Even when she reaches her hand out needing to be saved.

Thryaksha Ashok Garla, an eighteen-year-old, has been writing since she was a little kid. Having written over 300 poems, she touches upon themes such as feminism, self-reliance, love, lgbtq+, and mostly writes blues. Her poems have been published in various poetry anthologies. She's pursuing psychology. She's a voracious reader, a violinist, and dabbles in art. She can be reached at Instagram: @thryaksha_wordsmith and on her blog https://thryaksha.wordpress.com/.

Tikuli

Crossing the Threshold

In the half light of dawn the breeze –
laden with the scent of mango blossom –
drifts in from the courtyard,
calling her thoughts to the waiting river;
quietly she leaves her bed,
gathers her unkempt hair in a loose bun
then pauses for a moment,
listens to her husband's measured breathing,
then silently tiptoes out,
tucking in the corner of her sari at the waist
she hastily collects the fallen Parijatak in her pallu
placing a few in her hair at the same time,
the red from their stalks rising to her cheeks;
besides the well the empty pitchers wait,
nearby the battered clay stove
recalls her own scars,
for a split second, she wavers, then crosses
the threshold, her heart frantic with haste,
leaving behind the walls
that had risen around her brick by brick;
the river hears her hurried footsteps
with rapt attention, at its bend
under the shade of the mangroves,
a boat and a promise patiently wait
ready to carry her away.

The Convergence

She stands among the ancient trees,
hair fluttering protestingly over her full breasts,
strings of beads resting around her neck,
draped in red cotton her dark skin glistening in sweat,
her kohl eyes like fiery embers,
a sliver of sun on her forehead,
behind her, smeared in symbolic vermilion,
the Goddess sits cross-legged,
leaning against the matted roots of a tree,
defiant, wise, independent,
the power stemming from her womb,
non-conformist, non-submissive.
from a quiet corner I watch them,
fierce, unapologetic; both born of the soil,
somewhere beyond the hills a river turns red,
an embodiment of the eternal truth –
sa'ham asmi
the Aashad clouds gather
beating their ancient drums
as the earth receives its first rain

The Child Widow

Exhausted,
the sun dropped into the river,
vermillion flowed with the water
before being wiped away by the night
hunched over she sat at its bank,
tired, like a wilted flower,
her tonsured head shone
like the August moon,
slowly she rose to her feet,
a white shadow in the twilight,
and walked noiselessly away,
leaving behind the shards
of her broken childhood.

(All three poems were originally published in Cafe Dissensus Everyday, blog of Cafe Dissensus Magazine and later adapted for the poetry collection Wayfaring by Tikuli.)

Tikuli is an internationally published author and artist from Delhi, whose work has appeared in print and online literary magazines including Le Zaporogue, The Smoking Book (Poets Wear Prada Press, US), Levure Littéraire 10, The Enchanting Verses Literary Review, Cafe Dissensus, Mnemosyne Literary Journal, Dissident Voice, Peregrine Muse, The Peacock Journal & Silence Is White. Tikuli is the author of two poetry collections, Collection of Chaos and Wayfaring.
She blogs at Spinning a Yarn Of Life (tikulicious.wordpress.com).

Yūgen

I am the mirage of a dry oasis.
I am the noise you never see
I am the silent hallucination
I am the pause between your thoughts
I am the light between your darkness
I am the white space between double noughts
I am the lack of noise
that lives in graves
I am haunted and haunting at the same time

Tikuli

Coadunation (Kali)

Tikuli

Tina Sequeira
Pishachini

Lying on the floor
Wounded, naked, and numb
You called me
A slut
A bitch
A whore
And a cunt
Asked me to play by your rules
Or fuck back off to where I came from.

Close on the heels of the chase
You smirk, "Too easy a prey!"
Go ahead, my dear
Deem me a slut,
Shame me as much as you want
My choices and associations
Are none of your desires
My life—I own it
Write it and live it.

Does my direct gaze dent your pride?
Does my loud voice rattle your core?
"Too opinionated!", you cry.
I'd rather be a bitch
And stir a revolution
Than keep my gaze,
My tone down
Coz' down is where doormats belong
Not me, not any of my sisters.

Don't you dare brandish me a whore,
Nip me in the bud
Dim my shine

Or force me to cater to your calling.
For like a rose that blooms,
My curves will freely roam
And sway rapturously in the air
To the heart's fullest desire.

My cunt's not a curse
To thwart its life inside the cocooned womb
My cunt's not the cross
To exorcise me
Out of my maternal and marital home
My cunt's a fountain of hope for humankind
Let it flow naturally
Bleed equitably
Breaking glasses, ceilings, and ill-fate.

Call me
A slut
A bitch
A whore
A cunt
I'm all of this
And so much more
A Pishachini aroused
From the sacred Puja ashes.

Tina Sequeira is a marketer and moonlighting writer. Winner of the Rashtriya Gaurav Award (2019) in association with the Government of Telangana, the Orange Flower Award (2017) by Women's Web, Literoma Nari Samman Award (2020), and GrandQueens Leadership Award (2020) by Lions Clubs International, Tina has published over twenty short stories and poems in various anthologies and literary journals. She is the founder of Write Away.
Find her at 'Tina Sequeira' (www.thetinaedit.com) and on Twitter and Instagram at @thetinaedit.

Umara
Kaalratri

Kaalratri comes
To avenge the blood of her lost daughters
First forced, then hacked in a paddy field
Choking against the summer loo
Or in the bathroom of a sinking two-room space
In a colony where neighbours walk with ears sliced.
Kaalratri comes
On Durgasaptami every year
To the sacred dholak and appropriated temple rituals
Camouflaging as a fragrant night
Trails down these streets and strikes her flail upon inauspicious doors
Eager to stitch new ornaments to her garland of skulls.

Far towards the ghats
An Aghori sits by a half-burnt pyre abandoned too soon
He had witnessed the treachery
Them burning her, an already burnt.
He spreads his mat better and adjusts his limbs
High on hash to the gurgle of Ganga
He patiently waits for Kaalratri
He knows she will come
Years ago, he had seen her burn too...

Umara is a writer, editor, reviewer, and academic from Pondicherry/ Odisha. She completed her MA in English and Comparative Literature from Pondicherry University, 2016. Being a practising occultist of many years, she is also a Reiki Master, Pranic Healer, Angel Therapist, Wiccan, and Tarotist. Currently, she works as Senior Editor at SPi Global, Pondicherry. Her research interests include Dalit literature, indentured labour, memory studies, feminist spirituality, and various occult myths, theories, and practices.

urmila
She Laughs

Social media post "why do all films/visuals always show women being raped, tortured, abused. I know of so many women, women who laugh out loud. why do none show women laughing."

she laughs, the privileged one

never picked   then why
up   do you do
my own   all the cooking
glass of water
& now!

      it's written in the books
      the holy ones
      women are to cook
      for men
            i look at her disbelievingly
            she looks at me
            and laughs

my father   then why are
you
gave a   never seen
flat, a car   shopping
& a driver   meeting friends
when we got married

      he does not
      like it
         and laughs

she laughs: the not privileged one
covid
has made an animal
out of him

his eyes
devour my body
children, elders around
my husband
is a rapist
and she laughs

with the lockdown
deprived of beer
his anger rage
raises his hand
on me! (who else?)

and since
the shops opened
he drinks
and raises his hand
on me, the children
my husband
is a drunkard

          and she laughs

        and a woman suggested
        a Durga who is smiling
        laughing while killing
        the *bhasmasur*

and my mind goes
why?
do not the women here
have the goddess
the power
else how would they
deal with daily abuse?

● ● ●

The number
of abortions
by widows

Grandmother
in white

women
in *Lal alwan*
tonsured
in secret silent cold rooms
a man
with *ustara*

Sex
liked, abhorred
rape

unknown known
forced

Asuras
The helpers
Aborting
hope
pleasure too
showed its face
occasionally

(Lal alwan: red cloth, traditionally worn by widows in India. Ustara: blade. Asuras: mythical negative energy.)

Visible

Profiling
apparently as per the detective stories
(and police procedure, i understand)
there is a way of finding who the
murderer, attacker, rapist
is
profiling
sociopath, psychopath, loner
without family or close ties etc.
the tool to make invisible the visible

you
are educated, from a good family, your
mother loves you, so does your father
and your large joint family. you are
successful, drive a car, have a high
faulting job, friends, a fat bank balance

your hitting me daily
at night, during day
forcing yourself on me

is
Domestic
not an attacker, a rapist, or a murderer

neither is your family
for killing the fetuses

no profiling needed.

urmila is a Gender Consultant. Her work brings her closer to the issues women face. She recently started exploring her creative world through writing, among other things. Both short stories and poetry are her expression of the inner world.

Usha Akella
For a certain kind of woman
(for the ones I can't be)

*A woman will be exalted in heaven by the mere fact that she has
obediently served her husband.
They (women) pay no attention to beauty, they pay no heed to age;
whether he is handsome or ugly, they make love to him with the single
thought, 'He's a man!' Lechery, fickleness of mind and hard-heartedness
are innate in them;
After her husband is dead, she may voluntarily emaciate her body by
eating pure flower, roots, and fruits; but she must never mention even
the name of another man.
By being unfaithful to her husband, a woman becomes disgraced in the
world, takes birth in a jackal's womb, and is afflicted with evil diseases.
By following this conduct, a woman who controls her mind, speech, and
body obtains the highest fame in this world and the world of her husband
in the next.*
—*Manusmriti*

There's a certain kind of woman I fear,
wound in traditions and piety,
rouged with a meticulous attention
to refrain from bringing attention to herself,
tattoos of Brahmin caste and culture—
the botu, managlasutra, bangles, toe rings,
a high-necked blouse veils her flesh,
her gait like a lolling elephant,
her braid a flag of her piety and virtue,
oiled, flattened, obedient, not a wanton wisp flutters,
she is demurely beautiful; her laughter is neither loud
nor raucous, she addresses her husband as 'andi',
affectionately bossy, she fussily puts up with his less adorable traits,
so saccharine is her tone the air becomes diabetic,
she is modest, an empress of her domestic domain,
her intellect is well reined utilized only for earning,
her studious simplicity is practiced to perfection,
her plain face of no make-up is exhibit A.

She is emboldened in husband's bedroom like a Khajuraho statue,
in the morning she is virginal, her children are birthed
a gift from the Gods, not from the lust in her body,
she knows every Sanskrit sloka and mantra,
she observes fasts and vrats,
she is respectful to elders, she wins their approval,
especially the grand patriarchs
are managed with such efficient sweetness,
they become blind to her failing—the burnt dal is overlooked,
she is a perfect PRO,
beloved to all, she is faultless,
her husband is a little snug ring on her finger,
so smug, he doesn't know he is being worn,
thinking he wears her,
this is a couple who have a passport to Hindu heaven.

She can make a 7-layer kaaja to perfection,
a pulihaara and pulsu, have the right amount of tamarind,
a doting mother she keeps her children in line with a look,
she is known to the temple priests and volunteers,
weaving delicate jasmine garlands on weekends,
the Tulsi is sure to be in a pot by a window,
she keeps the flag of sanatana dharma flying high in the US,
she could be a badge for the BJP,
her girly voice puffs up a man's chest
and her recipe for womanhood tightens his loins in desire.

She is never bitter, she shuts out the 21st century,
she takes all of us 5 ½ centuries back,
she personally immolates other women who
are responsible for the air she breathes.

Instead of keys jangling at her hip
are many tiny sharp daggers,
she uses with precision to undermine other women,
she keeps a lot under lock,
her tongue is witty and sharp,

somehow, it is never noticed as bitchy,
she hoards goodwill and gifts from relatives
so precise are her feminine wiles and deliveries,
no one would suspect her
of anything but the finest sentiments and virtues,
it must be honey is in her veins, not blood,
she is a golden lotus, she is a curse to other women.

She lives by divide and rule, she mastered Chanakya,
she does what she has to, to survive,
she will never support an abused woman in her family,
maintaining a smirking silence carrying the torch of patriarchy,
she is the kind of woman who does not deserve a line of poetry,
so, this is poetry saying it in prose, as is,
she is the kind of woman who makes a woman like me necessary,

Thank you N.S. Sahasrabuddhe for December 25th, 1927.

Naming
(for Jyoti, Delhi rape survivor)

*We want the world to know her real name. My daughter didn't do
anything wrong, she died while protecting herself. I am proud of her.
Revealing her name will give courage to other women who have survived
these attacks. They will find strength from my daughter.*
        —Father of rape victim Jyoti[1], Delhi rape case, 2012 BBC Hindi.

She was returning home from watching *Life of Pi*,
the hero lived to tell the tale
in a boat shared with animals... was this a sign from
fate? Her journey in a bus with predators:

                            six men falling
                                        upon her like hyenas,
                            a wheel jack handle and metal rod
plunged
in her private parts, the intestines ripped out,
in a moving bus circumambulating Munirka,
bite marks across her body... death in a Singapore hospital.

Her mother's eyes were dark charcoal, unspilled lakes,
*She died but we die every day... Kudrat bhi ne hamare saath nahin
diya*[2]

                    When the dots finally connected they were black,
black gags, gnashes across their mouths, black dressed,
the women gathered in India Gate, Raisina Hill,
the drumbeat of marching feet in cities spelt *Justice...*

                        women as petroleum, she the wick
                                keeping the flame burning.

If this day is a fruit, it is a papaya, with a black heart

in the gaudy gold of a nation; if a flower, the frangapani,
its milky sap blistering a nation's veins; if a fish, *vaam,*
as her intestines like eels on the bus floor;
if a tree, the tamarind souring the breath of India.

                    And if a name: Jyoti   emerging like a lion from a
                    cave,
                            whisking the world like a tornado,
                    Enough!

*([1] By Indian law a rape victim's name is not published. The victim was
given the name Nirbhaya in the media. [2] Even God was not on our side.)*

Not merely in Dakshineshwar

It is said that far away in Dakshineswar
glittering black on passive white you stand,
your red tongue slipping out in shame,
the alphabet around your neck engraved on a skull,
the WORD is you, you remind us while worshipped
with conch bangles, gusty hibiscus,
sindoor, sandal paste, aarthi, diyas and incense,
I hear the cries of *maa jaago, maa jaago, mother rise, mother rise!*
pounding the air as if the very earth is a drum
beating to your awakening.

'Not merely in Dakshineshwar,' you say,
look again. I am everywhere. I rise
on the ash-smeared corpse of day in victorious black
when the day's destruction is done,
I reside in the pupil of your eye,
I am your sight that sees,
seeyourbreathcoilupasincensetojoinmyvoid,
see the minutes of your life weave into garlands
for my worship,
see your body as the altar,
see your poems dance on the cremation ground of your life,
it is my dance,' you say.
'See my mark branded on every Hindu woman's forehead—
menstrual blood celebrated!
See every baby encased in every woman's flesh as the universe
in my womb.
See History itself spat out of me.'

'My child, you say, when will your red chord of memory
coil back to me?
When will you wind your way back home?
When will you realize *Aham Brahmasmi?*'

Usha Akella has authored seven books. She earned an MSt. In Creative Writing from the University of Cambridge, UK. The Waiting (poetry) was published by Sahitya Akademi, (India's highest Literary authority). She was selected as a Creative Ambassador for the City of Austin for 2019 & 2015. She is the founder of 'Matwaala' the first South Asian Diaspora Poetry Festival in the US (www.matwaala.com). She has read in international poetry festivals all over the world.

Usha Kishore
Kali

How can I portray you as a goddess here?
They would not comprehend your mini skirt
of severed arms, your garland of demon heads,
your serpent bracelets, your vicious fangs
and lolling tongue seeking some twilight vein,
your dishevelled hair flying across the world.
They would not decipher a vampire goddess,
holding a decapitated head, a skull bowl,
a bloodied scythe. They would not fathom
a terrible tantric deity, anklets ringing across
eternity, marrying the sacred and the profane.

Perhaps they would appreciate if I portray
you as scantily clad, third world feminist,
flagrantly flaunting comely breasts,
slender waist and shapely thighs; your lithe
body, dark as night, revelling in sensuality;
your red eyes, as inebriate as the wine you
constantly consume. They would possibly
envisage you as polymorphous primeval energy,
devouring time in flickering tongues of flame;
female wrath trampling male divinity, inhabiting
the fringes of liminal nature; woman boldly
crossing boundaries, eluding all definition.

(From Immigrant, Eyewear Publishing, London, 2018)

Girl Trees
To the women of Piplantari

Today they are planting trees here, to celebrate
the birth of a baby girl, invoking mother-goddesses
lost in time. Their spirited talk about a greener future

revives the still air; their veiled giggles promises to
the tired earth mourning for green trees that once stood
and breathed. Elsewhere, they drown baby girls

in milk, sell them in *bazaars*, pluck them out
of their mothers' wombs, like fragile dreams.
I touch the earth, her drying skin watered by tears.

I hear the whimpering of foetuses inside her throbbing
womb, overflowing with new seed yearning to be born.
I hear stories pulsing in her lapis-blue veins.

I hear leafy whispers, rustlings, auguries of the birth
of a dark woman, saviour of the world. I hear cries
of unborn girls, with wombs as large as the universe.

Meanwhile, in the festive hamlet, rainbow saris flower
amidst the myriad saplings they carry for the little girl,
a miniature mother goddess chuckling in her cradle.

Today, the village common is a pulsating forest
of women, laughing, singing, dancing. Mother Earth
reborn, every girl becomes a tree, every tree a girl.

*(In Piplantari, Rajasthan in north-western India, local women plant 111
trees in the village common, each time a baby girl is born.)*

(From Night Sky Between the Stars, Cyberwit India, 2015.)

Indian born Usha Kishore is a British poet and translator, resident on the Isle of Man. She is currently a Research Scholar in Postcolonial Poetry at Edinburgh Napier University. Internationally published and widely anthologised, Usha's poetry is featured in the British Primary and Secondary syllabi and Indian Middle School and Undergraduate syllabi. Usha is the author of three poetry collections and a book of translation from Sanskrit. Website:www.ushakishore.co.uk Twitter:@kilipaatu

Vandana Kumar
The unshape of you

Some days I wake up
As Medusa's child
Fingers and thumbs
A runaway girl

Sacrificial mom
Doting daughter
The clothes in my wardrobe
Hang loose sometimes
Some days burst at the seams

Sometimes I show you my tattoo
A little glimpse of flesh
To go with it
I might like it
Done here a little
A little there
(The color of that bruised soul?
Now, that I hide)

I sleep at night
A lot like you do
I love my man
Yet fantasize that rank stranger

I let my hair down
Meet up with friends
You notice my wine
I play with the rim
You deduce I like it wild
Just because I know
The white from the red

And I tell you
It depends on my mood
Whether I trim
Or shave
Or just let it grow dense
I too have urges
Minus the bulges on parade

Will you call me a vixen?
Or one of you
Will you still dedicate?
A day for my ilk

(Published in the UK Based website "Destiny Poets" on March 2019)

Latest issue on the shelf!

Burn pages 45 and 46
That give vile tips
To conform to ugly standards
Of beauty

Burn pages 63 and 64
That teach you
How to sit with legs
Crossed at ankles
Not at knees
Especially when wearing
Short skirts
Particularly when you are in mood
To spread those legs
Fiddle with moistness
Leftover from last night

Burn also pages 77 and 78
That tells you a life
Without knowing
How to make pineapple upside-down cake
Isn't one worth it –at all!

And while at it
Don't leave out pages 21 and 22
That tells you
To put aside
Gripping novel at the bedside
To make those moves
Or find him
In arms of a mistress
In the morrow

In-between these pages
A lot of gloss
Samples of fairness creams
Bulging out of even pages

Do yourself a favor
Go burn
That woman's magazine today!!!

Vandana Kumar is a middle school French teacher, translator, and recruitment consultant in New Delhi. She contributes poems to online publications like 'GloMag'. She has also been published in international journals like Toronto based 'Scarlet Leaf Review' and Philadelphia based 'North of Oxford'. One of her poems was recently published in the Winter 2020 paperback edition of the Houston, Texas-based – 'Harbinger Asylum' which is available at amazon.com. She was recently published in the heritage newspaper 'Madras Courier.'

Vayu Naidu
Abhisekham

Water falls
Milk pours
Turmeric balms the black stone deity.
Saree weaves
Jasmines cluster
Diamonds wink
Flames dilate as
Oil wells from the brass lamp with five mouths.
Coins flick between nimble fingers of the 6:00 a.m pundit on
abhisekham duty.

Mother sits, hands clasped, facing the goddess.
As temple bells toll overhead
Her prayers heighten:
"For this girl, give her hope, husband, and fertility."
These words have passed her lips earlier.
This time after that prodigal return:
"where her eye is battered, o Ganga-goddess of all rivers, soothe it
with sight.
Let there be peace, with love."

Slow dissolve, our furrows deepen.
I see the last vestige of unconditional love flow
Into the pool of milk and turmeric, jasmine, oil, and ash
Rushing in the gutter by the feet of the goddess.

The song to Ganga
Finds a new meaning,
in Mother.
My birthday abhisekham passes.

Dr. Vayu Naidu's PhD from The University of Leeds was on transposing Ramayana and Mahabharata in English for Storytelling performance and Theatre and founded an intercultural touring company. Her novel Sita's Ascent (Penguin: 2013) is a reimagination of Sita's awakening and was nominated for the Commonwealth Book Award. Her second novel The Sari of Surya Vilas (Speaking Tiger; AffirmPress: 2017) is about the freedom from colonisation in the Madras Presidency. ABC book of the week August 2017. Her forthcoming novel is set in 17th Century India experienced through an immigrant woman who triumphs over tyranny through art. Follow her at 'Vayu Naidu' (www.vayunaidu.com).

Vineetha Mekkoth
Some Things Gather Dust to Remain

As she cleaned the prayer room
She found the pamphlet of the temple,
The one where years ago
Her husband had taken her
To do a yajna to beget a son.

She had been pregnant then.
"If the chromosomes decided the gender,
Would supplication help?" she wondered.
But being the typical submissive wife
She silenced her doubts rife.

Obediently she poured in the ghee
The sacrificial flames blazed high,
All she prayed was that
The new soul within her
Wouldn't suffer much strife.

"It's the woman's birth month
That decides the child's gender," he quipped.
"This Chinese calendar gives the days,
A woman should conceive to beget a son."
She wondered how there were Chinese women.

But questions were unwelcome.
She continued having the sacrificial ghee
Prayed day and night regularly.
Her daughters she hugged, they were her extensions
And shared her fears with family when rose her tension.

That was the day he hit her again
"Who asked you to tell her?"
"But she's your sister!"
He hit her again. "I want you to keep mum
No sharing anything without my permission."

Clutching her belly, she cringed.
Of her crime, she was ignorant.
As the first trimester drew to a close
Trips to scanning centers arose
"Is it a boy?" He enquired anxiously

"Can't be determined at this stage," they pronounced
They visited a large number of centres
All manners of external scans were followed
By invasive ones which broke her spirit
Yet behind him, she trudged meekly.

A doctor gave him her word
"I'll make your dream come true
Let your wife carry the foetus till the fifth month
Then scan and if it's a girl
An MTP, I'll do."

"You can try again after that
I understand your dream for a boy, son."
He looked at the doctor with brimming eyes
To him, she seemed a goddess in disguise
Only she understood his pangs

She gaped at the goddess
"What about me?" She asked
"Isn't it risky the later it gets?"
Her anxieties were dismissed as frivolous
"I'm aged and experienced," the doctor said.

Back home she lay deep in thought,
"Now what? Now what?
At five months the foetus is a baby!
Head, body, hands, legs, eyes, nose
Teeny little fingers and toes."

At five months this baby
Would move around
She would feel the kicking
And to kill the baby if it were a girl!
Just because it was a girl!

She screamed silently, then picked up the phone
"Darling! We can't continue this pregnancy."
"Hello! What? Why not?"
"Remember I had that morning-after pill
It had crossed the expiry date
The foetus might be affected."

Oh! How he raved and ranted!
She stood firm in her decision
No doctor could say that the baby would be perfect
"It might have brain damage or other issues," they said.

She had the MTP done
As he sobbed hysterically
At his dream undone.
In her heart, there was a dull silence
A permafrost that spread.

The temple pamphlet she folded
And kept on the shelf
Years had passed, the ache remained
But that paper she wouldn't throw away.
She didn't want to forget.

Burn

(Dedicated to the 19-year-old Dalit rape victim of Hathras, Uttar Pradesh, India.)

Will there be candlelight vigils for you Dalit girl?
Will anyone cry over your brutalisation?
Will there be any encounters to polish off the criminals
Disregarding their "upper caste" status and religion?
Will they even ever get punished for their cruelty?
Or will they win tickets to join the Parliament?
Will you be mourned for by anyone other than your family?
All women shudder at what you underwent.
Has it not been like this since time immemorial
Rape and brutalisation of women, more so of Dalit women?
Is not casteism the greatest inhuman burden
That all Hindu minds bear with or without trepidation?

Call a spade a spade
Call an illness by its name
Casteism is shit
Violence against women
Happens because you can get away with it
If you have the right connections
Sab kuch chalta hai
So much for greatness and equality
The future is bright
Shining
Blinding
But bright
Maybe we will all burn

Vineetha Mekkoth is a poet, writer, translator, editor from Calicut, Kerala working as Assistant State Tax Officer in the State GST Department. She has translated for the Kerala Sahitya Academy. Her poems, articles and short stories have been published online and in various anthologies. Her debut poetry collection 'Ashtavakra and Other Poems' was published in August 2017 and finds mention in The Journal of Commonwealth Literature, 2018, Vol. 53(4) p618.

Vinita Agrawal
Woman

Woman
Like a plastic palmyra showcased at the front door
A rag doll - gloved, thumb-printed, buttressed
bruised, soughed, oboe-d
and at the end of it all - grey like the ash of a rose.
Rabbit-like. Fearful, frightened.
Babbling, burbling, dripping
scurrying, stumbling, succumbing
until reduced to a sobbing choir of broken hummingbirds.
She is his colour-card for abuse
one shade for every kind;
to rape, demean, curb, thrash, burn, mutilate, violate, intimidate,
a fertile ground for the plough of his madness.
She is no one. She is nothing.
She is dry yellow grass, an invasive weed
sawdust, thorn, nettle.
an abandoned trellis on which he pegs his evils.
But really, she is none of these.
She is a cause to be fought for in her own voice.
Though sandpapered by scars of a thousand hard years
her resilience is still intact.
Woman - she shines in a light of her own - ever evolving
weaving a special bond with her sisterhood
no veil, no hijab, no purdah can conceal her strength
nothing can keep her down.
She is Ma Durga, Ma Kali, Ling Bhairavi
Jwala, Amba, Bhavani
the fierce rider of tigers, spewer of fire
killer of demons, drinker of blood.
She is the twin of every aspect that exists in the universe
the half of the whole called man
She is Shakti. The bearer of souls.
Because of her man exists.

Author of four books of poetry, Vinita is an award winning poet, editor, translator and curator. Joint Recipient of the Rabindranath Tagore Literary Prize 2018 and Gayatri GaMarsh Memorial Award for Literary Excellence, USA, 2015. She is Poetry Editor with Usawa Literary Review. She has edited an anthology on climate change titled Open Your Eyes (pub. Hawakal). She judged the RLFPA poetry contest (International Prize) in 2016 and co judged the Asian Cha's poetry contest on The Other Side ' in 2015. She has read at the FILEY Book Fair, Merida, Mexico, Kala Ghoda Arts Festival among others. She is on the Advisory Board of the Tagore Literary Prize. She has curated literary events for PEN Mumbai. She can be reached at www.vinitawords.com

Yamini Pathak
Rape Culture

In India, when the baby is born:
a.   His father brags, shares sweets with neighbors.
b.   Her mother apologizes, shares shame with her pillow.

When the kids return from school:
a.   Brother needs to study for a test.
b.   Sister brings snacks for brother. Practices rolling rotis for dinner. Studies for test.

Going to the movies:
a.   Brother escorts sister. A sister must be shielded from leering eyes.
b.   Sister's safe at home. Brother and his buddies thrust their hips, smack their lips at the buxom woman on the bus.

When it's time for college:
a.   Brother is the heir and hope of the family, will pin the moon and stars to our name.
b.   Surely not law school? Nobody wants to marry an argumentative girl.

Before and After:
a.   *Take the car keys, son. Avoid the cops if you've been drinking. See you in the morning.*
b.   *What was she wearing? How late was it? Does she have a boyfriend? Was she drunk?*

Yamini Pathak's poetry and nonfiction have appeared in Waxwing, Anomaly, The Kenyon Review blog, The Hindu newspaper, and elsewhere. Her chapbook, Atlas of Lost Places is published by Milk and Cake Press. A Dodge Foundation Poet in the Schools, she is poetry editor for Inch magazine (Bull City Press) and an MFA candidate at Antioch University, Los Angeles. Yamini is an alumnus of VONA/Voices (Voices of Our Nations Arts Foundation), and Community of Writers.

Zehra Naqvi
The Dark One

I am not death
I am rebirth.

Wheel of eternity
kaalchakra of certainty
borne of the banks of Ganges
sprung from the womb of *sangam*
—that meeting of a trinity of sacredness—
I am the destroyer and the purifier:
the creator of new worlds, new orders.

Crafted from light and darkness
etched out by sandstorm and flood
hardened and softened by turns, I am
kaalratri— keeper of secrets
and silence.

Born of the forehead of *Durga*
I am
the mind-sword, slayer of myth.
Saviour, punisher, and refuge
I am
The Dark One—black and blue

Blackest blue of deepest ocean
where reaches not one speck of light.
Devouring blue flame of water, ignited,
that sets aflame lungs, eyes afire.

Avenger, cleanser
restorer of cosmic order
I am the flickering tongue of *Agni*.

I am not death
I am rebirth.

Wrath and Fury, might unleashed;
a force of Nature alive.
Raging, destroying, creating
I am
Kali – the goddess of time.

(The poet reimagines herself here – beyond the confines of one's 'own'
religion and context — as the fiery goddess Kali.)

Desire

Black magic days give you away,
Witch
        — hiding in blinding sunlight—
wisps of smoke curling from your locks
winter's breath on your earlobes
fingers inching towards the broom
that twitches uneasily in an obscure corner
        waiting to come alive.
The winter wind blows, gnawing at your bones
teasing, pleading begging to be straddled
to sweep you into the steel grey sky
while you stir your cauldron
        —palms slick with cold sweat—
brewing up that which must not be named,
that which drives hearts insane
bubbling slowly over silver-blue flame:
        flame of ice and winter's breath.
Ice *burns*, scalds, claws and bites—
tugs viciously at your disguise
careful, witch, for the winter wind blows
        and your black magic shows.

Zehra Naqvi is an author and a journalist with a decade of experience, writing across a spectrum of subjects including gender, literature, socio-political issues, economics, philosophy, culture, and parenting. Her articles have been featured in national and international publications like Reader's Digest, Indian Express, The Hindu, The Quint, Financial Chronicle, Women's Web and Child Magazine. Her forthcoming memoir titled 'The Reluctant Mother: A Story No One Wants To Tell' is being published by Hay House.

Zilka Joseph

Havan

—Sacrifice; sacrificial fire used for Hindu ceremonies

he got angrier they lifted
    the blue plastic can
        from the kitchen
            floor my hand
                haldi-streaked
                    I cried out I backed
                      away ran toward
                      the bedroom the old lady
                      held onto my sari pallav
                          pulled
                      me hard she was seventy
                      but she was strong I could
                      see her betel-stained
                  teeth close to my face
              blood-red yellow bone
            cage door opening
        fingers like steel hinges
      creaking Krishna Krishna
pay my dowry

O Krishna

I have no children
      murmuring in the pipal trees
        rain of thin glass
           bangles breaking
             mouth full flood
               of kerosene
                  generous as love
                  blue god flesh
                  on fire like sindur
                    in my hair easily, caught
                  like ghee and grain
                  eaten whole
                  take it all take
             O witness
          union divine
       no holy Ganga water
     no sweetness
   like jasmine
or sandalwood this

burning   this flame   eternal

The Bharatnatyam Dancer

Imagine this: It's Shiva's Rudra tandav
my mother performs

frenzied
dance of destruction

her lotus feet

scorching
the earth with flame

not the great god's three wild locks
or river Ganga
bursting through matted curls

      but her thick black rope of hair
      whipping

the backs
of her knees. Her sari pleats
open and close

the pallav's silken sweep bound
in a belt of gold

How thunderous

her kohled eyes, how pure
the gestures of her ever-changing
mudras. But where was

your   fury   O sweet mother

Nataraj, where's your protective flame?
Did your three eyes
freeze unweeping

and deaf your holy ears

to her
to the sounds of a hundred brass
ghungurus

thrumming on her ankles

No No   you heard her feet the bells the beat of lighting feet
you heard

her desire you heard
her steps her dance shatter Mount Kailash
your home your god-abode your manly
kingdom
you heard the audience
roar

and knew all along   her father's will
that he would say to her

No more!   The tongue

the tongue of every ankle bell

ripped out   her heart a tomb

her art her fame
turned to cinders by you

you jealous, jealous lord of dance

What Burns

—for Jyoti Singh, raped on a bus in Delhi and who died of fatal injuries

Child of light, is there solace in darkness
of death? Will it be God's hands that will burn

10 P.M. Six men; a girl "blamed" for rape
So foolish to fight back! Resistance can burn

Look how her beauty attracts! To protect
the *diamond between her thighs,* we shall burn

Now rapists will *kill,* not just rape your girls
"dangerous if you hang us", his eyes burn

How safe we are our homes and the street
where "lawyers" can say— with petrol she'll burn

Only "20 percent of girls are good"
hood them and hide them, or it's you they'll burn

Best smother them small, in wombs or your home
no food, books, dowry, and no bra to burn

What do you want? To be God, man or beast?
your house, your goddesses, your crosses burn

Sweet mercy rains on the holy who pray
who never see women and children burn

Who will remember, as we turn to ash
poet, can true words make this darkness burn

("Havan" won the Michael S. Gutterman prize at the University of Michigan. It was published in Sharp Blue Search of Flame, Wayne State University Press. "The Bharatnatyam Dancer" was published in Sharp Blue Search of Flame, Wayne State University Press. "What Burns" (an earlier version) was published in Sharp Blue Search of Flame, Wayne State University Press).

Zilka Joseph was nominated twice for a Pushcart, for a PEN America, and a Best of the Net award. Her work has appeared in Poetry, Poetry Daily, Frontier Poetry, KRO, MQR, Ablucionistas, and in several anthologies. Her book Sharp Blue Search of Flame published by Wayne State University Press was a finalist for the Foreword INDIES Book Award. She teaches creative writing and is an editor and manuscript advisor.
www.zilkajoseph.com

Zinia Mitra
The Wail

Let me in
now that father is dead
I am still that frightened child
peeping through the gap
under your closed door,
my cheeks touching your lifeless floor.
I was scared of father
of his size (he was wise)
his black-framed square glasses,
his seriousness, his official files
that allowed no mistakes anywhere,
I played with flies, my page full of mistakes
was flung outside your closed door.
There would be a lot of rustle, cooker whistle
in the kitchen, cuttings and beatings and frying
when he was home.
I was the quiet sneaking child
roaming in the kitchen garden
waiting for father to go. I was slow.
I was scared of father
of his loud voice
his loud alcoholic friends
and when you whined and complained about me
of his abuses, of the cold floor
outside your closed door.
The lone hours of watching the moon
stiff from my bed pretending sleep
kept me awake for nights
and I could hear grandma's wails
see her frights
see her lost daughter shine in the moonlight
a mist-pale pale and white.
Her tears like fairies with wings

escaped the house playing flutes
there were noise of boots,
as father's alcoholic friends left the house.
You drowsed in your siesta
while grandma and myself collected *dumur*
from the forest nearby that smelled of *nagkesar*
dumur that you so liked to cook
but the look that you gave me, the look
stayed with me for years
whether I made love or war.
I did none of the things you thought I did
I was an obedient kid
but you whined and complained
and I hid
I was a ghost, most-ly
but now that father is dead
your footsteps unsure and lean
let me in.

(The Wail was published in Sahitya Akademi journal, September-October issue 2018. http://sahitya-akademi.gov.in/journals/indianliterature.jsp)

On Reading her Story

She stood at the crossroads of her life for him
she stood there denuded of the poundage of her everyday.
> He had asked her to leave her baggage behind
> promised her that they would start afresh
> that he would always be there for her
> she lugged the weight of the moments
> she couldn't have left behind.
All the raindrops on her leaves
all his poems they would read aloud
all the coffee bills they could laugh at
all her fresh ferns, spear grass,
train tickets and egret feathers,
a small water-bottle, some money

lipstick and comb,
also memories of scratches on her dry barks
yellow leaves that had collected at her feet
in short, her bare essentials and a part of Sukna Forest Range.
>   She waited for him there
>   through all the droplets of water
>   that formed in the mouth of the taps
>   fell one by one
>   she waited for him there
>   until she was hungry and not hungry anymore
>   she waited for him there
>   until the last train left the platform
>   until the bodies around wrapped blankets
>   turned dead on the benches
>   until she was unburdened of all the tearing noises the world
>   makes
until it was time to return home
until it was time to return home.

*(Originally published in Pangolin Review Issue 13, November 8, 2019,
https://thepangolinreview.wixsite.com/mypoetrysite)*

Tears

Tears moped the room
the day slid in again and broke its back on the floor.
Her shadow broke away by turns
negotiating with the heaviness of her eyelids
heavy like breasts swelled with milk
the pains swam from one lake to another
soggy with questions
the answers were perhaps packed
in the empty bottles under the bed
adding up every night like personal blemishes.
Her body felt like squeezing of damp laundry
before they are hung out to dry.
Back in the kitchen she could not chop the inside
or roast the insults

just anger boiling
boiling
without ever reaching a point.
The sunless day felt so blue
like the colour of her cheeks.
Her screams kept her from getting scared
at night
night was a time when her cheeks turned red
somewhere the whining cry of a child
hit against the walls
heavy
like her hours of unpaid dowry.

Zinia Mitra teaches at University of North Bengal, India. Her poems have been published in National and International journals, including Muse India, Ruminations,Contemporary Literary Review, Kavya Bharati, East Lit. Indian Literature, Coldnoon, Asian Signature, Teesta Review, Setu, Pangolin Review, Poetry Potion, Setu, Erothanatos. She writes from Siliguri, Darjeeling.

The Kali Team

Pushcart Nominee **Megha Sood**, Co-Editor of The Kali Project lives in Jersey City, New Jersey. She is an Assistant Poetry Editor at MookyChick and Literary Partner in the project *"Life in Quarantine"* with CESTA, Stanford University, USA. Her work has been widely featured in journals, newspapers, including Poetry Society of New York, WNYC, American Writers Review, SONKU, FIVE:2: ONE, KOAN, Kissing Dynamite, etc. Numerous of her works have appeared in anthologies by the US, UK, Australian, and Canadian Press. Three-Time State-level winner of the NJ Poetry Contest 2018/2019/2020. National Level Winner Spring Mahogany Lit Prize 2020. Chosen twice as the panelist for the Jersey City Theater Center Online Series *"Voices Around the World"*. Co-edited anthologies (*"The Medusa Project"*, Mookychick) and (*"The Kali Project"*, Indie Blu(e) Publishing).
Blogs at https://meghasworldsite.wordpress.com/.
Tweets at @meghasood16

Candice Louisa Daquin, Co-Editor of the Kali Project, has always held a dear place in her heart for India. Outraged by reports of young women being raped, Daquin approached Sood about co-editing an anthology of out-cry, feminist poetry from Indian women. Daquin feels creating platforms for important, often neglected voices is the greatest worth someone in publishing can be part of. Editor of SMITTEN, This Is What Love Looks Like (an anthology of poetry by women for women), which was Finalist in the National Indie Excellence Awards (2019) and Co-Editor of We Will Not Be Silenced (an anthology of poetry in response to the #metoo movement) and As The World Burns (an anthology of poetry and art in response to #Covid-19, #BLM, #Trump).

Tejinder Sethi is a bilingual poet currently residing in Bangalore. She freelances in creative writing. She has authored an e-book of Hindi Poetry, 'Cotton Blooms – Kapaas Ke Phool'. While most of her poems are a melange of her life experiences, the subject close to her heart is the narratives of India - Pakistan Partition. One of her soul stirring poems from the collection 'Kapaas Ke Phool' on the Partition of 1947, was awarded and featured by the Partition Museum, Amritsar. Her creations, Shaneel, A Journey to Nowhere, Tareekh, Golden Lotus, Voice Of Draupadi and others have been published in various anthologies and journals. Inspired by 'karumi' (lightness) and 'ma' (space/emptiness) in haikai aesthetics, she has recently transitioned from free verse to haikai verse. त्रिya is a digital space she's carved for the translations of her published haiku, tanka, haibun and tanka prose. You can reach her at tejisethi13@gmail.com

Indie Blu(e) Publishing

Indie Blu(e) Publishing is a progressive, feminist micro-press, committed to producing honest and thought-provoking works. Our anthologies are meant to celebrate diversity, raise awareness, and embolden our sisters and brothers to speak their truths. The editors all passionately advocate for human rights; mental health awareness; chronic illness awareness; sexual abuse survivors; and LGBTQ+ equality. It is our mission, and a great honor, to provide platforms for those voices that are stifled and stigmatized.

Kindra M. Austin is an author and co-founder of Indie Blu(e) Publishing. Austin is an advocate for mental health awareness, sexual trauma survivors, and for the LGBTQ community. She writes from the state of Michigan, where she was born and raised. Her debut novel was released in 2017; she has since written and published two other novels, as well as four poetry collections. Other Indie Blu(e) publications include contributions to We Will Not Be Silenced, and SMITTEN; Austin has also written for The Mansfield Pride magazine, an annual periodical out of Ohio. You can find her books at Amazon, Barnes and Noble online, and at other major online retailers.

Christine E. Ray lives outside of Philadelphia, Pennsylvania. A former Managing Editor of Sudden Denouement Publications, she co-founded Indie Blu(e) Publishing with Kindra M. Austin in September 2018. Ray is author of *Composition of a Woman* and *The Myths of Girlhood*. Her writing has also been featured in *As The World Burns: Writers and Artists Reflect on a World Gone Mad*, *SMITTEN This Is What Love Looks Like*, *We Will Not Be Silenced : The Lived Experience of Sexual Harassment and Sexual Assault Told Powerfully Through Poetry, Prose, Essay, and Art*, *Anthology Volume I: Writings from the Sudden Denouement Literary Collective*, *Swear to Me* (Nicholas Gagnier), and *All the Lonely People* (Nicholas Gagnier).
Read more of her work at https://braveandrecklessblog.com/.